"I am not a breakfast person, yet no food memory will live up to my experience at Big Bad Breakfast. I was in desperate need of comfort (from a hangover and a long flight), sustenance (when you're in the South, your belly knows it must be fed), and warmth (okay, maybe I'm being dramatic), and Big Bad Breakfast delivered. Was it the sweet, savory, gooey Sausage Cinnamon Rolls or the deeply dirty and delicious waffle–topped Pylon? Or maybe it was the indescribable power of true Southern hospitality. I revel in that meal, and any meal with John at the helm."

CHRISTINA TOSI

CHEF-OWNER OF MILK BAR AND AUTHOR OF *MOMOFUKU MILK BAR*

"They say breakfast is the most important meal of the day. With *Big Bad Breakfast*, John gives you 137 reasons why that's true, and shows you that breakfast is not only the most important, but also the most delicious meal of the day. Get ready for some of the best breakfast foods you've ever had."

AARÓN SÁNCHEZ

CHEF-PARTNER OF JOHNNY SÁNCHEZ AND COSTAR OF *CHOPPED*

"Mr. Currence won a James Beard award in 2009 for best Southern chef, and it's possible to eat brilliantly in Oxford for weeks, without repeating a course, in his restaurants alone. In fact I'd recommend this experience . . . . He's pushing the notions of what Southern food can be, pulling off impressive feats with a casual air of embarrassment."

NEW YORK TIMES

"Venerable food writer John T. Edge once told us we couldn't leave Oxford without stopping by Big Bad Breakfast—and boy, are we glad we listened to him. Chef John Currence is a great cook with a lot of soul."

SERIOUS EATS

BIG BAD
BREAKFAST

BIG BAD BREAKFAST

THE MOST IMPORTANT BOOK OF THE DAY

JOHN CURRENCE

PHOTOGRAPHS BY ED ANDERSON

TEN SPEED PRESS

BERKELEY

CONTENTS

To my amazing wife, Bess, mother to our daughter
and anyone who needs her love and guidance.

———————————————

To my mother, Becky, tireless, wise, and always fair.

———————————————

To the "Mother Hen" of BBB, Jill Stevens, mother to the throng of folks
who make the Big Bad Breakfast clock tick every day.

———————————————

To all three of you and to mothers everywhere.

ACKNOWLEDGMENTS

The greatest thanks goes to the staff at BBB, who make that mighty little machine grind every day. Those thanks extend to everyone who has punched the clock since June 2008, showed up hung over the morning after big football games or during "snow storms," floods, etc., to pour coffee, flip eggs, scrub pots, scrub toilets, massage biscuit dough, and perform countless other thankless duties in our obscure strip mall parcel, all for the greater good. Thank you all for believing in the mission of our place and giving it wings by preaching the word of what we are about and helping deliver one of the most divine breakfast experiences available.

Thank you to my partners at Fresh, Inc, for believing in me and putting up with me so that we could take Big Bad Breakfast on the road . . . and thrive.

Thank you to our countless regular diners and folks who try us once and go out and spread the word of what they have had. Thank you for understanding that we are human, we have flaws and occasionally make mistakes. Thank you for appreciating the fact that our people will fall all over themselves to make right whatever was wrong. Thank you for supporting us, loving us, and introducing us to your family and friends. Thank you for waiting out front on those long hot August mornings and cold January ones. Bless those of you who slide into Snackbar and suspend the reality of that wait with a Bloody Mary. Thank you all for loving what we do. Haters, well, you aren't reading this, but you can suck it.

Thank you to my family and friends who supported this little idea when it was just a seed. We took a huge risk putting BBB in what was, at the time, a strange and out-of-the-way location (with a giant parking lot). You helped me generate ideas, cobble together junk to decorate with, paint booths, hang lights, and polish the joint. Then you became the first wave of regulars.

Thank you to the whole staff at Ten Speed for carrying me through this. We bickered like an eighty-year-old couple and drank our way to common understanding in order to get through the process, and I loved every minute of it. You guys have been a dream.

Thank you to the teams at the Black Agency and Splinter Group for constant help with design, sinister-scheming, and overall spiritual fulfillment. You guys all make us better at every turn.

Thank you Mamie, my opinionated, bossy, whip-smart, beautiful, and entirely uncompromising three-year-old girl. Your frequent visits to my office upstairs while I was trying not to claw my eyeballs out writing this freaking book, making me spin you around in my office chair and draw Peppa Pig, preserved what little sanity I still have. The fact that you consider my food "shit" stings a little, but your smile soothes the ache immediately.

FOREWORD
BY JOHN BESH

WHEN IT COMES TO CHEFS, WE ENJOY BREAKFAST, ALTHOUGH MOST chefs seldom wake early enough to partake in the definitive morning meal. John Currence and I happen to be early risers who revel in the art of cooking, serving, and eating all things breakfast, to the point that it's become a competition when he stays at my house or I at his, to see who can wake earlier than the other and lay out a fabulous spread. This generosity has always been in evidence for as long as I've known John, though I'm not quite sure when or where it was that we first crossed paths. However, it was through the Southern Foodways Alliance that he and I first bonded and became the best of friends, especially after hurricane Katrina. Not having an ounce of mechanical ability, I have never been more impressed with any chef than I was with John, who hung up his toque, strapped on his tool belt, marshaled resources, and led a group of Southern Foodways Alliance volunteers in rebuilding the shrine to fried chicken in New Orleans, Willie Mae's Scotch House, on a dilapidated block of the Treme neighborhood. His deeds and gestures not only restored a restaurant but restored hope in a neighborhood most had forgotten, hope in the city, hope in humankind.

These noble deeds aside, John is not always the best of influences. Such was the case when I journeyed to Oxford with the intention of preparing a banquet to raise funds for the Southern Foodways Alliance. That morning when I first graced the doors of Big Bad Breakfast, the line proceeding out of it was too formidable so I entered through the employee entrance. With a day's work ahead of me to prepare for the banquet, I was just there for a quick "kitchen tour" and the idea of eating was far from my mind, yet apparently John had a different agenda. That agenda began with an innocent Bloody Mary, which John justified as "nothing more than a tomato salad" and "perhaps more healthy." Being an advocate of good health, I consumed and savored multiple "salads" until food began to appear, beginning with the most delicious biscuits, butter, and jam. (Without alcohol, John is one of the most articulate speakers: witty, bold, and irreverent. Yet add a few "salad" drinks to the mix and you've got the Ignatius Riley of Oxford, Mississippi, reciting an ode to biscuits, butter, and jam, each revered in equal proportions.) Then came the most beautiful sight— perfectly cooked house-cured bacon from the fattest hogs south of the Mason Dixon along with overflowing platters of plump, juicy, and sizzling house-made sausages (accompanied by another ode by John to all things hog), and paired with another "salad" or two. On the heels of the big buttery biscuits and platters of perfectly prepared pig came the creamiest cheese grits and a procession of eggs cooked every way imaginable (accompanied by a litany of organic egg anecdotes, stories, and poems), and of course a couple more "salads."

Hours into the not-so-petite affair, I looked at my watch only to discover that this never-ending breakfast had gone senselessly past the noon hour. With much work ahead of me, I made my feeble objections to the breakfast debauchery known to my dear host, only to have platters of spicy fried chicken, feather light flapjacks, crispy soft waffles, rich French toast, American toast, and every other high-caloric, high-carb delectable imaginable delivered, along with a couple more "salads" to wash it all down. Before long,

I thought maybe the key to my freedom was to admit defeat and graciously beg for mercy from the delicious torture, but that turned out to be no simple task and involved a couple more "salads." At that point, I came up with a plan not of escape or evasion but rather to prepare the night's meal while under the influence of Big Bad Breakfast, and shockingly, we managed to pull the dinner off. John and I built fires to cook on, made the most delicious food, set off unbelievably irresponsible fireworks, and left the happy guests reveling well into the morning hours. This, I promise, is no tall tale and I've left out or forgotten most of the really good stuff, but one thing that will never leave my memory was the elegant simplicity of John's food, hospitality, and generosity. John's food speaks of place, it speaks of people, and it speaks of fun-loving times with good friends and delicious memories.

FOREWORD
BY DAVID CHANG

OXFORD, MISSISSIPPI, IS WELL KNOWN AS THE HOME OF THE GREAT
William Faulkner, the location of the legendary Square Books bookstore, and the epicenter of Ole Miss football fandom—but it should also be known as a nexus of some of the most intense drinking anywhere in the planet.

So truth be told, my first time eating one of John's big bad breakfasts back in 2009, I was suffering one of the worst hangovers in my life. John swore to me that he had the cure. His prescription was a combination of bloody Marys, tomato gravy and biscuits, pimento cheese, bacon, and basically every delicious thing in this cookbook. But it was that goddamn Pylon that saved my life—an unholy combination of hot dogs, waffles, chili, and who knows what the hell it was. A few bites of that monster gave me the second wind I needed. I began to taste everything else around me and realized that this was one of the best breakfasts I've ever had in my life. Shit, I don't even drink coffee and for some reason the coffee made sense and all the food made sense and my mind righted itself and I found myself having one of those rare, magical moments one has over great food and great company.

It took me a second to realize that everything I was eating wasn't just hard-hitting breakfast deliciousness, but the byproduct of years of hard work and real learning that John had accumulated working in kitchens all over the South, from North Carolina to New Orleans. There were elements that he had carefully crafted and fussed over that no one else did . . . who

else makes their own bacon and sausage and those black pepper biscuits?!! The people around me were having as good of a time as I was.

That pure joy and excitement is the reason why I'm so happy to have this book in my hands. I really hope you get to visit Oxford, but until you do, use this book to familiarize yourself with one of the best places to eat anywhere. If you are a local and lucky enough to visit Big Bad Breakfast often, you are now holding the years of hard work that makes BBB look so easy, and you have the chance to add some of those kernels of culinary genius to your repertoire.

So maybe the The Pylon didn't save me, maybe it was the bloody Mary. Maybe it was the pimento cheese (seriously, pimento cheese needs to become a trend everywhere). The shrimp and grits will make you weep. Maybe I will never make The Pylon at home . . . that's okay. All the more reason to head back down to Oxford and go drinking with the great people down there. And be restored again the next morning at Big Bad Breakfast.

INTRODUCTION: A TESTAMENT TO THE MOST IMPORTANT MEAL OF THE DAY

1. GENESIS

In the beginning, God made heaven and earth. But before that, he surely ate breakfast, because that's a lot for a guy to do in one day . . . And there was much rejoicing.

Years later in Oxford, Mississippi, however . . .

My dear, sweet, wonderful, and insanely smart (though terminally naïve at times) wife, Bess, looked at me like I was fucking crazy. You see, this was the morning Big Bad Breakfast was scheduled to open—it was June 2008—and we were waiting for the health inspector to sign off on our permit so we could open the door to the 200 or so people waiting out front.

Bess's face was screwed up and her head cocked slightly. "Are you *kidding* me?" she asked, tornado swirling around us. My mother was in town, as were my two young nieces, Lucy and Frances, who were crawling up the walls, unfed, and in need of attention we could not give them. The staff scrambled, assembling *mise en place*, setting up stations, rolling silver, portioning jelly, polishing glassware, and placing merchandise. Myra, an unstoppable force of nature, was hand juicing her eighth or tenth case of oranges, a dishwasher was sweeping up sawdust, and Jason, our kitchen manager, scurried along behind the health inspector trying to explain the hurricane-like scene unfolding in our kitchen and prep space. Our managers were feverishly checking lists and Jill Stevens, our "mama hen," calmly glided through the chaos, directing the staff. I stood in the middle of it all and grinned at my wife.

"I am telling you, Bess, this is the place that will put us on the map," I said. "What are you talking about?" she shot back, as if I were having a complete mental breakdown. I had been in Oxford for sixteen years and had a half-dozen restaurants under my belt. We were not short on recognition: at City Grocery, we had been nominated for the James Beard Award several times and featured in every magazine and paper one could dream of. We were part of the ongoing conversation about Southern food and its place in our national cooking canon. So when I told her that this place—a breakfast and lunch counter that, if things didn't go the way we wanted that morning, might *never* open—was the spot that people were going to talk about, well, the comment did not compute.

Turns out, I was right—and Bess would remind me of my weird forewarning time and again in the following years, as Big Bad Breakfast grew, stretched it legs, and became the beast of a restaurant that it is now. It is not a restaurant that will vie for awards or be lauded in a roomful of puffy white men in tuxedos congratulating each other for being "swell at making food." It's a place that needed to exist. It's a place that I knew people wanted, even if they didn't know it themselves. It's a place that existed in my heart, moved to my brain, and then was born.

From the time I opened my very first restaurant, I wanted to have a breakfast place. I grew up in the last days of breakfast joints and lunch counters, of guys in crisp short-sleeved white work shirts and folded paper hats and perfectly coiffed waitresses in skirts, heels, and aprons, with pencils tucked neatly behind their ears. There were dozens of them when I was growing up in New Orleans in the late 1960s: Allgood's on the downtown/river corner of Prytania and Delachaise (we don't use *north, south, east,* or *west* in NOLA) was my absolute favorite. It looked like the New Orleans version of Edward Hopper's *Nighthawks.* Giant glass windows down the long side of the building offered an aquarium-like view of an ongoing, bustling breakfast service. Like many of the breakfast spots and old-line lunch counters, it had a chair-height bar that stretched down half of the room and offered a bird's-eye view of all of the cooking activity. Its Formica expanse was dotted like a minefield with sticky spots of syrup, jelly, and juice.

Allgood's was our go-to spot every time my grand-parents came to visit. They traveled by train, and the Southern Crescent line, which ran up the Eastern Seaboard from New Orleans to New York, left daily at a very early hour. Dad would get my brother, Richard, and I dressed, drive us to the station for a tearful good-bye on the platform, and then take us to Allgood's as a distraction/numbing agent.

The cooks used a cryptic, staccato gunfire of a language that was both exhilarating and terrifying for a wide-eyed eight-year-old. "I need a burger bridge party with a little moo, waxy, drag it through the garden. One mother and child, two babies, a hot blonde in the sand, and one black cow, break it and shake it!" (Four medium-rare burgers, dressed with cheese. One chicken and egg, two milks, a coffee with cream and sugar, and a chocolate milk shake with an added egg.) If all that stimulation wasn't enough, every corner and unused space was stacked with cake stands full of doughnuts, pies, cakes, Danishes, and muffins. They were temples to refined sugar production, a veritable nightmare for my mother, but a total amusement park

for my father, who would load us up with whatever we wanted before dumping the sugar-fueled demons on Mom as he sailed off to work.

New Orleans's Camelia Grill, K&B, Woolworth's, the Hummingbird, St. Charles Tavern, Ted's Frostop, and others like it all struck me the same way: the same sassy service ("You just warmin' dat chair or you gonna order somethin'?"); menus with an arbitrary mix of egg plates, burgers, bad steak, pancakes, (frequently wilted) chopped salad; flimsy flatware; and a variety of colored plastic tumblers. And the noises that accompanied the experience were universal, too: the barking of orders, low hum of conversation, clatter of plastic plates and cups dropping into bus tubs, and constant dinging of a bell signaling that food was ready to "walk." Those memories—moments of joy, fascination, mystery, and excitement—seared into my eight-year-old brain. I'd even argue that they're why I'm interested in this weird, wonderful business today: the New Orleans restaurants of my childhood planted a seed that would germinate years later, sprouting through the crusty surface of my ambition into an idea that flowered as Big Bad Breakfast.

2. EXODUS

Allgood's closed in the mid-1970s. (The hospital adjacent to it bought the building and knocked it down to build a hideous parking garage.) That was also the decade when the K&B and Woolworth's drugstore chains removed their lunch counters, and mom-and-pop breakfast places and diners began drying up as highway development gave rise to fast-food chains. My friend Jim Harrison explained it one night as the "parsimonious erosion of the American spirit."

Basically, dining out stopped being an experience of significance and became a simple fuel stop. We the people fell under the spell of convenient and consistent roadside food options. Independent mom-and-pops failed to compete, and home-style greasy spoons withered on the vine and died at an alarming rate. Regional cuisines, in all their beautiful, heterogeneous, immigrant-influenced glory—Mississippi Delta tamales, Illinois horseshoe sandwiches, Texan chicken-fried steak, and even New Orleans's ubiquitous po' boy—were overcome by the vomitous tidal wave of McDonald's, Denny's, Chili's, McAllister's, and Chick-fil-A. We as a nation were entirely guilty of buying into their convenience, economy, and sparkling media campaigns.

And breakfast suffered the worst. The egg muffins, non-biscuit biscuits, flavorless sausages and bacon, and precooked eggs all smashed, processed, extruded, and shoveled into each passing car bore no resemblance to the home- and diner-cooked breakfast classics that they had mutated from.

3. REVELATION

In the mid-1980s, the nation really started to right itself. Chefs all over the country began to push back against the trend of homogenization and dug into what made regional food in America special. Mark Miller set up shop in New Mexico and reinvented Southwestern cuisine, Dean Fearing elevated what we understood about Texas prairie fare, Frank Stitt gouged away at the food of the Deep South, Louis Osteen plumbed the depths of South Carolina Low Country cuisine, and Paul Prudhomme set off a bomb of interest in Cajun food. A nationwide movement was in the making, and I was lucky to find myself, and cut my teeth as a chef, right in the middle of it.

I rode the crest of that wave through the early part of my career and right into my first restaurant, City Grocery, which opened in Oxford, Mississippi, in 1992. And as limited a visionary as I was, I always wondered about breakfast. "We are told our entire lives that breakfast is the most important meal of the day," I thought, "so why isn't anybody treating it as such?"

In the years that followed the opening of City Grocery, I launched several other restaurants. Each time, I'd think about the breakfasts and brunches of my childhood— at Commander's Palace, Brennan's, Mr. B's, the Pontchartrain Hotel, Broussard's—and ponder doing something with breakfast myself. But I always backed out, fearing what would happen if I tried to assemble a team of restaurant folks who would have to regularly show up for work at 5 a.m. (In my mind, it was central casting of north Mississippi's most notorious reprobates, parolees, scallywags, vagrants, and ne'er-do-wells.)

But finally, in February 2008, I gave in to the longing. I got a call from my friend Pat Tatum, who had a piece of property off the beaten path in Oxford. Some other friends and I were boarding a plane for South America to hunt doves for a week. I explained my situation to Pat and asked if we could talk when I returned. He responded that several people had already expressed a desire for the space and that he needed a quick answer. Immediately (and futilely), I tried to dial my bride. As is normally the case, I was unsuccessful, so I called Pat back and told him I wanted to secure the space UNDER ONE CONDITION: that he not say a word to anyone before I got back home, knowing that if my wife found out I was opening another restaurant without consulting her, I would certainly find my shit out in the yard upon my return.

So I just stood there in the eye of the storm that was trying to get the restaurant open that first morning, with a health inspector who should have never passed us and two hundred or so people on the other side of giant plate glass windows. While I was entirely aware that my wife wanted to slap the shit out of me, all I could do was grin, knowing we were about to do something oddly profound. People were going to talk about it, love it, and clamor for it.

And Big Bad Breakfast has been just that. There has been more attention focused on that little fifty-four-seat space in Midtown, Oxford, than I ever dreamed of. And while calling it *the* thing to put us on the map might be considered hyperbole, it has a cult following like few other restaurants I have ever known. We opened a second location on the outskirts of Birmingham, Alabama, on the bet that the idea has legs and that we could develop a flock outside of Oxford. It has been successful enough that we are building a third location, and more are planned after that one is complete.

We make breakfast right at Big Bad Breakfast. We apply the same principles to breakfast as other establishments would devote to lunch and dinner. Our front-of-the-house staff is educated, warm, courteous, and thoughtful. In the kitchen, we make things from scratch that most people never dream of. We make our own jellies and jams from local fruits and berries, and cure and smoke our own meats. We have our corn grown and ground into grits to our specifications and our coffee blended just for us. There is a single person on the premises who only makes biscuits and another who spends most of his/her time squeezing fresh fruit juice.

Our staff at the Oxford, Mississippi, and Birmingham, Alabama, restaurants—both front and back of the house—work tirelessly to choreograph the daily ballet that is the Big Bad Breakfast service. A relentless barrage of people come through the doors, and the folks who work for us understand exactly how special what they are doing is and what it means.

We've put breakfast back exactly where it is supposed to be—revered, respected, and adored. At Big Bad Breakfast, even if absolutely nowhere else, we treat breakfast as THE MOST IMPORTANT MEAL OF THE DAY, and this is how we do it . . .

THE TEN COMMANDMENTS OF BREAKFAST

1. **THOU SHALT EMBRACETH THE DAY.** First, accept that every day is new, fresh, and unique. Position yourself in the kitchen with an attitude that reflects your solemn purpose: you are about to prepare THE MOST IMPORTANT MEAL OF THE DAY, likely for someone you care for (otherwise you would not be up and at 'em at the stove).

2. **THOU SHALT HOLD NO MEAL HIGHER THAN BREAKFAST.** Commit to raising this disregarded meal from the depths of neglect to the place of honor it deserves. Pledge to put the same effort and passion into preparing breakfast as you would lunch or dinner. In other words, make something other than just a plate of eggs.

3. **THOU SHALT GET THY MIND RIGHT.** This is fun, damn it. Plan ahead so you don't stress yourself out early in the morning: shop the day before, stock strong coffee, prep certain items in advance, and find some music that gets you going in the wee hours. All of these will make the chore at hand a little easier.

4. **THOU SHALT SLATHER WITH BUTTER.** It will not kill you (consumed in quantities within reason, that is). Just let go for a few minutes and enjoy life a little. No fat tastes better on toast with jelly or when cooking eggs (bacon fat included).

5. **THOU SHALT ANOINTETH WITH BLACK PEPPER.** Whenever pepper is called for in an ingredients list, use freshly cracked black pepper. (The only exception is when I specifically call for white pepper.)

6. **THOU SHALT MAKE FROM SCRATCH.** It will certainly take more time and effort, but the essence of Big Bad Breakfast is scratch cooking. It's what made grandmother's cooking "grandmother's cooking." As a matter of fact, I am certain that if my grandmothers and great-grandmothers had not succumbed to other, more natural afflictions, shame over what we accept as food these days would certainly have consumed each of them.

7. **THOU SHALT USE RESTRAINT WITH INGREDIENTS.** Lots of folks get the wrong idea about recipes and lean toward "the more flavors and ingredients I add, the more complex the end product." This could not be farther from the truth. The best cooking celebrates the elemental beauty of ingredients. You want to be able to taste everything in the dish, not create something that is just a muddle.

8. **THOU SHALT SEEKETH LOCAL WHENEVER POSSIBLE.** Honey, eggs, grits, bacon, sausage, jellies, coffee, flour—whatever it is, a local product is more often than not going to have a more singular character. Visit farmers' markets, bake sales, local farms, and locally owned grocery stores.

9. **THOU SHALT NOT OVERCOOK.** I am fascinated with the American worry about "undercooking things." Food can always be cooked more if it is not cooked enough, but YOU CAN'T FUCKING UNCOOK IT if you cook it too long. Granted, we shouldn't rub raw factory chicken on our toast right before we eat, but I have been making fresh mayonnaise and Caesar dressing with raw eggs for thirty-five years and nobody has ever been sick. Trichinosis is not carried by domestic pigs, and a piece of cooked pork that's still a little pink beats the crap out of a well-done, dried-out offering. Try the yolk runny, people. With a little salt, it transforms dishes from good to resplendent.

10. **THOU SHALT REMEMBER THE SABBATH, BUT COOK FROM THIS BOOK EVERY DAY.** You can make pancakes for your kids, freeze them, and rewarm them later. You can make a breakfast casserole or assemble sweet rolls the night before and just turn on the oven the next day. Breakfast is a fun meal, and most of the time, it doesn't require a ton of effort or mess. More often than not, it's just about clearing your eyes and committing to loved ones. Remember, breakfast is a joy, not a chore, and the possibilities are endless. It just comes at a weird time of day. And if that's the deal breaker for you, well, shit, make breakfast for dinner.

THE WELCOME BASKET

MY BUSINESS PARTNER IN BIRMINGHAM, NICK PIHAKIS, IS A GENIUS at opening and operating restaurants. (He has shit for taste when it comes to college football, but that's another matter.) We partnered up eight years after opening the original Big Bad Breakfast location in Oxford, Mississippi, and as he and I prepared to open our second location in Birmingham, Alabama, we spent months talking through what we would do to make Big Bad Breakfast even better. One of the ideas we struck on was to give a welcome basket. Nick had the brilliant idea of dropping something warm, sweet, salty, and satisfying in front of folks the minute they sat down. It was a wonderful idea and gave me pause to really reconsider the whole way we think about breakfast.

CHAPTER 1

We approach breakfast, more often than not, like a battle offensive rather than a meal. It is, for all intents and purposes, a surgical strike with the goal of consuming, as quickly as possible, whatever calories we need to get us to a midday meal. We're in a hurry. We're starting our day and have that day's agenda on our minds. There are kids to consider; their schedules, needs, and desires. Breakfast is rarely a meal we approach with the same care and aplomb as we do dinner. And for a restaurant, the service plan and organization is given a completely different consideration.

A restaurant's breakfast service is an immense challenge for any number of reasons, not the least of which is that it is, at least 99 percent of the time, the first meal of the day. If we're lucky, our guests have had a cup of coffee before arriving. People arrive hungry and eating is the matter at hand. Our protocol is to get them coffee, hot chocolate, or tea right away followed by food as soon as is humanly possible. When we're running efficiently in Oxford, the time between when an order is printed in the kitchen and when food lands on the table is about three minutes and forty-five seconds. When it's busy, that time can get upward of nine minutes. If it gets over ten, we're in trouble.

But what if the world could slow down and we could enjoy breakfast in the same way we do lunch or dinner? Maybe sit down to have a discussion about what we hope to accomplish that day, savor the nuanced flavors and textures assembled in the dish, and wax philosophical about a book we've recently read? Big Bad Breakfast was built to be that kind of place.

The welcome basket was conceived in hopes of changing our diners' mentalities. If we could place an offering on the table as soon as our guests sat down, giving them something fun to nibble on that would also buy us a few precious seconds to prepare their food, it could be a win-win for everyone. The reality, though, is that we couldn't change people's schedules and thought patterns. They want to eat in a hurry, and there's a ceiling to what you can charge for breakfast. And folks typically know exactly what they want to eat in the early hours of the morning. Fiddling with any of these cards would do nothing but bring the house down.

The welcome basket, as a result, remains a dream. We developed some ideas for it and all of them are perfect for a more laid-back setting. As it turned out, it would never work out for us, no matter how badly I wanted to change the world with our breakfast. In the restaurant business, things just move too fast in the mornings and folks have too much on their minds. At home, though, it's a different story. Imagine a basket being set in front of you before a special breakfast and you really had time to nibble and enjoy it. The recipes in this chapter are what I would put in it. Maybe you go after it one Saturday morning and offer it up to family and friends. Let me know how it works out. Twenty bucks says they put you up on their shoulders and carry you around the fucking block.

SAUSAGE CINNAMON ROLLS

MAKES 14 ROLLS

I have a primal weakness for the combination of sweet and salty flavors. I still remember the first time I combined some of my granddad's spicy breakfast sausage with pancakes and Karo syrup on my fork and took them down in one bite. I was a very young child, but I became a devout believer in the combination, immediately. Cinnamon rolls have been a special that has floated in and out of our repertoire for years, and one day it dawned on me that adding sausage to them might induce the same euphoric reaction I remember as a youngster. Guess what? Damn right they do! These rolls require a commitment, but you can bet your sweet ass they are worth all of the work.

DOUGH

1 (¼-ounce) package active dry yeast

1 cup warm whole milk (100°F)

4½ cups all-purpose flour

½ cup granulated sugar

⅓ cup unsalted butter, melted

2 eggs, at room temperature

1 teaspoon salt

FILLING

1 cup firmly packed light brown sugar

1 cup cooked breakfast sausage, crumbled

¼ cup unsalted butter, at room temperature

2½ tablespoons ground cinnamon

ICING

1½ cups confectioners' sugar

3 ounces cream cheese, at room temperature

¼ cup unsalted butter, at room temperature

½ teaspoon pure vanilla extract

⅛ teaspoon salt

¼ cup unsalted butter, at room temperature

Preheat the oven to 350°F.

To make the dough, in the bowl of a stand mixer, dissolve the yeast in the warm milk and whisk together well. Allow to stand in the bowl for 5 to 7 minutes, or until the mixture begins to look a little foamy on top. Add the flour, granulated sugar, butter, eggs, and salt. Attach the dough hook and knead the dough on low to medium speed until it begins to come together, about 2 minutes. Transfer the dough to a floured surface. Dust your hands lightly with flour and then knead the dough for 3 to 4 minutes until it's smooth and elastic. Form the dough into a large ball.

Transfer the dough to a medium bowl that is coated with cooking spray. Cover the bowl tightly with plastic wrap and let the dough rise in a warm place until doubled, about 1 hour. (At Big Bad Breakfast, we set the bowl on the stove top above a warmed oven. The radiant heat helps the dough to rise.) To test if the dough is ready, poke it with your fingertip. If the indention remains, it's ready.

Once your dough has risen, make the filling: In a small bowl, stir together the brown sugar, sausage, butter, and cinnamon. Set aside.

To make the icing, in a stand mixer with the paddle attachment, beat together the confectioners' sugar, cream cheese, butter, vanilla, and salt on medium speed until combined. Set aside.

To assemble the rolls, turn out the dough onto a floured surface and roll it into a 21 by 16-inch rectangle that's about ¼ inch thick. Spread the ¼ cup butter over the dough, then evenly sprinkle with the sausage filling. With the long side facing you, roll the dough into a tight log.

Using a sharp knife, cut crosswise into 14 slices (if you prefer smaller rolls, cut more slices). Place the cinnamon rolls in a lightly greased 15 by 11-inch glass baking dish. Cover loosely with plastic wrap and let rise, again in a warm place, until nearly doubled, about 30 minutes.

Once your cinnamon rolls have risen, bake them until golden brown, 18 to 20 minutes. The rolls should be brown on top with a light crust.

Take the rolls out of the oven and allow to cool for 8 to 10 minutes. With an offset spatula or icing paddle, spread the icing on them while they're still warm. The frosting should melt into the cinnamon rolls, but not run off completely. Serve immediately.

BUTTERMILK CAKE DOUGHNUTS

MAKES 15 TO 18 DOUGHNUTS

My brother, Richard, is my best friend. It definitely wasn't always that way, though. During our younger years, I treated him like a booger I couldn't flick off my finger. I was an asshole of a big brother. We were a lot like modern-day Republicans and Democrats. Whatever he chose to love, I immediately chose to hate, regardless of its empirical goodness or badness. I was a total turd.

We lived a half block from a local New Orleans bakery chain that made insanely good doughnuts, cakes, petits fours, pastries, and breads. Once every couple of weeks, Mom would give us a couple of bucks and send us off to buy breakfast. Invariably, Richard would order one of the colossal, baseball-size buttermilk cake doughnuts, and I would jump immediately into the Bavarian cream–filled doughnut. We would share a pint of Brown's Velvet Dutch Chocolate Milk, and for a moment there was peace between the two of us. I like to think there was a mutual admiration for the choices each of us made, but that was certainly never spoken.

This recipe produces doughnuts that are more bite-size—a better product, in my estimation, though they are outstanding no matter what shape they take. Just have the chocolate milk ready.

VANILLA GLAZE (OPTIONAL)

2 cups confectioners' sugar

1 teaspoon pure vanilla extract

2 to 4 tablespoons whole milk

Vegetable oil, for frying

1 cup all-purpose flour

2 teaspoons granulated sugar

1 teaspoon baking powder

½ teaspoon ground ginger

½ teaspoon ground nutmeg

¼ teaspoon baking soda

½ cup buttermilk

1 egg

Cinnamon sugar, confectioners' sugar, or vanilla glaze, for topping (optional)

To make the glaze, stir together the confectioners' sugar, vanilla, and 2 to 4 tablespoons milk, until the glaze reaches the consistency of heavy cream.

Pour 3 inches of oil into a deep skillet or countertop fryer and heat over medium heat to 350°F. Turn the heat to low and hold at this temperature.

To make the doughnuts, whisk together the flour, granulated sugar, baking powder, ginger, nutmeg, and baking soda in a large bowl, then make a well in the center. When the oil is hot, whisk together the buttermilk and egg in a separate bowl, then pour them into the well, stirring gently just until combined.

Drop the batter by rounded tablespoons into the hot oil, 8 to 10 at a time, being careful not to crowd the pan. Fry until golden brown on all sides (they should turn over by themselves as they cook), 2 to 3 minutes.

Remove from the oil with a slotted spoon. Drain the doughnuts on paper towels, then roll in cinnamon sugar or confectioners' sugar, or drizzle with the glaze while the doughnuts are still hot. These are best served immediately, but will still represent well for a couple of hours at room temperature.

BANANA PECAN COFFEE CAKE

MAKES ONE 8-INCH SQUARE CAKE

McKenzie's Bakery is a sadly shuttered chain of New Orleans bakeries. What was wonderful was that, unlike like many present-day chains, the McKenzie's stores each baked their own product daily from scratch. There was no central commissary that trucked products to the individual stores, and they did not work from homogenized premixed batches full of fillers, cheapened ingredients, chemicals, and preservatives. As a result, the neighborhoods lucky enough to house a McKenzie's always smelled delicious. It's a wonder there wasn't a Saturn's belt of obesity that developed around each of them.

Their banana nut coffee cake was a masterpiece of affordability. A 9-inch cake cost all of $1.99 and would feed me and my brother breakfast for at least two days, if not three. My version of McKenzie's coffee cake was on the original Sunday brunch menu at City Grocery, and I still like to throw it together when we have a houseful of guests.

Feel free to leave out the nuts and/or substitute chopped strawberries or blueberries for the banana. Whatever you do, just make it. It's too easy a crowd-pleaser.

Preheat the oven to 375°F. Grease an 8-inch square baking pan.

To make the cake, in a large bowl with an electric mixer, cream the granulated sugar and butter at medium speed until fluffy, about 5 minutes. Add the bananas, sour cream, and egg and mix until combined.

Stir together the flour, baking powder, baking soda, nutmeg, and salt in a separate bowl. Add the flour mixture to the banana mixture, and then the milk. Beat until well combined. Pour the batter into the prepared baking pan.

To make the topping, in a small bowl, stir together the flour, sugars, and cinnamon. With a pastry blender or your fingertips, work the cold butter into the flour mixture until coarse crumbs form. Sprinkle the topping over the batter, followed by the pecans.

Bake until golden brown across the top, 35 to 40 minutes. Drizzle with glaze and let cool for 10 minutes or slightly longer before cutting into squares or wedges. Serve immediately or cover with a cake cover or kitchen towel for up to 2 days.

CAKE

⅓ cup granulated sugar

¼ cup unsalted butter or margarine, at room temperature

2 soft, ripe bananas, mashed

¼ cup sour cream

1 egg

1¼ cups all-purpose flour

1 tablespoon baking powder

½ teaspoon baking soda

¼ teaspoon ground nutmeg

¼ teaspoon salt

¼ cup whole milk

TOPPING

¼ cup all-purpose flour

¼ cup firmly packed light brown sugar

2 tablespoons granulated sugar

½ teaspoon ground cinnamon

3 tablespoons very cold, unsalted butter, cut into pieces

⅓ cup toasted chopped pecans

Honey Buns glaze (optional, see page 18)

SOURDOUGH ENGLISH MUFFINS

MAKES FIFTEEN 3-INCH MUFFINS

Other than the fact that the first English muffin was created by Samuel B. Thomas, there is a lot of differing opinion on the origins of this breakfast bread. The only thing English about the muffin is the birthplace of its inventor. Thomas, by all accounts, was an Englishman living in the United States, and his first English muffin was probably the product of a failed crumpet recipe. Even so, his delicious yeast-leavened griddle cakes were a smash.

These muffins require a commitment to make a sourdough starter (which will take about a week to get rolling). Whether you make the starter and feed it for continued use or just make a single-use batch matters not. Either way, the starter, once seeded, will grow into the yeasty brilliance that makes these muffins truly delicious. If you commit to a starter, it can become sort of like a child. It requires a little bit of love and care every day and you'll find you want to put it in everything. It adds moisture and punch to cakes, makes delicious pancakes and dinner rolls, and little in this world smells better than a loaf of sourdough bread cooking. It needs the right ingredients, though. Unbleached all-purpose flour and unchlorinated water are keys to a healthy, bubbly starter.

A dear friend of our family makes these muffins every Christmas to give as gifts. Once you have the starter, the muffins couldn't be easier to make. Little smells better than these suckers cooking.

½ cup warm water
(108°F to 115°F)

½ cup warm milk
(108°F to 115°F)

1½ tablespoons sugar

1 (¼-ounce) package active dry yeast

1½ cups all-purpose flour

¾ cup sourdough starter
(recipe follows)

1½ cups bread flour

3 tablespoons unsalted butter, melted, plus more for cooking

2 teaspoons salt

Cornmeal, for dusting

Clarified butter (page 30), for frying

In the bowl of a stand mixer, whisk together the warm water, milk, sugar, and yeast and let stand until the yeast dissolves and gets foamy, 7 to 10 minutes. Whisk in ½ cup of the all-purpose flour and the starter to the yeast mixture and let stand for 10 minutes more.

Attach the paddle to the stand mixer, add ½ cup of the bread flour, the melted butter, and salt, and mix on medium speed until well blended, about 2 minutes.

Replace the paddle attachment with the dough hook. Add the remaining 1 cup all-purpose flour and the remaining 1 cup bread flour and knead the dough on low speed until a ball begins to form.

Continue to knead on low speed until the dough is soft and elastic and no longer sticks to the sides of the bowl, about 5 minutes more. If the dough is too sticky, add more flour, a little bit at a time, until no longer sticky.

Gather the dough into a round. Transfer to an oiled bowl and turn once to coat the dough with oil. Cover the bowl tightly with plastic wrap and let rise in a warm place until doubled, about 1 hour. To test if the dough is ready, poke it with your fingertip. If the indention remains, it's ready.

Dust a sheet of parchment paper with cornmeal. Turn out the dough onto a lightly floured surface. Punch it down and let rest for 10 minutes. Cut the dough in half and shape into 2 balls. Roll out one of the dough rounds until it's ¾ inch thick. Using a 3-inch round biscuit cutter (or whichever size you prefer), cut into rounds. Transfer to the parchment paper, spacing them about 3 inches apart. Dust the tops with cornmeal. Repeat with the second dough ball. Cover loosely with plastic wrap and let rise in a warm place until doubled, about 45 minutes.

Preheat the oven to 350°F.

Warm 2 tablespoons of clarified butter on a griddle or in a large skillet over medium heat. Working in batches, place the muffins on the griddle (or pan) and cook until golden brown, 3 or 4 minutes on each side. Once browned, transfer to a cookie sheet and bake for an additional 7 minutes.

Remove from the oven and allow to cool briefly until they can be handled. Split with a fork and serve immediately. Extra muffins can be refrigerated for up to 2 days or frozen for up to 8 weeks.

SOURDOUGH STARTER
MAKES 1½ CUPS

½ cup rye or whole wheat flour

½ cup unbleached all-purpose flour, plus more for feeding

1 teaspoon sugar

¾ cup distilled water, plus more for feeding

In a nonreactive bowl, or a large glass measuring cup or jar, stir together the flours and sugar. Stir in the distilled water until thoroughly combined. Cover loosely with a kitchen towel and let stand in a warm place (above 70°F) for 24 hours.

On the second day, bubbles should form; if they haven't, re-cover the starter and let stand for another day. Once bubbles form, feed the starter by discarding half of it, then stir in 1 cup all-purpose flour and 1 cup distilled water until thoroughly combined. On the third day, feed the starter twice, once in the morning and once in the evening. Continue feeding the starter twice a day until it bubbles vigorously after 8 hours of feeding and gives off a very nice sour, earthy smell. After 5 or 6 days, your starter will be ready to use.

Once ready to use, store the starter in the refrigerator. It will slow fermentation significantly and you will only need to feed it every 3 or 4 days. Mine lives in a mason jar and sits on our kitchen counter and I feed it every day. My wife hates our special relationship, but loves what we make together . . .

NOTES

1. You don't have to discard your starter as it grows, though it will grow exponentially if you do not, so consider this fair warning. This recipe will net you about 1½ cups of starter a day. If you are going to bake with starter regularly, find the volume that fits your needs and work from there.

2. If a light brown liquid accumulates on the surface, do not worry, just stir it in. It is an alcohol by-product of the fermentation process.

3. If any green- or blue-colored growth begins to form on top of your starter, discard the batch and begin again. These are mold spores and will not hurt you, but don't have an appealing flavor.

DRIED FIG CALAS

MAKES ABOUT A DOZEN CALAS

Cala is a sweetened rice fritter that we can thank the Creole cooks of seventeenth- and eighteenth-century New Orleans for gifting us. The cala is similar to the beignet, but its history tells a richer story of New Orleans. One might even argue that it is has a more important history than any other in the New Orleans food canon.

In the latter part of the eighteenth century, West African slaves were being brought to the States to help grow rice, a nonindigenous crop that was largely unfamiliar to Southern settlers. And so cala, a traditional dish of Western Africa, also made the trip.

The Code Noir—the French decree that governed how whites, slaves, and free blacks would live together in the French colonies—allowed free blacks to live very independent lives in New Orleans. Many of them were professionals and several even held spots in the local legislature. As part of the Code Noir, all slaves were guaranteed a day off each week, usually Sunday. Congo Square, which served as the slave market the rest of the week, became a hub of activity on Sundays, with music, dancing, and artisans selling their wares. It was an opportunity for slaves to generate income for themselves and their families. On Sundays, it was common to hear women wandering the French Quarter, singing, "*Belles calas, tout chauds!*" which translates as "Beautiful calas, very hot!"

The Code Noir also dictated that should a slave approach his master with the money to buy his freedom, the master was required to honor the purchase. It's more than conceivable that the humble cala led to the freedom of many a Louisiana slave.

Calas are delightful little bites. I add figs here, but you can substitute any reconstituted dried fruit or chopped fresh fruit. Calas need little more than a dusting of confectioners' sugar, though a drizzle of good cane syrup elevates them to another level. They are a delightful surprise that most folks have never had the pleasure of eating, and they couldn't be easier to make.

Vegetable oil, for frying
½ cup all-purpose flour
¼ cup granulated sugar
1 tablespoon baking soda
½ teaspoon salt
2 eggs, lightly beaten
3 tablespoons buttermilk
2 teaspoons pure vanilla extract
2 cups cooked, long-grain white rice
½ cup chopped dried figs
Confectioners' sugar, for dusting

Pour 3 inches of oil into a deep skillet or countertop fryer and heat to 350°F.

Stir together the flour, granulated sugar, baking soda, and salt in a medium-sized mixing bowl. Stir in the eggs, buttermilk, and vanilla until fully combined. Stir in the rice and figs until just combined. The batter should be relatively stiff.

Drop the batter by rounded tablespoons into the hot oil, 6 to 8 at a time, being careful not to crowd the pan. Fry until golden brown on all sides (they should turn over by themselves as they cook), 3 to 4 minutes. Remove from the oil with a slotted spoon and drain on paper towels. Dust the tops with confectioners' sugar while they're still warm. Serve immediately.

HONEY BUNS

MAKES 8 TO 10 BUNS

The world is a slightly sadder place than it once was, simply due to the fact that my grandparents' general store in Lenoir, North Carolina, is no longer around. McDonald's General Store was a slice of Americana that filled a need that has since been eliminated; a need for comfort, community, and commiseration that was taken out at the knees with the advent of drive-thru. Our McDonald's is where the locals used to come for coffee and ham biscuits, sit around the woodstove, and share the morning paper. Ladies came for sliced bologna, hoop cheese (similar to farmer cheese), bread, eggs, and milk, and the men would play checkers and argue about politics, Lions Club softball, and the "way young'uns act these days."

Every morning, the bakery truck delivered racks of bread and buns, cakes and pies. The prize among them was the tray of fresh honey buns. I must have plowed through a thousand of them during my summers with my grandparents. They are sticky, sweet, soft, chewy, and *always* better slightly warm. A honey bun is the ticket to a young'un's heart. Trust me.

DOUGH

3 (¼-oz) packages dry active yeast

½ cup warm water (115°F)

7½ cups all-purpose flour

2¼ cups scalded whole milk, cooled to 108° to 115°F

¾ cup granulated sugar

½ cup lard

3 eggs, lightly beaten

1½ teaspoons salt

CINNAMON SUGAR

½ cup ground cinnamon

1 cup granulated sugar

GLAZE (OPTIONAL, BUT YOU'D BE AN IDIOT TO LEAVE IT OUT)

1 cup confectioners' sugar

¼ cup honey

1 tablespoon pure vanilla extract

2 tablespoons whole milk

3 tablespoons unsalted butter, melted

Vegetable oil, for frying

Unsalted butter, for serving (optional)

To make the dough, in the bowl of a stand mixer, stir together the yeast and warm water and let stand until the yeast dissolves and gets foamy, about 5 minutes. Add 3¼ cups of the flour, the milk, granulated sugar, lard, eggs, and salt. Attach the paddle and knead the dough on low speed until fully combined, about 3 or 4 minutes. Replace the paddle with the dough hook. Slowly add as much of the remaining 4¼ cups flour as needed until the dough no longer sticks to the bowl, about 6 or 7 minutes. Transfer the dough to a floured work surface. Dust your hands lightly with flour, then knead the dough until it's smooth and elastic, about 5 minutes.

Form the dough into a large ball. Transfer the dough to a large bowl oiled generously with vegetable oil. Turn the dough ball to coat fully with the oil. Cover the bowl loosely with plastic wrap and let the dough rise in a warm place until doubled in size, about 1 hour. To test if the dough is ready, poke it with your fingertip. If the indention remains, it's ready.

To make the cinnamon sugar, in a small bowl, stir together the cinnamon and granulated sugar. Set aside.

To assemble the buns, turn out the dough onto a floured surface and gently roll it into a large log. Cut into 8 or 10 even-sized pieces. Roll each piece of dough into a ¾-inch-diameter log and roll that log in the cinnamon sugar. Coil the log like a garden hose on a nonstick baking sheet, and sprinkle again with the cinnamon sugar.

Cover loosely with plastic wrap and let rise in a warm place until doubled, about 45 minutes.

To make the glaze, in a small bowl, stir together the confectioners' sugar, honey, vanilla, milk, and melted butter. Set aside.

Pour 1 inch of oil into a deep skillet or countertop fryer and heat to 350°F. Place the buns in the hot oil, 2 at a time, being careful not to crowd the pan. Fry, turning once, until light brown on both sides, about 3 minutes per side. Remove from the oil with a large slotted spatula and drain on paper towels. While the buns are still warm, spread butter over the tops or drizzle with the glaze along with more cinnamon sugar.

BLUEBERRY MUFFIN TOPS

MAKES ABOUT 20 MUFFIN TOPS

There is an undeniable appeal to the top of a muffin. After all, the bottom is nothing but cake without icing. There are folks out there (like my wife) who are just as happy to eat any part of a muffin. And while I know I should be glad those folks exist because they up the percentage of muffin tops available for consumption, I can't help but feel like they're a little dead inside.

I wrote this recipe as part of a four-course dessert smorgasbord for Hogs for the Cause, an outstanding barbecue cook-off in New Orleans that raises money for children's cancer research. My buddy Stephen Stryjewski of Cochon fame assigned me the dessert course as a joke. To show I was a good sport, I made the most gigantic dessert course ever conceived. These muffin tops were part of the "Stoner Basket" that went to each table, along with brownie edges, chocolate potato chips, curried chocolate haystacks, and peach gummie sours. They were exactly the hit we had expected them to be. Your people will love them, too.

MUFFINS

6 tablespoons unsalted butter

⅓ cup whole milk

1 egg plus 1 yolk

1 teaspoon pure vanilla extract

1½ cups all-purpose flour

¾ cup plus 2 tablespoons granulated sugar

1½ teaspoons baking powder

½ teaspoon salt

2 cups fresh blueberries (frozen are acceptable if you must make these out of season)

TOPPING

4½ tablespoons unsalted butter, cut into bits and frozen

1 cup all-purpose flour

½ cup firmly packed light brown sugar

Preheat the oven to 350°F.

To make the muffin batter, melt the butter in a pan on the stove top over low heat or in a measuring cup in the microwave. Whisk in the milk, egg and yolk, and vanilla until well combined.

Stir together the flour, granulated sugar, baking powder, and salt in a large bowl. Pour in the milk mixture and stir together until just combined. Fold in the blueberries gently but thoroughly.

To make the topping, combine the frozen butter, flour, and brown sugar in a food processor and pulse until combined and it resembles a very coarse meal.

Spoon the batter 2 heaping tablespoons at a time onto a Silpat or a nonstick baking sheet, spread to about a ½ inch thick, and sprinkle generously with the topping. Bake until a cake tester comes out clean, about 15 minutes.

These are certainly best warm, but will remain almost as good for up to 2 days. Store at room temperature under a cake dome.

RUM RAISIN AND ORANGE SCONES

MAKES 18 SCONES

My parents are amazing and wonderful people. Both came from incredibly modest upbringings. Both are insanely smart and, as a result, successful. Both wanted as much as anything to treat my brother and me to things they were not afforded growing up. And while we weren't lavished with material goods, we were rich in experience.

We lived for several years in the mid–1970s in the UK. During that time, we traveled extensively, and eating was as much a part of our education as anything. On a trip to London, Mom and Dad decided we needed to experience high tea at the Savoy Hotel. It was truly a quintessential moment; it was also entirely lost on a couple of hyperactive, self-interested young boys who would rather be looking at mummies and dinosaurs at the Natural History Museum.

Even worse were the dry scones and tasteless clotted cream we had to choke down. The two of us could not have behaved worse, staging our protest by overreacting to these unpalatable "treats." We were both dragged by the ear from the tearoom of that beautiful hotel by our furious and embarrassed parents. That moment framed my opinion of the scone as the scourge of the pastry world.

Well, it turns out that scones, in the hands of a loving Southern cook, are an absolute delight. The flavor combinations you can dream up for scones are endless, but this recipe combines a couple of my favorites. Straight out of the oven, these are almost impossible to beat.

½ cup raisins

½ cup rum

2½ cups all-purpose flour

¼ cup granulated sugar

1 tablespoon baking powder

½ teaspoon coarse salt

½ cup cold unsalted butter, cut into small pieces, plus 2 tablespoons melted

½ cup buttermilk

1 tablespoon finely grated orange zest plus ¼ cup orange juice (from 1 orange)

1 egg yolk

Coarse or sanding sugar, for sprinkling

Honey Buns glaze (optional, see page 18)

Set the racks in the upper and lower thirds of the oven and preheat to 400°F. Line 2 rimmed baking sheets with parchment paper.

Combine the raisins and rum in a sauté pan and warm over medium heat for 3 minutes. Set aside and allow to steep while you make the dough.

In a large bowl, whisk together the flour, granulated sugar, baking powder, and salt. With a pastry blender or your fingertips, work the cold butter into the flour mixture until it resembles coarse meal; a few pea-size pieces of butter should remain. With a fork, stir in the buttermilk, orange zest and juice, plumped raisins, and egg yolk until just combined.

Turn out the dough onto a floured surface and knead several times. The dough should just barely hold together and large pieces of butter should be visible throughout. Pat the dough into a 7-inch square. Cut into 9 smaller squares, then cut each square in half on the diagonal. Transfer the scones to the prepared baking sheets.

Brush the tops with the melted butter and sprinkle with coarse sugar. Bake until the tops are golden brown, 15 to 17 minutes. Let cool briefly on wire racks and then drizzle with glaze. Serve warm.

MONKEY BREAD

I firmly stand behind the conviction that there are moments when only the most ridiculous store-bought products will suffice. There are times when only French's yellow mustard or the cheapest hamburger dill pickles will make a certain recipe work. My enormously sweet buddy Chris Sheppard and I spent a boozy hour in NOLA recently expounding the virtues of Miracle Whip to a couple of bewildered young line cooks. And monkey bread is one of those recipes that calls for an ingredient that some people might deem unthinkable: refrigerated biscuit dough.

We worked on this recipe for weeks when we got ready to open City Grocery for brunch service. We tried different biscuit recipes and cooking methods, but until I threw up my hands one day and sent someone to buy a store-bought can of biscuit dough, it didn't come close to working. On first test run, while not perfect, the Pillsbury Grands monkey bread blew any of the scratch biscuit attempts out of the water.

¾ cup granulated sugar

1½ teaspoons ground cinnamon

½ teaspoon ground nutmeg

¾ cup chopped mixed nut topping (see Note)

½ cup dried currants

½ cup diced Granny Smith apple

2 (16-ounce) cans biscuits, each biscuit cut into quarters

1¼ cups firmly packed dark brown sugar

1 cup (2 sticks) unsalted butter, melted

2 teaspoons pure vanilla extract

Preheat the oven to 350°F. Lightly oil a 9-inch round or square cake pan.

Combine the granulated sugar, cinnamon, and nutmeg in a gallon-size zip-top plastic bag. In a bowl, toss the nuts, currants, and apple with 2 tablespoons of the sugar mixture, then spread in the bottom of the prepared pan.

Add the biscuits to the bag, seal the bag, and toss to combine well. Layer the biscuit pieces and sugar mixture evenly in a single layer in the pan on top of the nuts, currants, and apple. Don't be concerned if the biscuits don't fit perfectly. They will expand to fill out the pan.

In a small saucepan, warm the brown sugar, butter, and vanilla over medium heat until it reaches a very low simmer. Turn off the heat and pour the sugar mixture evenly over the biscuit pieces. Bake until golden brown and puffed up nicely, about 25 minutes. Remove from the oven and allow to cool for 3 or 4 minutes, then turn out onto a large serving plate. Serve warm and pull off the individual pieces to eat.

NOTE: Chopped mixed nut topping is available in the bakery aisle of the grocery store.

BAKED CORNMEAL AND BUTTERMILK DOUGHNUTS

MAKES 18 TO 20 DOUGHNUTS

Phoebe Lawless is as cool as the other side of the pillow. If you are ever anywhere within a hundred miles of Durham, North Carolina, do yourself a favor and go see her at her über bakery, Scratch. Then call me and tell me you are naming your next child after me.

In 2009, Phoebe came to Oxford to cook a breakfast for the Southern Foodways Symposium. She offered versions of Appalachian livermush and a baked doughnut I am still thinking about all these years later. I like this doughnut because it is, arguably, a healthy alternative to their delicious, fried cousins. I was inspired by Phoebe's recipe, and while my ham-fisted attempt is admittedly a pale imitation of Ms. Lawless's masterpiece, it'll do in a pinch. These are great plain, dusted with powdered sugar, or drizzled with glaze.

You'll need a nonstick doughnut pan to bake these in. Alternately, a mini Bundt pan will work, or you can partially fill openings in a muffin pan and bake.

1½ cups sugar

½ cup unsalted butter, at room temperature

3 eggs

2½ teaspoons pure vanilla extract

Zest and juice of 1 lemon

½ teaspoon almond extract

3 cups all-purpose flour

1½ cups cornmeal

1 tablespoon baking powder

¼ teaspoon baking soda

½ teaspoon salt

¼ teaspoon ground cinnamon

Pinch of ground cloves

1¼ cups buttermilk

Honey Buns glaze (see page 18)

Preheat the oven to 350°F.

In the bowl of a stand mixer fitted with the paddle attachment, cream the sugar and butter at medium speed until light and fluffy, about 7 minutes. Add the eggs, one at a time, beating for 30 seconds after each addition, until fully combined and smooth. Add the vanilla, lemon zest, lemon juice, and almond extract and beat until combined.

In a large bowl, stir together the flour, cornmeal, baking powder, baking soda, salt, cinnamon, and cloves. Add the dry ingredients to the batter ½ to ¾ cup at a time, mixing on medium until fully combined, about 30 seconds or so after each addition.

Add the buttermilk and mix until fully combined, about 30 seconds.

Spoon the batter into a nonstick doughnut pan and bake until the tops are golden brown, 17 to 20 minutes. (You may need to bake the doughnuts in batches.) Remove from the oven, allow to cool, and turn out of the pan. Drizzle with glaze and serve immediately.

THE INCREDIBLE, EDIBLE, OMNIPRESENT EGG

WE ONCE FOUND AN EMU EGG IN THE PARKING LOT BEHIND CITY
Grocery. (At least we assume it was an emu egg—it may have been
the egg of a pterodactyl or some kind of giant man-eating reptile.)
Of course, we had no real idea of how it got there, nor did we care.
The mystery was as much a part of the excitement of finding this
giant, weird-as-fuck, alien egg thing in the 110°F parking lot behind
the restaurant and in relative proximity to the Dumpster.

For anyone who has been living under a rock since
Kitchen Confidential was published, kitchens are
filled with reprobates, derelicts, and potheads. I tell
you this only to make it easier to understand that the
immediate impulse from my fellow kitchen pirates
that day was to cook and eat the monster egg. So, we
cracked it open (the shell was as thick as a quarter)
and scrambled it with salt, pepper, some onions
and peppers, and hot sauce. It was categorically
unremarkable, apart from the fact that we had found
it in the parking lot. The girls at work that day were
thoroughly disgusted. I am pretty sure one got sick at
the sight of us eating this thing. Had we found *anything*
else out is the parking lot behind the restaurant, we
would have never dreamed of cooking it, but the egg . . .
well, it just couldn't be denied. The moral of the story
is that the plebeian egg has an undeniable magic. We
could not ignore its siren song that day in the parking
lot, even if we had wanted to.

We're not the only ones to have noticed the magic of
eggs. Until recently, the egg was mostly relegated to
breakfast, with the occasional addition to a salad or
cheeseburger here and there. But in the past several
years, as people have continued to dig more deeply
into regional cuisine—whether from here in the States
or from western Europe or Asia—eggs have seen a
resurgence. Eggs are an inexpensive and easy way to
add twists and turns to noodle bowls, posoles, rice
dishes, and more. The explosion of quail and duck eggs
on restaurant menus (their flavors are indiscernible
from chicken eggs) has just added to this flurry of
interest. The beauty of the egg is in is elemental
simplicity. In its most basic form, it's pure protein, but
perfectly cooking an egg could not be more challenging

to the untrained hand. More than one chef has been
made or broken by the egg. There was a time when
cooks' dexterity with the humble egg established the
hierarchy in the professional kitchen: candidates for
kitchen jobs used to be judged on egg preparation in
cooking interviews. Culinary myth has it that the one
hundred folds in a chef's toque (that tall white hat that
you associate with French kitchens) represent the one
hundred ways a chef should know how to prepare an
egg. (I'm not sure I buy that—*Larousse Gastronomique*,
considered by most to be the bible of classical French
cooking, contains just fifty or so egg recipes.)

In all fairness, cooking eggs is not that hard in the grand
scheme of things. What it requires is thoughtfulness,
care, respect, and patience. These are all hallmarks of
a good cook and the things most easily dismissed by
the folks who will never develop into good cooks. So
while it can define a person's ability to one degree or
another, egg cookery is not all that daunting if you are
willing to be patient and caring. You don't have to be a
professional chef to cook an egg right.

In this chapter, we will examine some of the most
frequently used techniques to cook eggs. Let there be
no mistake about it: cooking eggs well takes patience,
practice, and persistence. Like all cooking, if you don't
really enjoy what you're doing, it will show in the final
product. With eggs, this is particularly true. They are
a fragile protein. A certain amount of their finickiness
depends on the age of the egg and, believe it or not, the
freshest of eggs are *not* always the easiest to cook.
Stick to these few tips, and with a little practice, you
can go toe-to-toe with any Waffle House egg cook.

TOOLS AND INGREDIENTS FOR COOKING EGGS

- An 8-inch nonstick pan is the best home tool for egg cooking. In our restaurants, we use very inexpensive aluminum pans that we burnish constantly with steel wool to keep the surface perfectly smooth. When they are taken care of properly, they function like Teflon and shine like a mirror. But we take care of them obsessively—the slightest deviation from regular, diligent care for an aluminum pan and you might as well be cooking in rusty cast iron. So stick with Teflon at home. An 8-inch pan easily cooks two fried eggs (three will cook in it, too, but it'll get a little crowded). You can scramble enough eggs in it to serve two people and it can accommodate a giant fluffy American omelet for one.

- A heatproof silicone spatula is excellent for manipulating your eggs without scratching the surface of your pan. Get one with a wide head. It will help you flip fried eggs, fold omelets, and scramble.

- I use clarified butter for cooking eggs. Lots of high-volume breakfast places use a neutral vegetable oil and/or butter-flavored shortening, and frankly, almost any fat will work. I don't know that my grandmother ever cooked an egg in anything but the leftover bacon fat that was stationed on top of her stove, and even olive oil adds a very nice flavor to cooked eggs from time to time. However, anything that has any residual solids in it (for example, bacon fat or unfiltered oils such as first-pressed olive oil or natural peanut oil) has the potential to make your eggs stick to the pan, so go with filtered oils or clarified butter if you want to avoid sticking. The bottom line is that the purer the fat, the better.

EGG TECHNIQUE

- There is just one thing to remember when cooking eggs: low and slow is always better. Eggs don't take that long to cook, and if cooked over too much heat, they brown in an instant. The edges of fried eggs get lacy and crisp (unless, of course, that's what you are going for, in which case, let that fire rip). Take it slow (which means adding a few seconds to your cooking time) and you will make professional-grade egg dishes every time.

- Crack your eggs lightly on a flat surface. If you crack them on the edge of a bowl you run the risk of shell shards falling into the egg mixture. If broken lightly, the shell's interior membrane will, more often than not, retain all the shell pieces and keep you from having to fish them out of your eggs. If you do get shell pieces in your eggs, wet your fingers before trying to retrieve them. The shell pieces won't slide away from you and will be easier to fish out.

Clockwise, from top left: Fried Egg, sunny-side up (page 30), Fried Egg, over-easy (page 30), Scrambled Eggs (page 31), Poached Egg (page 31)

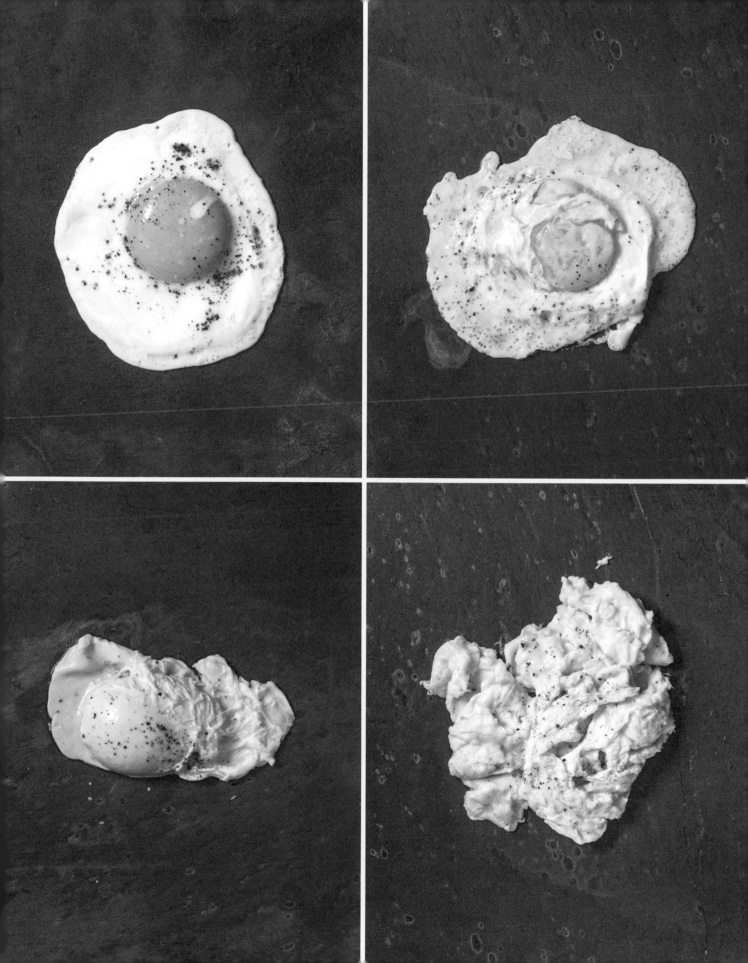

FRIED EGGS
MASTER RECIPE

SERVES 1

2 tablespoons clarified butter (see box) or your preferred cooking fat	2 eggs
	Salt and black pepper

For over-easy, over-medium, and over-hard eggs, warm an 8-inch nonstick skillet over low heat for 1 minute. For sunny-side up eggs, use an ovenproof skillet and preheat the broiler. Pour in the butter, swirl to coat the pan, and warm for 1 minute more.

Meanwhile, crack the eggs into a small bowl and check to make sure there is no shell. Slowly and carefully pour the eggs from the bowl into the pan and allow them to sit, undisturbed, for 1 minute. As the whites begin to set, agitate the pan gently in a circular motion. Sprinkle with salt and pepper and continue to agitate the pan.

TO MAKE SUNNY-SIDE UP EGGS, after about 2 minutes, when the whites are cooked almost through (they will still be slightly clear and runny on the top), place the pan directly under the broiler for 20 to 30 seconds to finish cooking the top side of the whites. Serve immediately.

TO MAKE OVER-EASY EGGS, after about 2 minutes, when the whites are cooked almost through (they will still be slightly clear and runny on the top), flip the eggs and continue to cook for 10 to 15 seconds more. The yolk should be very soft to the touch if poked with your finger. Serve immediately.

TO MAKE OVER-MEDIUM EGGS, after about 2 minutes, when the whites are cooked almost through (they will still be slightly clear and runny on the top), flip the eggs and continue to cook for 30 seconds. Flip back to the first side and the yolk should feel a little firmer to the touch than it was when first flipped, but it shouldn't be hard. Serve immediately.

FOR OVER-HARD EGGS, after about 2 minutes, when the whites are cooked almost through (they will still be slightly clear and runny on the top), flip the eggs and continue to cook for 1½ minutes. Flip back to the first side and cook for an additional 30 seconds, until the yolk is cooked solid and is firm to the touch. Serve immediately.

CLARIFIED BUTTER

Butter is composed of three parts: butterfat (that's the good stuff), water, and milk solids (that's what turns black in the pan when it gets too hot). Clarified butter is available for purchase in specialty food stores, or you can just make it yourself. When making clarified butter, the object is to separate those three elements and isolate the butterfat for cooking.

To clarify butter, place cold butter in a stainless steel saucepan over low heat. Melt the butter and allow the butter to cook over very low heat for 30 minutes. There is no need to stir or agitate the butter once it's melted; just keep your eye on it. The melted butter will initially be cloudy, but as it gently simmers, the water will boil off. As soon as the water evaporates, most of the milk solids will begin to sink to the bottom of the pan and the butterfat will appear to be clearer. A thin layer of the milk solids will accumulate around the surface of the butter; remove it with a spoon. Turn off the heat and allow to cool briefly. Carefully tip the pan and pour the butterfat into a heatproof container, being careful that the milk solids don't begin to run off as well. When you can't pour off any more of the butterfat, put the pan down and skim the rest of the butterfat off with a ladle or spoon. Discard the milk solids. Once cooled, clarified butter can be stored just like any other butter. Refrigerate in a nonreactive container for up to 2 months.

SCRAMBLED EGGS MASTER RECIPE

SERVES 1

2 eggs

2 tablespoons whole milk

Pinch of salt

Pinch of black pepper

1 tablespoon clarified butter (page 30) or your preferred cooking fat

Crack the eggs into a small bowl and beat well with the tines of a fork. You want to thoroughly mix the yolk and white to get an even color to your eggs. (Alternatively, a whisk or an immersion blender does a nice job. I'm just old-fashioned and watched my mom, dad, and grandparents beat eggs my whole life with a fork, so I feel obligated to keep the tradition alive.) Once done, beat in the milk, salt, and pepper.

Warm the clarified butter in an 8-inch nonstick skillet over low heat for 1 minute. Pour in the eggs and allow to sit, without stirring, for 15 seconds. With a silicone spatula, push the eggs from one side of the pan gently toward the other side, then tilt the pan and allow the uncooked eggs to fill the void. Allow the eggs to sit again, without stirring, for 15 seconds, then push the eggs to the opposite side and tilt the pan again. You want large fluffy curds to form as you scrape the pan. Run your spatula around the edge of the pan, and cook just until the eggs are almost set but still a tiny bit runny, another 10 to 15 seconds. Remove them to your plate. The eggs retain heat and will continue to cook after being removed from the stove. Serve immediately.

POACHED EGGS MASTER RECIPE

SERVES 1

3 tablespoons white vinegar

1 tablespoon salt

2 eggs, cracked into a shallow bowl

Bring 8 cups of water to a boil in a shallow, straight-sided 12-inch frying pan. Lower the heat to a gentle simmer. Add the vinegar and salt and stir until combined. Position the bowl with the eggs so that it's just above the water's surface, then tilt it in a single motion and gently pour the eggs into the water. Allow the eggs to sit, undisturbed, for a moment until the whites begin to turn milky. (Believe it or not, the eggs will separate from each other naturally.) Gently move the eggs around the pan with a spoon until the whites have cooked through but the yolks are still soft, about 2 minutes. (A certain amount of the white will naturally separate from the eggs while gently stirring, but most will remain attached to the yolk.) Remove the eggs and serve.

NOTE: No bullshit—eggs can be poached up to an hour in advance, plunged into a bowl of ice water to stop them from cooking, and returned to simmering water for about 20 seconds to warm again when ready to serve. I prefer them straight out of the poaching water because they are slightly less rubbery, but cooking in advance is great for when you're serving a crowd.

BIG BAD BREAKFAST EGG BAKE

SERVES 1

In an attempt to create something that was arguably "healthy," we came up with this little gem. It is a wonderful spoonful of everything that's great about breakfast, but baked, rather than fried. (Keep in mind that the public perception of health and actual healthiness, as far apart as that can be, makes serving a "healthy dish" both a challenge and a *great* sleight of hand.) We use a tinned Charlotte mold for this dish, but an 8-ounce, ovenproof ceramic cup works just as well.

1 slice whole wheat bread

¼ cup diced country ham or cooked bacon (chopped into ¼-inch bits)

¼ cup Garlic Cheese Grits (page 187)

¼ cup grated Parmesan cheese

¼ cup grated sharp cheddar cheese

1 tablespoon chopped fresh herbs of your choosing

2 eggs

Salt and freshly cracked black pepper

Preheat the oven to 350°F. Spray a 10-ounce Charlotte mold or an 8-ounce ceramic ovenproof cup with nonstick spray.

Toast the bread and cut into two 3-inch rounds. Place one toast round in the bottom of the cup, followed by half of the ham, half of the grits, and a pinch each of the Parmesan, cheddar, and herbs. Add another layer of toast, followed by the remaining ham and grits, and a pinch each of the Parmesan and cheddar. Crack the eggs over the top, season with salt and pepper, and sprinkle with the remaining herbs and cheeses. Place the cup on a small baking sheet and bake until the cheese is melted and bubbly and the visible egg whites are just cooked, about 8 minutes. If you like your eggs completely set and hard, bake for 12 to 14 minutes. Serve immediately.

"BROILED" TOMATO BENEDICT

SERVES 2

In the summer, my grandmother would make broiled tomatoes for breakfast for my grandfather. When I was a kid, they were a profound curiosity. I really didn't understand why people ate tomatoes—for breakfast . . . or ever, for that matter. To my tiny brain, they just seemed like they weren't finished growing. The insides were full of seeds, disgustingly mushy, and looked like some kind of unborn alien.

Oddly, though, I was intrigued with the way the leaves and stems smelled. I loved brushing up against them. They were scratchy and made me itch, but exploded with the craziest, green-smelling perfume whenever you did. When we picked tomatoes, that smell got all over my hands and I would smell it for hours. To this day, I love that smell like none other, and it carries me back, every time it hits me, right to my grandparents' garden in Lenoir, North Carolina, at the bottom of the hill next to the creek. And while I was completely rapt with that smell as a boy, it never got me over my disgust with the fruit itself—that would take years. I was a stupid child.

Like so many other things, I ultimately came to love tomatoes as much as I loved their smell. I use them everywhere I can now. This dish is a mash-up of my grandmother's breakfast plate and a traditional-ish Benedict. It's a little bit of a mindblower, if you like such things.

For this recipe, I actually do a slow roast on the tomatoes that takes about three hours to accomplish. The process slowly draws the water out of the tomatoes, concentrating the natural sugars and intensifying their flavor. You might want to make extra tomatoes if you're going to do this. They are a great side with steak, go very well in a salad, and are an outstanding addition to an omelet. Like anything tomato-based, these are best in the summer, but in the winter, with a decent hothouse tomato, you can achieve a more than adequate outcome. (These can be made the night before and rewarmed easily.)

2 ripe slicing tomatoes

Salt and pepper

1 teaspoon fresh thyme leaves

2 cloves garlic, thinly sliced

2 teaspoons olive oil

3 tablespoons water

4 cups fresh spinach, stems removed

4 slices thick-cut sourdough bread

4 slices bacon, cooked until crispy

4 Poached Eggs (page 31), warmed

2 tablespoons Herb Pistou (recipe follows; optional)

¼ cup Hollandaise (page 56), warmed

Tabasco pepper sauce, for garnish

Pinch of smoked paprika

Preheat the oven to 275°F. Line a baking sheet with parchment paper.

Core the tomatoes and cut in half across the equator. Squeeze out the seeds and place the halves, cut side up, on the prepared baking sheet. Season the tomatoes with salt and pepper and sprinkle with the thyme. Lay the garlic slices on top of the tomatoes and drizzle with the olive oil. Bake, rotating the baking sheet every 30 minutes, until the tomatoes are golden and very soft, about 3 hours. Allow to cool to room temperature. (If you make extra, store them chilled in a covered plastic container for up to a week.)

Warm the water in a large sauté pan over medium heat for 45 seconds. Place the spinach in the pan and turn the heat to low. Begin turning the spinach carefully. The spinach will wilt in a matter of a few minutes. As soon as it has completely wilted, remove to a strainer and press out as much of the water as you can. Set aside and keep warm.

CONTINUED

To serve, toast the bread and cut into 4 (3-inch) rounds. Place 2 toast rounds on each plate and put a warmed roasted tomato half on top of each toast. Crumble the bacon over the tomatoes, then evenly layer the spinach over the tomato halves. Place a poached egg on top of each tomato and spoon the pistou over the eggs. Pour the hollandaise over the eggs and pistou, splash with a little Tabasco, and sprinkle with smoked paprika.

HERB PISTOU
MAKES ABOUT ½ CUP

1 cup torn fresh basil leaves

1½ teaspoons fresh parsley leaves

1½ teaspoons fresh chopped chives

1 teaspoon fresh thyme leaves

1 teaspoon fresh rosemary leaves

3 tablespoons grated Parmesan cheese

2 tablespoons chopped plum tomato

1 tablespoon extra-virgin olive oil

Zest of ½ lemon

1 teaspoon minced garlic

1 teaspoon black pepper

¼ teaspoon salt

Combine all of the ingredients in a food processor and process until smooth. Store in a covered plastic container and refrigerate for up to 2 weeks.

NORTH MISSISSIPPI EGGS BENEDICT

SERVES 2

Like most folks, I grew up eating eggs Benedict on English muffins of varying quality. There wasn't a single commercial kitchen making English muffins in New Orleans when I was growing up, so every one I ever ate was from the grocery store, which I will admit isn't *all* terrible. As a matter of fact, until you have actually had a sourdough English muffin made from scratch, there are a couple of grocery store brands that are altogether respectable. That reality was shattered for me by a friend who started delivering homemade muffins some twenty years ago. I am now completely spoiled and little else will suffice.

It dawned on me one day while we were working on the "Bene" section of the first Big Bad Breakfast menu that a split buttermilk biscuit would make a reasonable substitution for an English muffin. With the addition of some thin slices of our house-cured country ham, we could make a North Mississippi version of the classic Benedict. Know what? I'm a smart son of a bitch. As if it weren't good enough on its own (it is), a drizzle of Red-Eye Gravy on the plate adds another layer and compliments the smoky ham perfectly.

2 fresh Black Pepper Buttermilk Biscuits (page 183)

2 tablespoons unsalted butter, at room temperature

8 thin slices country ham (or pit-smoked ham)

4 Poached Eggs (page 31), warmed

¼ cup Red-Eye Gravy (page 198; optional, but you're terminally foolish to leave it out), warmed

½ cup Hollandaise (page 56), warmed

Generous pinch of Barbecue Dry Rub, homemade (recipe follows) or store-bought, or smoked paprika, for sprinkling

Split the biscuits and toast lightly. Butter the warm biscuits as soon as they come out of the oven. Place 2 ham slices on each buttered biscuit half and toast lightly again. Place a poached egg on each biscuit half and drizzle with the gravy. Spoon the hollandaise over the eggs and sprinkle with the dry rub. Serve immediately.

BARBECUE DRY RUB
MAKES ABOUT 1 CUP

1½ tablespoons smoked paprika

1½ tablespoons kosher salt

1½ tablespoons dark brown sugar

1 tablespoon ground coriander

1 teaspoon dried thyme

1 teaspoon dried oregano

2½ teaspoons garlic powder

2½ teaspoons onion powder

1½ teaspoons ground cumin

1 teaspoon black pepper

½ teaspoon cayenne pepper

¼ teaspoon mustard powder

¼ teaspoon chili powder

¼ teaspoon ground cinnamon

Stir together all of the ingredients in a bowl until fully combined. Store in an airtight container in a cool, dry place for up to 6 months.

BIG BAD BREAKFAST QUESADILLA

MAKES 1 QUESADILLA; SERVES 1 ADULT OR 2 YOUNG'UNS

As I was searching for documentation of the days when I first started making this delicious snack, I ended up reading through a couple of my college journals, which, for the record, is a patently stupid fucking thing to do—well, for me at least. Apparently, about five or six years of my life was spent going in and out of agonizing and earth-shattering heartbreak like an Olympic downhill skier goes in and out of those goddamned flags. I was a monumental idiot and disgustingly melodramatic.

In the midst of the drama, I was introduced to the beauty of the quesadilla by a girlfriend who did a particularly shitty number on my heart. Remember, this is the early '80s I'm talking about. The quesadilla was still slightly exotic, or at least Chili's and Applebee's had not yet made it a household word. I was in my early twenties and had the propensity to fall in love hard and ridiculously fast (think of how fast the human eye blinks, the speed of a bullet, how quickly the government will decide to overspend the annual budget . . . you get the idea). This breakup was particularly painful, but at least I pulled the recipe for making a quesadilla from the wreckage. Tortilla consumption helped me through the brief healing process.

The quesadilla, unlike the wretched woman who first shared it with me, was a blessing and became a go-to snack around my house. The jump to making it a breakfast item clearly took Socratic reason and vision, so here it is. Quick, easy, and delicious, may it heal your wounded chubby little heart, too. It's one of the few things my three-year-old maniac agrees to eat regularly, so if you don't need it for medicinal purposes, hopefully it will make you a kitchen hero to your little one(s).

2 eggs, well beaten

¼ teaspoon ground cumin

2 tablespoons whole milk

2 tablespoons clarified butter (page 30) or your preferred cooking fat

¼ cup diced yellow onion

1 (10-inch) flour tortilla

½ cup grated cheddar or Monterey Jack cheese

⅓ cup diced tomato

2 tablespoons chopped fresh cilantro

2 tablespoons minced pickled jalapeño (optional)

¾ teaspoon Southwest Seasoning (page 44)

⅓ cup chopped roasted chicken

2 tablespoons olive oil

¼ cup Basic Salsa (recipe follows) or your preferred salsa

Sour cream, for garnish

In a bowl, stir together the eggs, cumin, and milk. Warm the clarified butter in an 8-inch nonstick skillet over low heat for 1 minute. Sauté the onion for 1 minute, or until softened and transparent. Pour in the eggs and allow to sit, without stirring, for 15 seconds. With a silicone spatula, push the eggs from one side of the pan gently toward the other side, then tilt the pan and allow the uncooked eggs to fill the void. Allow the eggs to sit again, without stirring, for 15 seconds, then push the eggs to the opposite side and tilt the pan again. Run your spatula around the edge of the pan, and just as the eggs are almost set but still a tiny bit runny, remove them to your plate.

Spread the tortilla on a flat surface and sprinkle ¼ cup of the cheese over one half of the tortilla, followed by the tomato, cilantro, jalapeño, Southwest Seasoning, chicken, and the scrambled egg. Top with the remaining ¼ cup cheese and fold over the uncovered half of the tortilla to create a half moon.

Warm the oil in a 10-inch sauté pan over medium heat for 30 seconds and gently place the quesadilla in the pan. Cook, pressing like you would a grilled cheese sandwich, until the bottom is golden brown, about 2 minutes. Flip and brown the second side, pressing again, until golden brown, about 2 minutes more.

Slide the quesadilla onto a cutting board and cut into 4 wedges. Garnish with the salsa and a dollop of sour cream. Serve immediately.

BASIC SALSA
MAKES 1½ CUPS

½ cup diced tomato

3 tablespoons diced yellow onion

2 tablespoons minced jalapeño

2 teaspoons lime juice

1 teaspoon ground cumin

1 teaspoon minced garlic

1 teaspoon black pepper

½ teaspoon salt

Pinch of ground cinnamon

Stir together all of the ingredients in a nonreactive bowl until well combined. Cover and refrigerate for at least 1 hour or up to 4 days.

LOUISIANA
CRAB CAKE BENEDICT

SERVES 4

I'm going to go ahead and say it: New Orleans doesn't do a very good version of the crab cake (for the most part). We make them, however, nonetheless. In New Orleans, we lean too much on bread crumbs as a binder and bell pepper and onion as filler, so the crab part of the cake frequently gets lost. In my best estimation, it's a version of the stuffed crab, just without a shell.

I went to college in Virginia, where I had the distinct pleasure of enjoying crazy good Eastern Shore crab cakes. A couple of my friends' moms and grandmoms made crab cakes for me time and again. As many and as fast as I ate those delicious cakes, those ladies knew how much I loved them, and like good moms, they loved feeding hungry boys, especially the ones who liked their cooking. Virginia crab cakes are little more than crab, egg, mustard, a hint of Old Bay seasoning, and a mild suggestion of cracker crumbs, so pretty much all you get is a mouthful of crab and whatever they dress them with.

The Big Bad Breakfast crab cakes are unapologetically more in the bready, New Orleans style. My justification is that cooking them this way makes a fantastic base for a Benedict, with the cake becoming a crabby English muffin substitute, topped with a poached egg.

CRAB CAKES

¼ cup plus 3 tablespoons Creole mustard or whole-grain Dijon mustard

3 tablespoons diced red bell pepper

3 tablespoons diced green bell pepper

2½ tablespoons heavy cream

1 tablespoon freshly squeezed lemon juice

2 egg yolks

1 shallot, minced

1 teaspoon diced seeded jalapeño

1 pound lump crabmeat, picked over for shells

¾ cup panko bread crumbs, plus more for coating

Salt and black pepper

5 tablespoons extra-virgin olive oil

8 Poached Eggs (page 31), warmed

1 cup Hollandaise (page 56), warmed

Pinch of cayenne pepper

3 tablespoons chopped fresh chives

In a bowl, whisk together the ¼ cup mustard, bell peppers, cream, lemon juice, yolks, shallot, and jalapeño. Fold in the crabmeat gently but thoroughly, followed by the bread crumbs. Season with salt and pepper. Cover and refrigerate for 30 minutes before forming into cakes.

Divide into 8 portions. Form each portion into 2½-inch patties that are about ¾ inch thick. Place the bread crumbs on a plate and coat each cake with the bread crumbs.

Warm the oil in a sauté pan over medium heat for 1 minute. Place the crab cakes in the pan and cook, turning regularly, until golden on both sides, about 3 minutes per side. Divide among 4 plates.

Top each crab cake with a poached egg. Stir together the hollandaise and remaining 3 tablespoons mustard and spoon over the cakes. Dust lightly with cayenne pepper and sprinkle with chives for garnish. Serve immediately.

CHORIZO MIGAS

SERVES 4

In the late 1970s and early 1980s, the Mexican Rio Grande Valley was as good a place as anywhere on the planet for dove hunting. Getting there was ridiculously easy and affordable, so Americans with an interest in high-volume dove hunting (Mexico had no federally imposed limit on the number of birds you were allowed to kill) flocked there by the hundreds. My dad, brother, myself, and a group of twenty or so friends were among them, every Labor Day, for about ten years. The only hiccup on these trips was that we regularly dealt with Mexican authorities, who more often than not required slight lubrication to keep certain wheels (like the ones on the trucks we drove around in) turning. You see, when they figured out that Americans with disposable income were heading their way regularly, they realized making a little pocket money by inconveniencing those folks would be easy. And it was.

Other than that, the morning-after hangover was the worst of our issues. The landscape in south Texas and in the Mexican border towns was dotted with mom-and-pop roadside joints serving a bevy of Mexican breakfast specialties. A greasy plate of chorizo-laced migas, it turned out, frequently kicked the crap out of what a bottle of aspirin could otherwise do and became the breakfast item of choice. These are like a plateful of breakfast tacos, minus the hassle of trying to fold it all up and get it in your mouth. As much as I love finger-fed food, I'll happily shovel up a plate of migas any day of the week, especially if it helps shoo away a lingering case of Tequila influenza. Throw back a Michelada and a Shot (page 224) should more drastic measures be required.

The Southwest Seasoning yields more than the amount needed—use leftovers to give chili or salsa an extra little kick.

Vegetable oil, for frying

7 (6-inch) corn tortillas

6 eggs, well beaten

½ cup whole milk

2½ teaspoons Southwest Seasoning (recipe follows)

3 tablespoons clarified butter (page 30) or your preferred cooking fat

6 ounces beef chorizo

½ cup diced yellow onion

½ cup diced green bell pepper

1 serrano chile, seeded and minced

1 tablespoon minced garlic

¾ cup diced fresh tomato

Salt and pepper

¼ cup chopped fresh cilantro

⅓ cup crumbled Cotija cheese

Valentina hot sauce or your preferred hot sauce (optional), for drizzling

Pour 2 inches of oil into a 4-inch-deep, straight-sided frying pan and warm over medium heat to 375°F.

Slice 3 of the tortillas into ½-inch strips and fry until crispy and golden, 30 to 45 seconds. Remove from the oil with a slotted spoon, drain on paper towels or a cooling rack, and set aside. Fry the remaining 4 whole tortillas until crispy, about 1 minute. Remove, drain, and set aside as well.

In a large bowl, stir together the eggs, milk, and Southwest Seasoning with a fork, and set aside. In a large sauté pan, heat the butter over medium heat for 1 minute. Add the chorizo and cook, stirring constantly for 4 minutes. Add the onion, green bell pepper, serrano, and garlic and sauté until the onion begins to soften, about 3 minutes. Stir in the tomato and season lightly with salt and pepper.

Pour the egg mixture into the pan and allow to sit, without stirring, for 20 seconds. With a silicone spatula, push the eggs from one side of the pan gently toward the other side, then tilt the pan and allow the uncooked eggs to fill the void. Allow the eggs to sit again, without

CONTINUED

stirring, for 20 seconds, then push the eggs to the opposite side and tilt the pan again. Run your spatula around the edge of the pan, and just as the eggs are almost set but still a tiny bit runny, stir gently, trying to keep curds as large and fluffy as possible, for another 20 seconds. Remove from the heat and stir in the fried tortilla strips.

Place the whole fried tortillas on each of 4 plates and spoon the egg mixture over them. Sprinkle with the cilantro and Cotija. Drizzle with hot sauce, dig in, and kiss that hangover good–bye.

SOUTHWEST SEASONING
MAKES ABOUT ⅓ CUP

1 tablespoon chili powder

1 tablespoon paprika

1½ teaspoons ancho chile powder

½ teaspoon cayenne pepper

1½ teaspoons salt

1½ teaspoons black pepper

2 teaspoons ground cumin

2 teaspoons garlic powder

1 teaspoon ground coriander

Stir together all of the ingredients in a stainless steel bowl. Store in an airtight container in a dry place for up to 6 months.

DOUBLE-BOILED EGGS WITH BLACK TRUFFLE

SERVES 4

10 eggs, well beaten

¼ cup unsalted butter, cut into small pieces

¼ cup mascarpone cheese, at room temperature

Salt and black pepper

2 tablespoons chopped fresh chives

4 thick slices crusty bread, toasted and buttered

2 tablespoons excellent-quality extra-virgin olive oil

3 tablespoons grated Parmesan cheese

½ ounce French black Piedmont or Italian white Alba truffle (see Note)

Truffles, I think, are largely misunderstood. Most folks never get the opportunity to eat the real thing, which is truly exquisite. Fresh truffles are a form of underground fungus, dug from the roots surrounding trees with which they share a symbiotic relationship, most frequently oak, pine, hazelnut, beech, and poplar. French and Italian truffles are far and away the most prized. Fresh ones, while unsightly in appearance, are firm and aromatic little nuggets. They are best sliced or grated over something warm, when they just release their scent.

Truffles are extremely rare and during the season, fresh ones from Europe will sell for well over $1,000 per pound. It is an ingredient of truly cult status. While there are dozens of species of truffles out there that are harvested, only a fistful produce the aromas and "flavors" the lucky few who can get their hands on them seek. There is a load of "truffle" crap out there on the market assembled from inferior-quality truffles, including truffle oil, canned truffle slices, shavings, and cheeses meant to satisfy folks who don't know the difference between a good truffle and, well, everything else out there.

For my fiftieth birthday in the Tuscan countryside, my friends Ashley Christensen and Wright Thompson arranged the purchase of a white Alba truffle that was bigger than a golf ball and smaller than a baseball. We double-boiled about a dozen eggs with a touch of mascarpone and some extra-virgin olive oil from the farm we were on, shaved the whole freaking truffle, and had the breakfast of our lives. When we were done we sat in silence for fifteen minutes, the perfume of fresh truffle in the air, and tried to think of a happier food moment. No one could.

Set up a double boiler if you have one. If not, fill a large saucepan with 2 inches of water and bring to a simmer over medium heat. Combine the eggs and butter in a stainless steel bowl. Set the bowl over (but not touching) the simmering water and stir the eggs slowly and constantly with a silicone spatula or wooden spoon as they slowly warm. Hold the edge of the bowl with a kitchen towel and carefully let the steam out from under the bowl from time to time while you stir. After about 5 or 6 minutes, the eggs will begin to turn cloudy and cook. Remove from the heat for a few seconds and stir, allowing the eggs and the bowl to cool briefly. Return to the heat and continue stirring for a couple of minutes and remove from the heat again as the eggs cook a little more. Repeat this process several times until the eggs begin to firm up, but still appear a little wet and glisten brightly. Stir in the mascarpone, season with salt and pepper, and remove from the heat for the last time. Stir in the chives. Arrange the toasted bread on a platter and slowly spoon the eggs over the bread. Drizzle with the oil, sprinkle with the Parmesan, and immediately shave the entire truffle over the eggs. Sprinkle with a touch more salt and eat as quickly as possible.

NOTE: Truffles are not always easy ingredients to find—just ask the pigs and dogs tasked with sniffing around hardwood tree roots to locate them. Urbani Truffles in New York (www.urbani.com) keeps a steady supply and an excellent selection. Make no mistake, they are *extremely* pricey, but certainly worth the occasional splurge. My advice: Buy a Microplane grater if you don't already have one. It will increase the surface area of what you are shaving and spread the aroma and flavor much better than a traditional truffle slicer.

SHRIMP BREAKFAST ENCHILADAS

SERVES 8

In the universe of near-perfect flavor combinations—think peanut butter and jelly; lamb and mint; bacon, lettuce, and tomato—corn and cumin ranks near the top of my list. Whether in a posole or a salsa in tortilla wraps, I love it. Corn fails to get its due most of the time, especially when it comes to accelerating the flavor of a dish. If you don't believe me, the next time you make a pot of chili, make it without masa. When it is just about done cooking, taste the chili; then add the masa and taste it again. They're two completely different animals.

Corn tortillas work the same way in enchiladas. While you can get an altogether acceptable dish making this with flour tortillas, corn tortillas are the rocket ship to Planet Delicious. Combine corn tortillas with the cumin-flecked shrimp, scrambled eggs, and enchilada sauce and just try to stop eating this when it comes out of the oven. This dish is great for a group, as you can make it as long as 24 hours in advance and then slam it in the oven just a few minutes before breakfast the next day. You'll have a no-fuss breakfast dish just like that.

2 tablespoons olive oil

1 pound medium, fully peeled shrimp

2 teaspoons black pepper

1½ teaspoons salt

1¾ teaspoons ground cumin

Juice of 1 lime

6 eggs, well beaten

4 tablespoons whole milk

2 tablespoons clarified butter (page 30) or your preferred cooking fat

16 (6-inch) corn tortillas

2 cups grated cheddar or Monterey Jack cheese, plus some for sprinkling over the top

½ cup chopped fresh cilantro

1 cup thinly sliced yellow onion

Enchilada Sauce (recipe follows)

Preheat the oven to 350°F.

Warm the olive oil in a nonstick sauté pan over medium heat for 1 minute. In a large bowl, toss the shrimp with the pepper, salt, and 1 teaspoon of the cumin until evenly coated. Place the shrimp in the hot pan and cook, stirring, until the shrimp just turn opaque and firm, about 2 minutes. Remove the shrimp from the pan immediately and set aside to cool in a bowl. Drizzle the lime juice over the warm shrimp and toss to combine. Reserve the pan to cook the tortillas in.

In a separate bowl, stir together the eggs, milk, and the remaining ¾ teaspoon cumin with a fork. Season with salt and pepper.

Warm the clarified butter in a second medium nonstick pan over medium heat for 30 seconds. Pour in the eggs and allow to sit, without stirring, for 20 seconds. With a silicone spatula, push the eggs from one side of the pan gently toward the other side, then tilt the pan and allow the uncooked eggs to fill the void. Allow the eggs to sit again, without stirring, for 20 seconds, then push the eggs to the opposite side and tilt the pan again. Stir the eggs gently for 15 seconds, but you want to keep the curds as large and fluffy as you can. Run your spatula around the edge of the pan, and just as the eggs are almost set but still a tiny bit runny, remove them to a plate to cool.

Chop the cooled shrimp into bite-size pieces. Warm the sauté pan that you used to cook the shrimp and warm the tortillas, one by one, for 20 seconds on each side. Set aside and cover with a kitchen towel.

Wipe a 13 by 9-inch casserole dish with olive oil. Working in batches, assemble the enchiladas. Lay 1 tortilla on a flat surface and spoon 2 tablespoons of egg, several pieces of shrimp, a large pinch of cheese, a pinch of cilantro, and several slices of onion down the center. Roll the tortilla up so that the seam side is down and the enchilada holds itself closed. Place the enchilada in the prepared dish. Continue assembling the enchiladas with the remaining ingredients and pack them together snugly in the dish until all of the enchiladas are rolled and packed in the dish. Pour the Enchilada Sauce over the top and sprinkle with extra cheese.

Bake until the topping bubbles and exposed cheese begins to brown lightly in spots, about 15 minutes. Serve immediately or refrigerate for up to 24 hours and rewarm in the oven for 30 minutes at 325°F before serving (in which case, take the enchiladas out of the fridge and allow to come to room temperature for at least 2 hours before baking).

ENCHILADA SAUCE
MAKES ABOUT 2½ CUPS

3 tablespoons olive oil

1½ tablespoons all-purpose flour

3 tablespoons chili powder

1 tablespoon ancho chile powder

¼ teaspoon cayenne pepper

2 cups chicken stock

2 teaspoons dried oregano

2 teaspoons ground cumin

¾ teaspoon salt

Juice of 1 lime

Warm the oil in a small saucepan over medium heat for 1 minute. Whisk in the flour until well combined. Add the chili powder, ancho chile powder, and cayenne, combine well, and stir constantly for 2 minutes. Whisk in the stock, oregano, cumin, and salt and bring to a simmer. Cook, stirring constantly, until the sauce thickens slightly, about 10 minutes. Remove from the heat, cool briefly, and stir in the lime juice. Season with salt and allow to cool.

"DOUBLE OYSTER" HANGTOWN FRY

SERVES 2

I fell in love with Hangtown fry the very first time I read its description on a menu. It's basically scrambled eggs with fried oysters, bacon, and hot sauce. By all accounts, the dish has its origins in California around the time of the 1849 Gold Rush. The fable goes that a miner, having recently struck it rich, walked into a saloon, dropped his gold on the bar, and asked for the most expensive thing they could make. In the remote mining town at the time, bacon, oysters, and eggs would all have been brought in carefully from far away and at great expense. Combining the three in a single dish would have been the height of luxury, or so the story goes. Sounds a little farfetched, but why the hell should we complicate history with facts and reality?

For the version we serve at the restaurant, we give it a south Louisiana twist and "double" the oyster by adding roasted salsify, also known as "oyster root" because of its tender texture and creamy flavor. This addition is optional, but delicious if you can get your hands on it.

SEASONED FLOUR

1½ cups all-purpose flour

1 teaspoon salt

1 teaspoon black pepper

1 teaspoon paprika

¾ teaspoon garlic powder

¾ teaspoon onion powder

¼ teaspoon cayenne pepper

EGG WASH

¾ cup whole milk

3 eggs

1 teaspoon salt

1 teaspoon black pepper

SEASONED CORNMEAL

1½ cups cornmeal

1 teaspoon salt

1 teaspoon black pepper

1 teaspoon paprika

¾ teaspoon garlic powder

¾ teaspoon onion powder

¼ teaspoon cayenne pepper

FRY

2 (8-inch) pieces salsify, peeled (optional)

1½ tablespoons olive oil

Salt and black pepper

Vegetable oil, for frying

8 freshly shucked oysters or pre-shucked if fresh are not available

5 eggs

½ cup whole milk

2 teaspoons Creole seasoning

¼ cup chopped bacon

¼ cup diced yellow onion

3 tablespoons diced red bell pepper

1 teaspoon minced garlic

1 serrano chile, thinly sliced

Your preferred hot sauce, for serving

Preheat the oven to 175°F. In three separate shallow bowls, stir together the ingredients for the Seasoned Flour, the Egg Wash, and the Seasoned Cornmeal.

To make the fry, rub the salsify pieces with the olive oil and sprinkle with salt and pepper. Place on a baking sheet, cover with aluminum foil, and roast until a knife pierces the flesh easily, about 20 minutes. Allow to cool briefly, then cut into ½-inch pieces. Set aside.

Line a baking sheet with paper towels. Pour 2 inches of vegetable oil into a shallow skillet and heat over medium heat to 375°F. One at a time, pat the oysters dry and dredge in the Seasoned Flour, then dip into the Egg Wash, and finally dredge them in the Seasoned Cornmeal. Drop the oysters into the skillet, 1 at a time, being careful not to crowd the skillet. Fry until golden brown, 2 to 3 minutes. Remove from the oil with a slotted spoon and drain on the prepared baking sheet. Transfer the baking sheet to the oven to keep warm.

In a bowl, stir together the eggs, milk, and Creole seasoning with a fork. Heat a separate skillet over medium heat for 1 minute. Add the bacon and cook until just about crispy, about 4 minutes. Remove from the pan with a slotted spoon and drain on paper towels. In the same pan, add the onion, bell pepper, and garlic and sauté until the onion begins to soften, about 3 minutes. Add the salsify and cook just until warmed through. Pour the egg mixture over the vegetables and bacon and allow to sit, without stirring, for 15 seconds. With a silicone spatula, push the eggs from one side of the pan gently toward the other side, then tilt the pan and allow the uncooked eggs to fill the void. Allow the eggs to sit again, without stirring, for 15 seconds, then push the eggs to the opposite side and tilt the pan again. Run your spatula around the edge of the pan, and just as the eggs are almost set but still a tiny bit runny, add the bacon. Season lightly with salt and pepper.

To serve, spoon the eggs onto a platter and top with the fried oysters, serrano, and a few drops of hot sauce.

SUMMER VEGETABLE QUICHE

SERVES 4 TO 6

In the 1980s, a satirical paperback titled *Real Men Don't Eat Quiche* was published that lampooned the confusion over gender stereotypes. An unfortunate side effect was that quiche got a terrible rap and became *fooda non grata* on the nation's menus. I grew up in the crosshairs of this book, and while I never did eschew the occasional slice of quiche, I was definitely aware of, influenced by, and a victim of the stereotypes this silly little book brought about.

The reality is that quiche is not only great, it's also an extremely economical and health-conscious meal, especially for feeding a family. It's economical because a few eggs and some vegetables and leftover meat can go a long way, and a couple or three can be made all at once, then wrapped and frozen. It's healthy in that you can load it with fresh vegetables and herbs and have an altogether "good for you" meal that's delicious and filling. So arm yourself with pie shells, eggs, and whatever suits your taste because, by God, real men *do* eat fucking quiche. They also wear Lacoste shirts and Fred Perry tennis shoes and none of that shit defines who anyone is. Christ, am I glad I got that off my chest.

PIECRUST

1½ cups all-purpose flour

½ cup cold butter, cut into small pieces

½ teaspoon salt

2 tablespoons ice water

FILLING

½ cup sliced asparagus, cut ¾ inch thick

⅓ cup diced red bell pepper

⅓ cup diced zucchini

⅓ cup (¼ inch) diced fingerling potatoes

¼ cup diced yellow onion

3 tablespoons extra-virgin olive oil

2 teaspoons minced garlic

1½ teaspoons salt

1½ teaspoons black pepper

½ cup whole milk

3 eggs

2 tablespoons heavy cream

2 teaspoons fresh thyme leaves

3 tablespoons water

2¾ cups fresh spinach, stems removed

¾ cup grated Gruyère or Swiss cheese

Preheat the oven to 350°F.

To make the piecrust, combine the flour, butter, and salt in a food processor and pulse until the mixture is the texture of a coarse meal. Drizzle in the ice water and pulse just until the dough comes together, being careful not to overwork the dough. Transfer the dough to a work surface and flatten into a disk. Cover with plastic wrap and refrigerate for 30 minutes.

To make the filling, in a bowl, combine the asparagus, bell pepper, zucchini, potatoes, onion, oil, garlic, 1 teaspoon of the salt, and 1 teaspoon of the black pepper and toss to coat well. Place on a baking sheet, cover with aluminum foil, and roast until softened, about 20 minutes. Allow to cool briefly, then pour off any excess liquid.

In a separate bowl, whisk together the milk, eggs, cream, thyme, the remaining ½ teaspoon salt, and the remaining ½ teaspoon black pepper.

Warm the water in a large sauté pan over medium heat for 45 seconds. Place the spinach in the pan and turn the heat to low. Begin turning the spinach carefully. The spinach will wilt in a matter of a few minutes. As soon as it has completely wilted, remove to a strainer and press out as much of the water as you can.

Turn out the dough onto a floured surface and roll it into an 11-inch round that's about ¼ inch thick. Lay into a 10-inch pie pan and crimp the edges. Poke the pie crust all over with the tines of a fork. Place a piece of parchment paper in the bottom of the pie shell and add 1½ cups of dried beans on top of the parchment. Place in the oven for 12 to 15 minutes, or until the edges just begin to brown lightly. Remove the parchment and the beans.

Spread out the roasted vegetables in the piecrust, followed by the spinach and half of the cheese. Pour the egg mixture over the top and sprinkle with the remaining cheese.

Bake until the quiche is firm in the center and lightly browned, 30 to 35 minutes. Allow to cool briefly before slicing and serving. Wrap any remaining quiche in plastic and store chilled for up to 3 days. Rewarm before serving.

NOTE: You can substitute a 10-inch store-bought piecrust for the homemade piecrust if you wish.

TUGBOAT GALLEY EGGS AND DIRTY RICE

SERVES 4

3 tablespoons olive oil

8 ounces ground pork

Salt and black pepper

8 ounces chicken livers, chopped

½ cup unsalted butter

2 cups diced yellow onion

1 cup diced celery

¾ cup diced green bell pepper

1½ tablespoons minced garlic

2 cups long-grain white rice

1 tablespoon Creole seasoning

6 tablespoons white wine

4 cups chicken stock, plus ½ cup as needed

¼ cup chopped fresh parsley

8 Fried Eggs (page 30) or Poached Eggs (page 31), warmed, for serving

4 slices whole wheat bread, toasted and buttered, for serving

Your preferred hot sauce, for serving

The morning after I graduated from high school, my dad packed my bags and sent me off to work as a deckhand on one of his boats for the summer. You see, my dad had worked offshore during the summers to pay his tuition at Tulane University Law School. I wasn't being asked to do the same, but I think he thought it would help me build some desperately needed character. He drove me to the town of Lockport, Louisiana, where I was put in a carryall and sent down Bayou Lafourche to an industrial stain on the map called Port Fourchon. There's little more in Fourchon than offshore workers, marine repair technicians, welders, and hustlers trying to make a buck. Frank Bourge was my boat captain, and when I arrived on board he cuffed me by the neck and gruffly informed me that as the "new guy" I was the de facto cook.

It would be my first cooking job . . . on a tugboat . . . with a bunch of crusty Cajuns . . . in the middle of the Gulf of Mexico. Potential for drowning: high. I was taught how to make rice and coffee, given a copy of the *Joy of Cooking*, and instructed to look up *chicken* in the index if we had chicken in the freezer, and cook chicken. I cooked a lot of rice that summer. Cajuns eat it for every meal and love it with fried eggs and hot sauce. I leaned on that combination hard. At some point, I started adding leftovers in with the rice to punch up the sustenance. Though I never actually made dirty rice, per se, while on the boat, if I could go back, this is exactly what I would make for my first breakfast with those guys.

Preheat the oven to 350°F.

Warm the oil in a sauté pan over medium heat for 1 minute. Add the pork, season with salt and pepper, and cook, stirring constantly, until browned, about 4 minutes. Transfer the cooked pork to a plate and set aside. Pour off all but 2 tablespoons of fat from the pan and discard. To the same pan, add the chicken livers, season with salt and pepper, and sauté until firm, about 3 minutes. Set aside with the pork.

Melt the butter in an ovenproof saucepan over medium heat. Add the onion, celery, bell pepper, and garlic and sauté until softened, about 3 minutes. Stir in the rice until well coated with butter.

Return the pork and chicken livers to the pan and stir in the Creole seasoning. Deglaze the pan with the wine and add the 4 cups of stock. Cover the pan with aluminum foil and bake for 20 minutes, then remove the pan from the oven and remove the foil. Taste the rice. If it is still a little undercooked, add an additional ½ cup of stock, stir the rice, re-cover with foil, and put back in the oven for an additional 6 minutes. Remove and stir in the parsley. Season to taste with salt and black pepper.

Serve the dirty rice warm, topped with the eggs, toast, and a splash of hot sauce.

EGGS SARDOU

SERVES 2

Benedict egg dishes are by no means unique to New Orleans. However, we like to think we elevated, celebrated, and perfected them. To the best of my knowledge, Antoine's Restaurant claims responsibility for the invention of eggs Sardou. They were named for the French playwright Victorien Sardou, who penned a play called *La Tosca* that would later become an opera of the same name at Puccini's hands. (Now that I have opened that door, I am certain that New Orleans's food-history elite will burn my fucking house down over the dish's "actual" provenance.)

My earliest memory of eggs Sardou were of the version from Brennan's on Royal Street in New Orleans—one of the most notable breakfast restaurants in the city. I am old enough to remember when breakfast at Brennan's was a splendid affair. The men came only in jacket and tie, and *everyone* drank Champagne and slurped up rich demiglaces at otherwise inconceivable hours of the morning. It was the only way to fully surrender to the experience.

My first taste of their hollandaise made a junkie of me. The creamed spinach, which I associated with the scum at the bottom of a Dumpster and thought I despised, was in fact resplendent. And the oddly salty and interestingly textured artichoke hearts, which I normally would have pushed to the side of my plate with a curl of my lip, were an utterly integral part of this weird culinary experiment. It was the United Nations of egg dishes that made me question my shitty, little food attitude. I loved it and it was composed pretty much of all of the things I would have just classified as shit, but just couldn't when faced with this breakfast leviathan. It may have been the moment this "foodie" was born.

Now to drown myself for uttering that word.

CREAMED SPINACH

3 tablespoons unsalted butter

6 cups firmly packed spinach

2 tablespoons all-purpose flour

1½ cups whole milk

½ cup grated Parmesan cheese

2 or 3 dashes of Tabasco pepper sauce

Salt and pepper

FOR SERVING

1 tablespoon unsalted butter, at room temperature

2 English muffins, split

4 large canned artichoke bottoms, rinsed well

4 Poached Eggs (page 31), warmed

1¼ cups Hollandaise (recipe follows)

Espelette or cayenne pepper, for sprinkling

To make the creamed spinach, melt 1 tablespoon of the butter in a large sauté pan over low heat. Add the spinach and cook, stirring constantly, until fully wilted, about 5 minutes. Remove from the heat, allow to cool briefly, and squeeze out any excess water. In a small sauté pan, melt the remaining 2 tablespoons butter over medium heat, add the flour and whisk to form a roux. Continue to cook, whisking constantly, until the roux turns a light gold and gives off a slightly nutty aroma, about 5 minutes. Whisk in the milk and the wilted spinach, turn the heat to low, and simmer until the sauce thickens, about 10 minutes. Stir in the Parmesan and Tabasco and season with salt and pepper. Set aside.

Preheat the broiler. Butter the cut sides of the English muffins. Place the artichokes and English muffins on a baking sheet. Slide the baking sheet under the broiler and toast the artichokes and muffins for about 1 minute on each side, being careful not to burn them.

Place 2 English muffin halves on each plate. Top each muffin half with an artichoke, followed by the creamed spinach. Place a poached egg atop the spinach and spoon over the hollandaise. Sprinkle with a pinch of espelette and serve warm.

CONTINUED

HOLLANDAISE

MAKES 1¼ CUPS

4 egg yolks

2 tablespoons water

1½ teaspoons freshly squeezed lemon juice

½ teaspoon kosher salt

½ teaspoon white pepper

4 dashes of Tabasco hot sauce

Pinch of cayenne pepper

1 cup clarified butter (page 30)

Fill a large saucepan with 2 inches of water and bring to a simmer over medium heat. Whisk together the egg yolks, water, lemon juice, salt, white pepper, Tabasco, and cayenne in a stainless steel bowl. Set the bowl over the simmering water (but not touching it) and whisk constantly until the eggs thicken to the consistency of thickened heavy cream (it should barely leave a trail when the whisk is dragged through it), 7 to 10 minutes. Drizzle in the clarified butter, whisking vigorously, until fully incorporated, about 1 minute. Season with salt and set aside in a warm place but not over direct heat (on the stove top, with the oven on). Be very careful because the hollandaise will separate if it gets too hot or too cold.

SPICY BOUDIN AND POACHED EGGS

SERVES 4

Boudin was the first exotic south Louisiana foodstuff I ever fell in love with (unless you consider oysters "exotic," which I guess is entirely subjective, but I digress). Pork liver is not something most boys jump to stuff down their gullets, but somehow, as a young teenager, I was completely nuts about my first taste of boudin, a spicy pork and liver sausage filled out with rice and green onion. The combination of a salty cracker, the spicy boudin, and the sting of French's yellow mustard was a gustatory hand grenade for me. It was love from first bite.

Turns out that adding a runny poached egg and some Indian fry bread to that equation improves that result even more. Making boudin may seem like a commitment—it requires a meat grinder and sausage stuffer to complete—but it is entirely worth it, I promise. It's one of those things that will raise an eyebrow, but is quick to please.

When it comes time to consume, though, please step away from the fancy virgin Spanish mustard seed mustard and pick up the cheapest yellow mustard you can get your hands on. Also, a plastic knife spreads it as well as anything else.

4 pieces Indian Fry Bread (recipe follows)

4 links Poached Boudin, homemade (recipe follows) or store-bought

Yellow mustard, for drizzling

4 Poached Eggs (page 31)

Chopped green onions, green part only, for garnish

Several dashes of your favorite hot sauce (optional)

Place the fry breads on 4 plates. Slice the boudin lengthwise and lay on top of the fry breads. Drizzle the yellow mustard over the boudin and top with a poached egg. Sprinkle with green onion and hot sauce. Serve immediately.

POACHED BOUDIN
MAKES 12 LINKS

1 pound fatty pork shoulder or butt, cut into 1–inch cubes

2 teaspoons salt

2 teaspoons black pepper

8 ounces pork liver or chicken liver, cut into 1–inch pieces

1¾ cups diced yellow onion

2 bunches green onions, green part only, sliced

1½ tablespoons minced garlic

1 tablespoon chopped fresh parsley

6 cups cooked long-grain rice

1 tablespoon Creole seasoning

4 feet of 1–inch hog casings

1 (12-ounce) can cheap beer

1½ cups water

Place the pork, salt, and pepper in a medium Dutch oven. Add just enough water to cover and bring to a boil over high heat. Turn down the heat to low and simmer, covered, until the pork is tender and falling apart, about 45 minutes. Add the liver and simmer until the liver is firm to the touch, about 5 minutes more. Remove the pork and the liver from the pot. Strain and reserve the broth.

Set up your meat grinder with the medium die. While the pork and liver are still warm, stir them together in a bowl with half of the yellow onion, half of the green onions, half of the garlic, and half of the parsley and run through the meat grinder, working in batches. In a large bowl, stir together the ground meat mixture with the rice; remaining yellow onion, green onions, garlic, and parsley; and Creole seasoning. Once the mixture is fully combined, add about 1½ cups of the reserved broth or just enough broth to make a moist sausage that will hold together when squeezed in your hand.

CONTINUED

Place the sausage in a sausage stuffer and feed the casing onto the stuffing tube. Squeeze all of the air out of the sausage casing, then tie a knot at the very end. Begin cranking the handle (assuming you have a manual stuffer) and form 4-inch links, twisting each link several times as each is formed. When you reach the end of your sausage, squeeze the air out of the back end of the sausage and tie the casing off.

To poach the boudin, combine the beer and water in a large, straight-sided frying pan and bring to a boil over medium heat. Drop the boudin links into the pot, cover, and poach for 7 minutes. Remove and keep warm until ready to use.

Boudin can be poached and frozen, or it can be refrigerated after encasing and poached up to 3 days later.

INDIAN FRY BREAD

If you don't want to use lard, you can use all vegetable oil to make the fry bread.

MAKES 4 ROUNDS

2 tablespoons lard, plus more melted lard for frying

Vegetable oil, for frying

1⅓ cups all-purpose flour

2 teaspoons powdered milk

2 teaspoons baking powder

¼ teaspoon salt

⅔ cup whole milk

Melt the 2 tablespoons lard in a saucepan over low heat for 5 to 7 minutes.

Preheat the oven to 175°F. Line a baking sheet with paper towels. Pour 3 inches of vegetable oil and more lard into a Dutch oven or countertop fryer and heat over medium heat to 350°F.

Sift together the flour, powdered milk, baking powder, and salt into a large bowl.

Pour the milk and the 2 tablespoons melted lard over the flour mixture all at once and stir the dough with a fork until it starts to form one big clump.

Dust your hands generously with flour. Using your hands, mix the dough, trying to incorporate all of the flour and forming a ball. You want to mix the dough well, but you do *not* want to knead it. The inside of the dough ball should still be sticky after it's formed, while the outside should be well floured.

Divide the dough into 4 pieces. Using your floured hands, shape, stretch, and pat each dough into a 4-inch disk that's about ½ inch thick. When the oil is hot, carefully place the disks into the oil and cook, turning every 30 seconds or so, until browned, about 3 minutes. Remove from the oil with a slotted spoon, drain on the prepared baking sheet, and cover with a kitchen towel. Transfer the baking sheet to the oven to keep warm.

HILLBILLY EGGS HUSSARDE

SERVES 2

I'm not sure where I first bumped into this one. When I was growing up, the brunch restaurants in New Orleans had very similar egg menus, so it could have been a number of places. Eggs Hussarde are a New Orleans invention by all accounts and another in the lexicon of great egg dishes claimed by Brennan's. Despite their fancy-sounding name, they're really just eggs Benedict with the addition of *marchand du vin*, a mushroom demiglace. Whoever penned the recipe probably just added leftover sauce from Saturday's dinner to a Benedict and a classic was born. I've always been partial to this dish, but since we don't regularly make *marchand du vin* at the restaurant, we sub in Red-Eye Gravy for a "hillbilly" Hussarde.

2 tablespoons olive oil

2 cups mixed sliced white and shiitake mushrooms, stems removed

Salt and black pepper

2 cups Red-Eye Gravy (page 198)

2 teaspoons fresh thyme leaves

2 tablespoons unsalted butter, at room temperature

2 English muffins, split

4 slices smoked ham

4 Poached Eggs (page 31), warmed

1½ cup Hollandaise (page 56), warmed

¼ cup sliced green onions, green part only

Preheat the oven to 350°F.

Warm the oil in a saucepan over medium heat for 1 minute. Add the mushrooms, season lightly with salt and pepper, and cook, stirring, until the mushrooms soften, about 2 minutes. Add the gravy and thyme, turn the heat to low, and simmer for about 10 minutes.

Butter the cut sides of the English muffins. Place the ham and English muffins on a baking sheet. Slide the baking sheet into the oven and lightly toast the muffins and warm the ham, about 3 minutes. Remove from the oven and cool briefly.

Place 2 English muffin halves topped with a slice of ham on each plate. Spoon the mushroom gravy over the ham. Place a poached egg atop each muffin half, spoon over the hollandaise, and sprinkle with the green onion.

SHAKSHOUKA

SERVES 6

My dear friend and amazing chef Alon Shaya invited me along on a trip to Israel with the equally amazing chefs Mike Solomonov and Ashley Christensen. Preparing for the trip, I wanted to research the Holy Land and its food, so when I hit the ground, I had a grasp on what I could expect. I know a number of people who have made trips there before and all came back blown away. I wanted to suck in every ounce that I could while I was there and I thought going in prepared would help. (A gross miscalculation, it turns out, as there is absolutely no way to prepare yourself for how amazing the food and flavors are in the Holy Land.)

One of the more glaring things about Israel is how similar to the South it is in its ethnic diversity. It is made up of dozens of different immigrant populations that have converged on this region and created a Middle Eastern gumbo of people and, hence, food. One of the dishes I became fascinated with was shakshouka. So much so that I started cooking it before I left, based on certain principles I surmised would define the dish. I never found a version that knocked my socks off while I was there (though I ate a truckload of other amazing food), and I like our version of it better than any I have yet had.

2 pounds fresh San Marzano tomatoes or ripe Roma tomatoes

3 tablespoons extra-virgin olive oil

Salt

3 tablespoons clarified butter (page 30) or your preferred cooking fat

1 yellow onion, diced

1 large red bell pepper, diced

3 cloves garlic, thinly sliced

2 teaspoons za'atar (see Note)

1½ teaspoons ground cumin

2 teaspoons paprika

1 teaspoon red pepper flakes

Black pepper

1½ cups crumbled feta or queso fresco

6 eggs

½ cup chopped fresh cilantro

Warmed buttered pita bread, for serving

Preheat the broiler. Toss together the tomatoes and oil in a bowl. Season lightly with salt and place on an oiled baking sheet. Slide the baking sheet under the broiler. Turn the tomatoes continually until all sides are blistered and browned, but not burnt, 4 to 5 minutes. Remove from the oven and set aside. When cool enough to handle, remove the tops and coarsely chop. Reserve the tomatoes and their juice.

Turn off the broiler and preheat the oven to 375°F.

Warm the butter in a large skillet over medium-low heat for 1 minute. Add the onion and bell pepper and gently cook until very soft, about 3 minutes. Add the garlic and cook until fragrant, about another 30 seconds. Stir in the za'atar, cumin, paprika, and red pepper flakes, and blend completely. Stir in the tomatoes and their juice and season with salt and black pepper. Turn the heat to low and simmer until the tomatoes thicken, about 15 minutes. Stir in the feta.

With a large serving spoon, make 6 indentations in the tomato sauce, evenly spaced around the pan. Gently crack the eggs into the indentations and season the eggs with salt and pepper. Slide the skillet into the oven and bake until the eggs are just set, 5 to 7 minutes. Remove from the oven and sprinkle with the cilantro. Scoop portions from the pan and serve with the pita.

NOTE: Za'atar is actually a couple of things. It is, on one hand, a regional blend of spices (heavy on sumac and thyme) that takes on different flavor profiles depending on the locale and the cook blending it. On the other hand, it is a plant from the oregano family. In the Bible it was referred to as hyssop and is mentioned as a medicinal herb and cleanser. It has a delightful flavor that's like a cross between the pepperiness of savory, the earthiness of thyme, and the sweetness of rosemary. Recipes for blending your own za'atar are available all over the Internet.

OMELETS AND FRITTATAS

I WORKED WITH A GERMAN CHEF NAMED UDO WALTER AS A YOUNG
and *very* inexperienced man early in my career in New Orleans. Chef
Udo was exacting. He was demanding. He had a mean streak in him
as wide as the autobahn. When you weren't looking, he would turn up
your oven to 500°F and yell at you when things burned. He threw hot
pans of broken butter sauce back at cooks who tried to send them
out unnoticed. He tossed piles of prep in the garbage if the brunoise,
julienne, or bâtonnet cuts were not precise. There were times I wanted
to drive my chef's knife as deeply into his heart as I could with one hand
and high-five everyone else in the kitchen with the other.

On occasion we would host a buffet breakfast for
French Quarter tourists and the omelet station was
the dreaded assignment. Prep was brutal. There were
dozens of things to chop, dice, and sauté for fillings.
And, worst of all, you knew that Chef Udo was going to
park on the station and not only watch every movement
you made, but dump anything not 100 percent perfect
in the trash as you would invariably sink deeper and
deeper into the weeds trying to keep up. The backdoor
trading that went on to get out of the assignment
was remarkable. Cooks traded shifts, money, parking
privileges, post-shift beers, anything they could think
of that had value to get out of working the omelet
station. This is where I raked it in.

I loved working omelets. I loved the challenge. I loved
learning, if even through negative reinforcement. I loved
the satisfaction and pride that came along with doing
it right. And, mostly, I loved doing the thing that none
of the other cooks could or wanted to do. Anyone can
produce, without much difficulty, a browned and dried-
out omelet, and most diners will never bat an eye.
But regularly producing a well-cooked omelet takes
practice, patience, concentration, diligence, respect,
and love. This is by no means to say that only pros can
pull it off. But it is to say that without employing the
above-listed attributes, you can fucking forget it.

There are thousands of men and women at the stoves
of Waffle and Huddle Houses nationwide who never
had a German chef on their ass, and yet you can find
as well-prepared an omelet in one of their restaurants as
you will anywhere in the world (and, honestly, better than
most). It's their thing, and it can be yours. The secret,
like so many other things in the kitchen, is simply caring.

So, Udo Walter, the omelet recipes in this chapter
are for you. Thank you for being my taskmaster and
showing me the importance and pride that can come
from performing the most seemingly menial of tasks.
Your message was not lost on at least one young man.

But before you quickly turn the page away from this
chapter, thinking it's all going to be complicated
technique and weeks of practice, I'll let you in on a
secret: you can make an omelet from whatever you
want. At Big Bad Breakfast, much of the time we
just use leftovers from the night before. We have
made shrimp and grit omelets, fried chicken omelets,
cheeseburger omelets, and even a cinnamon roll
omelet for one particular wise guy. (You know who you
are.) The chapter starts out with two master recipes for
basic omelets that you can customize with whatever
fillings and garnishes you want, followed by recipes for
some of our favorite omelet combinations.

Here's another secret: if you don't want to go to the
trouble of making an omelet, you don't even have to
do the complicated rolling part. Just make a "skillet
scramble," which uses the same ingredients you might
find in an omelet but the eggs are lightly scrambled,
instead of worrying yourself to death with classic
omelet technique. Finally, before you begin cooking
from this chapter, you may want to review the tools,
ingredients, and techniques for cooking eggs (page 28)
in chapter 2.

FRENCH-STYLE OMELET MASTER RECIPE

SERVES 1

3 eggs

3 tablespoons whole milk

2 teaspoons mixed chopped fresh herbs of your choosing

Pinch of salt

Pinch of black pepper

2 tablespoons clarified butter (page 30) or your preferred cooking fat

½ cup filling of your choice, plus ¼ cup for the top (optional)

Whisk together the eggs, milk, herbs, salt, and pepper in a bowl until well combined and the whites are no longer stringy and the egg begins to hold bubbles when whisked, about a minute or so. Warm the butter in a nonstick 10-inch skillet over low heat for 1 minute. Pour the egg mixture into the pan and allow to sit for about 30 seconds. Stir the eggs with the back of a fork, while continually swirling the pan in a circular motion, so the uncooked egg fills the cracks left by the cooked egg being pulled away from the surface. After about 1½ minutes, when the egg is about 70 percent cooked, stop stirring, but continue swirling the pan for another 30 seconds. When the egg is almost fully cooked, but still slightly moist, remove the pan from the heat and cool briefly. Hold the pan firmly by the end of the handle. With short but firm motions, strike the handle of the pan close to the pan end and the omelet should slide up the side toward you. Place ½ cup of the filling in the center of the omelet, fold the third of the omelet rising up the side of the pan over onto the filling, and then roll the folded side and filling over onto the third of the omelet remaining in the center of the pan. Slide the omelet onto a plate, top with the remaining filling, and serve immediately.

AMERICAN-STYLE OMELET MASTER RECIPE

SERVES 1

2 eggs

3 tablespoons whole milk

Pinch of salt

Pinch of black pepper

2 tablespoons clarified butter (page 30) or your preferred cooking fat

½ cup filling of your choice, plus ¼ cup for the top (optional)

Combine the eggs, milk, salt, and pepper in a blender and blend on the highest speed for 3 minutes. (While you may be tempted to use a whisk or even a fork instead, a blender is the key to this omelet.) Meanwhile, warm the butter in an 8-inch nonstick skillet over low heat for 1 minute. Pour the eggs directly into the pan and allow to sit for 15 seconds. Turn the heat to medium and start swirling the pan vigorously over the heat. Continue until the eggs are about 85 percent cooked, about 2 minutes; the omelet should be nice and fluffy. Flip the omelet with a spatula (or a flick of the wrist, if you have that move in your arsenal) and return to the heat for 10 seconds. Place the ½ cup filling on one half of the omelet and gently fold over the other half to cover the filling. Slide onto a plate, top with the remaining filling, and serve immediately.

NOTE: You can increase the recipe and make a larger "batch" of omelet mix in the blender. If doing so, measure out a scant 1 cup of egg mix per omelet.

Top: French-Style Omelet; bottom: American-Style Omelet

FRENCH OMELET WITH GRUYÈRE, ASPARAGUS, AND AMERICAN BACON

SERVES 1

One of the few things the French know absolutely nothing about is the beauty of smoky pork belly. As a matter of fact, good people, bacon is ours and ours alone. Sorry, Canada, with your unsmoked impostor "bacon"—you lose. Italy, you're close with your pancetta, but no cigar. American smoked bacon, simply put, kicks ass. There are dozens of things in the French culinary canon that would blast right into the stratosphere with the simple addition of a little American bacon. And not that they aren't perfectly sublime without it, but a kiss from our side of the pond would change the game completely. The traditional French omelet, without equivocation, is one of those things. There, I said it and I'm proud. Dear France, we are here to help you.

I'm also on the record as saying that too many chefs rely on bacon as a crutch, and I stand by that statement. Sadly, lots of folks have misinterpreted my message and think that I actually *dislike* bacon. This could not be further from the truth. I love bacon, I just abhor the overuse of it in an effort to "Southernize" things.

In this recipe, bacon punctuates classic French ingredients and adds a smoky note to an already good omelet. And as much as the bacon helps the overall flavor of the omelet, it's actually the traditional fresh thyme that really provides the knockout punch. Knowing the French are not fans of people (particularly Americans) tinkering with their traditions (especially their food), I hope I have not made myself unwelcome in France with my clumsy, but brilliant, American nuance. I just wanted to help.

FILLING

½ cup asparagus tips, trimmed to 1 inch pieces

¼ cup thin-sliced bacon, chopped (a smoky-flavored bacon is ideal)

3 tablespoons sliced shallot

2 teaspoons fresh thyme leaves

Salt and black pepper

OMELET

3 eggs

3 tablespoons whole milk

Pinch of salt and black pepper

2 tablespoons clarified butter (page 30) or your preferred cooking fat

⅓ cup grated Gruyère cheese

Set up an ice bath by adding ice and cold water to a large bowl.

To make the filling, in a small saucepan, combine 6 cups of water and enough salt to bring the water to the salinity of seawater. Bring to a boil. Add the asparagus tips and cook for 1 minute, then remove and plunge into the ice bath to stop the cooking. Remove from the ice bath and set aside.

Warm a skillet over medium heat for 1 minute. Place the bacon in the pan and cook, stirring constantly, until lightly brown, about 2 minutes Add the shallot and cook, stirring, until it begins to turn transparent, about 1 minute. Stir in the asparagus and thyme and season lightly with salt and pepper. Remove from the heat, cover, and set aside.

To make the omelet, whisk together the eggs, milk, salt, and pepper in a bowl until well combined and the whites are no longer stringy and the egg begins to hold bubbles when whisked, about a minute or so. Warm the clarified butter in a nonstick 10-inch skillet over low heat for 1 minute. Pour the egg mixture into the pan and allow to sit for about 30 seconds. Stir the eggs with the back of a fork, while continually swirling the pan in a circular motion, so the uncooked egg fills the cracks left by the cooked egg being pulled away from the surface. When the egg is about 70 percent cooked, about 1½ minutes, stop stirring, but continue swirling the pan for another 30 seconds. Remove the pan from the heat briefly and place the filling and cheese in the center of the omelet. Fold the sides of the omelet to cover the filling. Slide the omelet onto a plate, seam side down, and serve immediately.

BIG BAD BREAKFAST CHILI AND CHEESE OMELET

SERVES 1

Decades ago, you didn't have to stand in line for hours to get a stool at the Camellia Grill on Carrollton Avenue in New Orleans. Nattily dressed black men with clean crisp aprons, paper caps, black bow ties, and perfectly pressed shirts served cheeseburgers, club sandwiches, milk shakes, and breakfast plates. A friend that rode the school bus with me had family who owned the restaurant, and once in a while, we were sent on the streetcar up St. Charles Avenue for a special treat: dinner at Camellia Grill. At eight or nine years old, being sent off alone on the streetcar for dinner was about as exciting as it got.

My favorite dish on these trips was the chili cheese omelet. It was a behemoth of egg and molten cheese, with gooey cheddar running from every little opening and topped with a giant ladle of bean-filled chili. It was, quite simply, awesome. It was my Matterhorn. I remember lying on the floor of the trolley as it trundled back down St. Charles Avenue on more than one occasion after trying to take it down.

This is my nod to a gentleman named Bat who used to take care of us every time we came in. He was kind and treated us like adults. He was the architect of the second best milk shake I ever had (Dad's being the top of the heap) and always treated us to some Life Savers on our way out the door. I am certain Bat has gone on to his great reward, and I am also certain he is making someone smile wherever he is.

Our chili is made without beans, though a can of them tossed in the pot would not hurt the outcome at all. Beans are just a bold choice at the beginning of the day.

2 eggs

3 tablespoons whole milk

Pinch of salt

Pinch of black pepper

2 tablespoons clarified butter (page 30) or your preferred cooking fat

¾ cup Breakfast Chili (recipe follows), warmed

⅓ cup grated sharp cheddar cheese

¼ cup sliced green onion, green part only

½ serrano chile, sliced (optional)

Combine the eggs, milk, salt, and pepper in a blender and blend on the highest speed for 3 minutes. Meanwhile, warm the clarified butter in an 8-inch nonstick pan over low heat for 1 minute. Pour the eggs directly into the pan and allow to sit for 15 seconds. Turn the heat to medium and start swirling the pan vigorously over the heat. Continue until the eggs are about 85 percent cooked, about 2 minutes; the omelet should be nice and fluffy. Flip the omelet with a spatula or a flick of the wrist and return to the heat for 10 seconds. Place ½ cup of the chili on one half of the omelet, top with the cheese and half of the green onions, and gently fold over the other half to cover the filling. Slide onto a plate and top with the remaining ¼ cup chili. Sprinkle the serrano and remaining green onion on top. Serve immediately.

CONTINUED

BREAKFAST CHILI
MAKES ABOUT 8 CUPS

2½ tablespoons vegetable oil

2 pounds 85 percent lean ground beef

1 tablespoon salt

1½ tablespoons black pepper

1½ cups small diced yellow onion

2½ tablespoons minced garlic

1 tablespoon hot chili powder

2 teaspoons paprika

2 teaspoons ground cumin

1½ teaspoons cayenne pepper

2 cups chicken stock

2 cups tomato sauce

¼ cup masa (see Note)

Warm a Dutch oven over medium heat for 1 minute. Add the oil and warm for 1 minute more. Add the beef and season lightly with salt and black pepper. Cook, stirring constantly to break up the meat, until the meat is completely browned, 8 to 10 minutes. Remove the meat with a slotted spoon to a bowl and reserve. Pour off all but 4 tablespoons of the fat from the pot.

In the same pot, add the onion and garlic and sauté, stirring constantly, until the onion is almost transparent, about 3 minutes. Return the beef to the pot and stir in the salt, black pepper, chili powder, paprika, cumin, and cayenne followed by the stock, tomato sauce, and masa. Continue stirring until fully blended. Turn the heat to low, cover, and simmer for 25 minutes, stirring every 5 minutes or so. Uncover the pot and simmer for 12 minutes more, or until the chili thickens.

Refrigerate in a plastic container for up to 1 week, or freeze for up to 6 months.

NOTE: Masa is wet ground cornmeal available at most grocery stores.

THE "J.Y.D." AN AMERICAN OMELET

SERVES 1

I am certain there was a time when the Denver omelet was a thing of beauty. More often than not these days, when presented with one, it is as exciting as a new season of *The Real Housewives*. Ham is usually as cheap and flavorless as imaginable, there's a smattering of bell peppers, and perhaps mushrooms and a cheese food product. I look at it as being one of the worst symptoms of breakfast neglect in restaurants these days. You can sneak poor pancakes and waffles by unnoticing guests, but a Denver omelet with anything but the freshest ingredients is glaringly shit.

For this one, we use the best country ham we can get our hands on, a selection of mushrooms, and sautéed-to-order bell pepper, onion, and tomato. A touch of *real* American cheese adds a wonderfully gooey and slightly sweet end to this little beast. It is the middle finger to lazy, bullshit omelets, just like J.Y.D. (The Junk Yard Dog) was to pro wrestling in the 1970s . . .

FILLING

1 tablespoon unsalted butter

3 tablespoons diced Benton's country ham (or a quality smoked ham of your choice)

3 tablespoons diced green and red bell pepper

2 tablespoons diced yellow onion

¼ cup stemmed and sliced shiitake mushrooms

3 tablespoons diced fresh tomato

1 tablespoon mixed chopped fresh herbs of your choosing

Salt and black pepper

1½ tablespoons white wine

OMELET

2 eggs

3 tablespoons whole milk

Pinch of salt

Pinch of black pepper

2 tablespoons clarified butter (page 30) or your preferred cooking fat

⅓ cup grated real American cheese (see Note)

To make the filling, melt the butter in a sauté pan over medium heat. Add the ham and cook, stirring constantly, until the edges begin to brown slightly, 30 to 45 seconds. Add the bell pepper and onion and cook, stirring, until the onion turns transparent, about 1 minute. Add the mushrooms and cook, stirring, until the mushrooms soften, about 1 minute more. Add the tomato and herbs and season lightly with salt and pepper. Add the wine, toss very briefly, then cover and remove the pan from the heat. Set aside.

To make the omelet, combine the eggs, milk, salt, and pepper in a blender and blend on the highest speed for 3 minutes. Meanwhile, warm the clarified butter in an 8-inch nonstick pan over low heat for 1 minute. Pour the eggs directly into the pan and allow to sit for 15 seconds. Turn the heat to medium and start swirling the pan vigorously over the heat. Continue until the eggs are about 85 percent cooked, about 2 minutes; the omelet should be nice and fluffy. Flip the omelet with a spatula or a flip of the wrist and return to the heat for 10 seconds. Place the filling on one half of the omelet, top with the cheese, and gently fold over the other half to cover the filling. Slide onto a plate and serve immediately.

NOTE: Real American cheese is actual cheese, not the highly processed, individually wrapped cheese "food," like Kraft singles. It is traditionally a blend of Colby and cheddar, and it is sliceable and grateable.

PEPPER AND CHORIZO FRITTATA

SERVES 2

I've eaten frittatas my whole adult life, but it wasn't until a few years ago that I truly came to appreciate them. On a chilly winter night, I stumbled into a place in Washington, D.C., called Estadio, sidled up to the kitchen bar, and watched a couple of guys bang out these suckers with laserlike precision for an hour. These guys sautéed, swirled, stirred, scraped, and flipped through dozens of those eggy Frisbees, each looking more perfect and delicious than the last.

I came home convinced I would re-create those beautiful little works of art, having watched, mesmerized, as long as I had that one night. But when the first frittata I stuck in the oven looked deflated and bland, I became a little despondent. Luckily, much to my surprise, it was absolutely perfect by the time I pulled it out of the oven. Turns out these little suckers are all about trust, preparation, and submission. A perfect frittata is easy to make—just don't be afraid to use a heavy hand with your cooking fat, prep all of your ingredients before you start cooking, and submit to swirling your creation without scraping and scrambling it. A frittata is basically a quiche with no crust, so it's perfect for all of you weirdos out there with carb issues.

Secret: A little fatty dairy makes these beasts roar. By adding cream and whole milk you are technically moving it toward a custard—and that's what sets these guys apart from a simple open-faced omelet. It adds to the fluff and smoothness of the final product, so armed with that info, fire away!

6 eggs, well beaten

¼ cup whole milk

¼ cup heavy cream

½ teaspoon salt

½ teaspoon black pepper

¼ teaspoon ground cumin

1 tablespoon unsalted butter

4 ounces spicy Mexican chorizo, crumbled

¾ cup sliced red and green bell pepper

3 tablespoons diced yellow onion

2 teaspoons minced garlic

1 jalapeño, seeded and diced (optional)

½ cup grated cheddar cheese

Preheat the oven to 325°F.

In a stainless steel bowl, whisk together the eggs, milk, cream, salt, pepper, and cumin until well combined. Set aside.

Warm a 10-inch sauté pan over medium heat for 30 seconds, then melt the butter. Add the chorizo and cook, stirring constantly, until fully cooked, about 3 minutes. Remove with a slotted spoon and drain on paper towels.

Pour off all but 2 tablespoons of the remaining fat from the pan. In the same pan, combine the bell pepper, onion, garlic, and jalapeño and sauté until softened, about 2 minutes. Pour off and discard any excess fat. Return the chorizo to the pan, then pour the egg mixture evenly over the chorizo and vegetables. Begin swirling the pan vigorously and while doing so, sprinkle ¼ cup of the cheese over the top and swirl into the frittata. As the eggs begin to set, after a couple of minutes, sprinkle the remaining ¼ cup cheese over the top and slide the pan into the oven. Bake until the center sets up and the edges pull away from the sides of the pan, 8 to 10 minutes. Allow to sit for 2 minutes, then turn out onto a plate, slice into wedges, and serve immediately.

ROASTED POTATO AND ADOBO FRITTATA

SERVES 2

The best frittatas I have ever eaten always involved potatoes. And though I never understood the magic in the combination of roasted potatoes and eggs, I have always love blending those two things on a plate. As I was writing this and considering it, it struck me how much I loved the terrible fried potato things on fast-food breakfast menus served with egg biscuits or sandwiches or how perfectly a gigantic pile of hash browns or tater tots (which are potato-esque, at least) goes with a plate of eggs. Suddenly, the roasted potato frittata made all the sense in the world. Amazing how these things will escape a weak mind from time to time. For this one I toss the potatoes in an adobo rub, which is particularly good with potatoes but also goes nicely on grilled fish, pork, and chicken, if you have any extra.

The nice thing about a frittata is, you can substitute just about anything you have on hand—meat, vegetable, herb, or cheese—to come up with hundreds of different combinations.

1 cup (½-inch) cubed, red-skinned potatoes, skin left on

2 tablespoons olive oil

2½ teaspoons black pepper

2 teaspoons salt

½ cup Adobo Rub (recipe follows)

6 eggs, well beaten

¼ cup whole milk

¼ cup heavy cream

½ teaspoon Tabasco pepper sauce

1 tablespoon unsalted butter

3 tablespoons chopped bacon

¼ cup slivered yellow onion

2 teaspoons minced garlic

¼ cup coarsely chopped fresh cilantro

½ cup grated fontina cheese

Preheat the oven to 325°F. Line a baking sheet with aluminum foil or parchment paper.

Toss the potatoes with the oil, 2 teaspoons of the pepper, and 1½ teaspoons of the salt in a stainless steel bowl. Pour the potatoes onto the prepared baking sheet and bake until the potatoes just begin to brown lightly, about 25 minutes. Remove from the oven and dump the potatoes into the same bowl they were marinated in, add the Adobo Rub, and toss to coat the potatoes well. Return the potatoes to the baking sheet and bake until they are easily pierced with a fork, about 8 minutes more. Remove from the oven. Set aside and allow to cool to room temperature.

In a separate stainless steel bowl, whisk together the eggs, milk, cream, Tabasco, the remaining ½ teaspoon salt, and the remaining ½ teaspoon pepper until well combined. Set aside.

Warm a 10-inch sauté pan over medium heat for 30 seconds, then melt the butter. Add the bacon and cook, stirring constantly, until fully cooked and almost crispy, 4 to 5 minutes. Remove and drain on paper towels. Pour off all but 1½ tablespoons of the bacon fat from the pan and return to the stove over medium heat.

In the same pan, combine the onion and garlic and sauté until softened, about 2 minutes. Pour off and discard any excess fat. Return the bacon to the pan, then pour the egg mixture over the bacon and aromatics. Sprinkle the cilantro and cooked potatoes on top. Begin swirling the pan vigorously, sprinkle ¼ cup of the cheese over the top, and swirl in completely. As the eggs begin to set, sprinkle the remaining ¼ cup cheese over the top and slide the pan into the oven. Bake until the center sets up and the edges pull away from the sides of the pan, 8 to 10 minutes. Allow to sit for 2 minutes, then turn out onto a plate, slice into wedges, and serve immediately.

CONTINUED

ADOBO RUB

MAKES ABOUT 1 CUP

2 tablespoons vegetable oil

3 dried guajillo chiles

2 ancho chiles

1 dried chile de árbol

¼ cup diced yellow onion

1 tablespoon plus 1 teaspoon
freshly squeeze lime juice

1 tablespoon minced garlic

2 teaspoons ground cumin

2 teaspoons ground
coriander

1 teaspoon salt

1 teaspoon sugar

Warm the oil in a large skillet over high heat for 1 minute. Working in batches, add the chiles and fry until they begin to brown lightly, about 2 minutes on each side. Remove and drain on paper towels. Place the chiles in a saucepan and add enough water to cover. Bring to a boil, then simmer for 20 minutes. Drain the chiles, reserving the cooking liquid, and allow them to cool briefly. When they're cool enough to handle, remove the stems, seeds, and any remaining white membrane.

Place the chiles in a blender and add just enough of the chile water to make a smooth puree. Add the onion, lime juice, garlic, cumin, coriander, salt, and sugar and blend until smooth. Add more water as needed. Adobo rub should be the consistency of a loose paste. Store in a glass container and refrigerate for up to 6 weeks.

NOTE: This recipe makes more than needed for the frittata. Rub it on chicken or pork for a slow roast that comes out spectacular, or stir a little into sour cream with a touch of lime juice for a really nice dip.

OPEN-FACED STEWED OKRA AND TOMATO FRITT-OMELET WITH SWISS CHEESE

SERVES 1

I'll eat good stewed okra and tomatoes out of a Dumpster. That's what my editor calls hyperbole. However, I've not yet found myself in a Dumpster–okra situation, so until that day, none of us knows if it's actually hyperbole or not.

I love stewed okra and tomatoes that much. There is a primal beauty to this dish that is absolutely transcendent. It completely connects with the season, the earth, the palate, the soul, and even the history of Southern food. Okra is a vegetable that, unlike many others, has to have its flavor coaxed from it. Unlike corn or peppers, whose flavors jump out at you immediately, okra has to be cooked slowly and carefully to fully unleash its wonderfully complex flavors. When paired with the natural sweetness of summer tomatoes, okra's flavors are explosive. It has a sweetness and a tartness. It is crunchy and smooth. It is spicy and earthy, and for me at least, it carries me to a very happy place in my life every time I taste it. Okra was a family favorite when I was little, especially toward the end of summer when it could literally go from "just about ready to pick" in the morning to "too tough to cook" in the afternoon.

Technically, this is more a frittata than an omelet, but since the filling is on top rather than cooked inside, I just call it the Fritt-Omelet, the love child of the frittata and omelet. When it is topped with the slight tang of a little Swiss cheese and a splash of hot sauce, little can touch it.

Leftover okra and tomatoes can be eaten over rice or just warmed and served with sautéed fish, roasted chicken, sliced pork . . . hell, anything. It's really that good.

3 eggs

3 tablespoons whole milk

1 tablespoon heavy cream

½ teaspoon salt

1 teaspoon black pepper

2 tablespoons clarified butter (page 30) or your preferred cooking fat

2 tablespoon chopped fresh parsley

½ cup grated Swiss cheese

¾ cup Black Pepper Stewed Okra and Tomatoes (recipe follows), warmed

Preheat the oven to 350°F.

Combine the eggs, milk, cream, salt, and pepper in a blender and blend on the highest speed for 30 seconds. Warm the clarified butter in a small ovenproof sauté pan over medium heat for 30 seconds. Add the egg mixture, 1 tablespoon of the parsley, and ¼ cup of the cheese and start swirling the pan vigorously over the heat. Continue for 1½ minutes, stopping occasionally to allow the eggs to set up for a few seconds. Once the eggs have almost cooked completely, flip the omelet over with a spatula or the flick of the wrist, top with the remaining ¼ cup cheese, and place the pan in the oven for 1 minute to melt the cheese. Remove from the oven. Slide the Fritt-Omelet out of the pan onto a plate, spoon the warm okra and tomatoes over the top, and sprinkle with the remaining 1 tablespoon parsley. Serve immediately.

CONTINUED

BLACK PEPPER STEWED OKRA AND TOMATOES

MAKES 4 CUPS

1 tablespoon bacon fat or unsalted butter

1 tablespoon olive oil

½ cup small diced yellow onion

1½ teaspoons minced garlic

3 cups sliced small okra

3 tomatoes, cored, seeded, and chopped

2½ teaspoons black pepper

Salt

¼ cup white wine

¼ cup chicken stock, plus more if needed

1 tablespoon fresh thyme leaves

½ teaspoon Tabasco pepper sauce

Warm the bacon fat and olive oil in a saucepan over medium heat for 1 minute. Add the onion and garlic and sauté until tender, 2 or 3 minutes. Add the okra, tomatoes, and black pepper and season with salt. Allow to simmer, stirring constantly, until the okra softens and gets stringy, 7 to 8 minutes. Add the wine, stock, thyme, and Tabasco, turn the heat to low, and gently simmer, stirring occasionally, until the okra is tender, 15 to 20 minutes. Add more stock or water to keep the okra moist, if needed. Remove from the heat and allow to cool to room temperature. Store in a plastic or glass container and refrigerate for up to 4 days.

HERBOLACE, AKA THE ORIGINAL FINES HERBES OMELET

SERVES 1

The omelet has a long and debated history. The French certainly want to lay claim to having invented—or at least perfected—the dish, but in fact, the earliest known recipe for an omelet-like dish appeared in England in the late 1500s. The dish was called an herbolace and it was a baked pan of mixed eggs with torn herbs and a touch of ginger.

I think one of the most wonderful gifts that age and experience delivers men and women in my profession is an appreciation for the beauty of minimalism. As young, inexperienced chefs, many of us slouched toward creating recipes with dozens of ingredients, laboring under the impression that the more we could work into a recipe, the more complex it would become. But as with mixing colors, the more we mix, the muddier things tend to get.

The *fines herbes* omelet is a study in minimalist beauty. Butter, eggs, salt, and a blend of herbs in the right hands are all that is needed for one of the finest bites one can have. This recipe calls for the addition of a little bit of minced ginger and a touch of white pepper, both of which add a little spice and brighten the herbs. Then I go off script and add some sautéed tomato and onion for a hint of acid and some added substance.

1 tablespoon olive oil

3 tablespoons minced shallot

1 teaspoon minced garlic

¾ cup diced tomato

Salt and black pepper

2 eggs

3 tablespoons whole milk

1½ tablespoons mixed chopped fresh herbs of your choosing

2 teaspoons minced fresh ginger

White pepper

2 tablespoons clarified butter (page 30) or your preferred cooking fat

½ cup grated Gruyère cheese

Warm the oil in a small sauté pan over medium heat for 30 seconds. Add the shallot and garlic and sauté until the shallot begins to turn transparent, about 1½ minutes. Stir in the tomato, season lightly with salt and black pepper, and cook until the tomatoes begin to soften slightly, about 1 minute more. Remove from the heat and set aside.

Combine the eggs, milk, herbs, and ginger in a blender and season lightly with salt and white pepper. Blend on the highest speed for 3 minutes. Meanwhile, warm the clarified butter in an 8-inch nonstick pan, over low heat for 1 minute. Pour the egg mixture directly into the pan and allow to sit for 15 seconds. Turn the heat to medium and start swirling the pan vigorously over the heat. Continue until the eggs are about 85 percent cooked, about 2 minutes; the omelet should be nice and fluffy. Flip the omelet with a spatula or a flick of the wrist and return to the heat for 10 seconds. Place one-third of the tomato mixture on one half of the omelet, top with three-quarters of the cheese, and gently fold over the other half of the omelet to cover the filling. Slide onto a plate and sprinkle with the remaining cheese and tomato mixture. Serve immediately.

SHRIMP AND BACON OMELET WITH SOFT CHEESE AND PESTO

SERVES 1

Challenge: In five seconds or less, think of anything that smells better than bacon, onion, and shrimp cooking together in a skillet . . . you lose. There is nothing. Unless you put all of that in an omelet and add a little La Tur and some fresh pesto. Then, well, I was wrong, but I am willing to bet *that* was not what you were thinking.

La Tur is a soft, slightly stinky Italian cheese I became acquainted with a few years ago. It is wonderfully affordable (like so many delicious Italian things that are not called truffle), and with some pesto, it will make one of the finest omelets you've ever had or I'll give you your money back. You can take *that* to the bank.

FILLING

1 tablespoon cold, cubed unsalted butter

¼ cup chopped bacon

¼ cup sliced red onion

Pinch of red pepper flakes

½ cup peeled and chopped medium Gulf brown shrimp

Salt and pepper

OMELET

3 eggs

3 tablespoons whole milk

Pinch of salt

Pinch of black pepper

2 tablespoons clarified butter (page 30) or your preferred cooking fat

3 tablespoons Herb Pistou (page 36) or store-bought basil pesto

3 tablespoons La Tur, Brie, or Époisses, or 4 tablespoons grated Swiss or Gruyère cheese

To make the filling, melt the butter in a sauté pan over medium heat. Add the bacon and cook, stirring constantly, until almost crispy, about 3 minutes. Remove with a slotted spoon and drain on paper towels. Pour off all but about 1 tablespoon of the fat from the pan.

In the same pan, add the onion and red pepper flakes and cook until the onion begins to turn transparent, 2 to 3 minutes. Add the shrimp, season lightly with salt and pepper, and stir until the shrimp just turn opaque, about 1½ minutes. (Do not fully cook the shrimp because the carry-over heat will finish them off.) Stir in the reserved bacon. Transfer the filling to a small bowl and set aside.

To make the omelet, whisk together the eggs, milk, salt, and pepper in a bowl until well combined and the whites are no longer stringy and the egg begins to hold bubbles when whisked, about a minute. Warm the clarified butter in a 10-inch nonstick skillet over low heat for 1 minute. Pour the egg mixture into the pan and allow to sit for about 30 seconds. Stir the eggs with the back of a fork, while continually swirling the pan in a circular motion, so the uncooked egg fills the cracks left by the cooked egg being pulled away from the surface. When the egg is about 70 percent cooked, about 1½ minutes, stop stirring, but continue swirling the pan for another 30 seconds. Remove the pan from the heat briefly and place the filling, 1 tablespoon of the pistou, and the cheese in the center of the omelet. Fold the sides of the omelet to cover the filling. Slide the omelet onto a plate, dollop with the remaining 2 tablespoons pistou, and serve immediately.

SHRIMP FRIED RICE OMURICE

SERVES 1

Europeans aren't the only ones with a tradition of omelet cookery. In Japan, tamagoyaki is a classic rolled omelet, often served with mirin and bonito flakes. Omurice is another version that mimics Western omelets and is filled with fried rice and topped with ketchup (usually copious amounts). I was fascinated with this immediately because, as a kid, I loved ketchup on eggs (or well, let's be honest, on fucking everything) . . . so this was an excuse to eat ketchup on eggs as an adult *and* make use of leftover fried rice.

For this treatment, we use shrimp fried rice, though any leftover fried or even white rice would suffice. The leftover Soy-Sriracha Ketchup also goes great on burgers and fried chicken.

FRIED RICE

1½ tablespoons vegetable oil

1 tablespoon sesame oil

3 tablespoons diced yellow onion

2 teaspoons minced garlic

3 tablespoons diced carrot

3 tablespoons English peas

⅓ cup peeled and chopped medium shrimp (or whole, fully peeled tiny shrimp)

1 cup cooked long-grain white rice

1 tablespoon soy sauce

OMURICE

3 eggs

¼ cup heavy cream

½ teaspoon ground ginger

½ teaspoon white pepper

¼ teaspoon salt

1½ teaspoons clarified butter (page 30) or your preferred cooking fat

½ teaspoon sesame oil

4 tablespoons Soy-Sriracha Ketchup (recipe follows), for serving

To make the fried rice, heat a wok or skillet over medium-high heat for 30 seconds. Add the vegetable and sesame oils and heat for 15 seconds more. Add the onion and garlic and stir vigorously for 5 seconds so the garlic doesn't burn. Immediately add the carrot and peas and continue to cook, stirring, until the carrot begins to soften, 1 to 2 minutes. Add the shrimp and cook, stirring, until they begin to turn opaque, about 1 minute. Add the cooked rice and sauté, stirring and turning the rice over constantly, until completely warmed through, about 30 seconds. Stir in the soy sauce, remove from the heat, and set aside.

To make the omurice, whisk together the eggs, cream, ginger, white pepper, and salt in a bowl until well combined. Set aside. Warm the clarified butter and sesame oil in a 10-inch nonstick skillet over medium heat for 30 seconds. Add the egg mixture and as soon the egg begins to cook, give it a couple of good stirs with a silicone spatula. Swirl the pan and stir conservatively, as you would for a French omelet (see page 66). As soon as the egg is almost fully cooked, after about 3 minutes or so, pull from the heat and tap the handle of the pan so the omelet climbs the far lip of the pan. Fill the center of the omelet with the fried rice and drizzle with 1 or 2 tablespoons of the Soy-Sriracha Ketchup. Fold the front lip of the omelet over the rice and roll the omelet over onto the back lip to seal it. Carefully slide onto a plate and top with the remaining 2 or 3 tablespoons Soy-Sriracha Ketchup. Serve immediately.

SOY-SRIRACHA KETCHUP

MAKES ABOUT 1 CUP

¾ cup tomato ketchup

1½ tablespoons soy sauce

1 tablespoon Sriracha

1 tablespoon chopped fresh cilantro

2 teaspoons freshly squeezed lime juice

2 teaspoons honey

1 teaspoon ground ginger

1 green onion, white part only, minced

Salt and black pepper

Combine all of the ingredients in a stainless steel bowl. Cover and refrigerate for 30 minutes. Season with salt and pepper. Store in a glass jar and refrigerate for up to 1 month.

LOW COUNTRY CAST-IRON SKILLET SCRAMBLE

SERVES 1

I started visiting Charleston, South Carolina, when I was in college in Virginia and North Carolina. I immediately liked it because the Low Country, as it is known, with its watery grassland, was a more regal-looking version of the marsh I grew up in hunting and fishing in south Louisiana. Charleston itself reminds me of old New Orleans, its European-style townhouses stacked side by side and a "Creole" cuisine steeped in tradition and history. As much as I felt a bond with the city, I was always oddly ill at ease there and came to feel like it was New Orleans with a stick up its ass. Years later, a friend would clap me on the shoulder as I mused over this and said, "Remember, New Orleans was settled by the Spanish and French, Charleston was settled by the English. Think about that, why don't ya!" The folks of the area do a Low Country boil that is a less spicy version of a Cajun shrimp boil. This is a tip of the hat to what my buddies in South Carolina do.

¼ cup fresh or frozen corn kernels

2 teaspoons olive oil

Salt and black pepper

¼ cup clarified butter (page 30) or your preferred cooking fat

2 tablespoons chopped yellow onion

2 teaspoons minced garlic

½ cup diced andouille sausage

⅓ cup medium shrimp, peeled

¼ teaspoon plus a pinch of Old Bay seasoning

½ cup Potato Hash (recipe follows)

¼ cup diced tomato

2 eggs, well beaten

¼ cup grated cheddar cheese

3 tablespoons sliced green onion, green parts only

Preheat the broiler.

In a small ovenproof skillet (see Note), stir together the corn and olive oil and season with a pinch of salt and black pepper. Broil, stirring every 30 or 45 seconds, until the corn begins to brown lightly, 5 to 6 minutes. Remove from the oven and set aside. Do not turn off the broiler.

Warm the clarified butter in a 6-inch cast-iron pan over medium heat for 1 minute. Add the onion and garlic and sauté until the onion begins to turn transparent, about 1 minute. Add the andouille, shrimp, ¼ teaspoon Old Bay, and Potato Hash, season with salt and pepper, and sauté, stirring constantly, until the shrimp turn opaque, 2 to 3 minutes. Stir in the broiled corn and diced tomato and cook, stirring, until warmed through, about 30 seconds.

Add the eggs and slowly scramble with a silicone spatula, scraping up large curds from the bottom of the pan. Just as the eggs are almost set but still a tiny bit runny, after about 2 minutes, turn off the heat and sprinkle with the cheese. Slide the pan under the broiler and broil until the cheese melts, 10 to 15 seconds. Remove from the oven and sprinkle with the green onions and a pinch of Old Bay. Serve immediately in the cast-iron skillet.

NOTE: If you don't have an ovenproof skillet, cook in a nonstick pan until the eggs are just done. Transfer the scramble to an ovenproof dish, sprinkle with cheese, and finish under the broiler.

CONTINUED

POTATO HASH

MAKES 2 CUPS

2 cups diced baking potato, cut into ½-inch cubes

Salt and black pepper

2 tablespoons bacon fat or your preferred cooking fat

¼ cup diced yellow onion

Set up an ice bath by adding ice and cold water to a large bowl. Place the potato in a medium saucepan with 2 cups of water and 2 tablespoons of salt. Bring to a boil over medium heat and cook until the potatoes can be easily pierced with a knife, 2 or 3 minutes. Drain the potatoes, then plunge into the ice bath for a minute or so to stop the cooking.

Warm the bacon fat in a nonstick sauté pan over medium heat for 1 minute. Add the onion and cook, stirring, until transparent, about 2 minutes. Add the potatoes, stirring to combine, and season immediately with salt and pepper. Continue to cook, slowly stirring, until lightly browned, 5 to 6 minutes. Serve immediately or set aside for a Skillet Scramble (pages 87 to 93).

THE STORY OF THE SKILLET SCRAMBLE

The idea for the scrambles we developed at the restaurant was to create a less fussy, more rustic omelet. We make a variety of them by building on basic ingredients, such as eggs, hash brown potatoes, and onions, and adding themed ingredients to create dishes like the Low Country Cast-Iron (page 87), the Creole (page 91), and the Yard Work (page 93) Skillet Scrambles. They are fun, attractive, and filling.

Even better, I have this weird love of serving food in the vessel it has been cooked in. To me, it delivers 100 percent of the possible flavor as well as added curb appeal when the cook-soiled, war-torn cast-iron pan slides right in front of the guest when it hits the table . . . kinda like eating at home.

Finally, one of the challenges of serving eggs can be to deliver them hot, but an even greater challenge is to deliver them hot but not dried out. You can achieve this with the use of warmed miniature cast-iron skillets. Warm them up in the oven beforehand, then when you put almost cooked eggs in them, they finish cooking them (and keep them warm) just as they arrive at the table.

Lodge Cast Iron makes a 6-inch skillet that is readily available on the Internet in some retail outlets, and at the Lodge Outlet stores, but if this is not an option, a similar-sized ovenproof ceramic dish will work just as well. Alternatively, scale up the Skillet recipes and make 2 or 3 in a pie pan or 6 to 8 in a baking dish.

CREOLE SKILLET SCRAMBLE

SERVES 2

This one could not be a more natural combination for me. It combines all of the elements of crawfish étouffée (one of my favorite dishes) with a little andouille sausage (one of my desert island selections) and eggs (one of my favorite ingredients). The result is a trifecta of south Louisiana deliciousness . . . a bitchin' bayou breakfast. (Add another BBB to the books.) There really is no good substitute for crawfish tails, but in a pinch, chopped shrimp or lobster tails might do. Frozen craw-fish should be thawed overnight in the refrigerator.

5 eggs

¼ cup whole milk

¼ teaspoon plus 2 pinches of salt

1 teaspoon plus 2 pinches of black pepper

2 teaspoons plus 2 pinches of Creole seasoning

1½ tablespoons olive oil

¼ cup diced andouille sausage

¼ cup diced yellow onion

2 teaspoons minced garlic

¼ cup diced celery

¼ cup diced red and green bell pepper

½ cup chopped tomato

½ cup frozen cooked crawfish tail meat, thawed

1 tablespoon freshly squeezed lemon juice

½ cup Potato Hash (page 87)

½ cup grated cheddar cheese

3 tablespoons chopped green onion, green part only

1 tablespoon chopped fresh parsley

Preheat the broiler.

Whisk together the eggs, milk, 2 pinches of salt, 2 pinches of black pepper, and 2 pinches of Creole seasoning in a bowl until well combined. Set aside.

Warm the oil in a 10-inch, nonstick sauté pan over medium heat for 1 minute. Add the andouille sausage and sauté, stirring, until the sausage begins to brown, about 2 minutes. Remove with a slotted spoon and drain on paper towels.

In the same pan, add the onion and garlic and sauté until the onion begins to turn transparent, about 1 minute. Add the celery and bell pepper and sauté until tender, about 2 minutes. Add the tomato, remaining 1 teaspoon pepper, and remaining ¼ teaspoon salt and stir until warmed through, about 45 seconds. Add the crawfish and remaining 2 teaspoons Creole seasoning, stir until combined, and cook until warmed through, 30 to 45 seconds. Stir in the lemon juice, then add the Potato Hash, stir until combined, and cook until warmed through, about 30 seconds.

Pour in the egg mixture and allow to sit, without stirring, for 15 seconds. Stir from time to time gently with a silicone spatula, scraping up large curds from the bottom of the pan and tilting the skillet to let loose, uncooked egg run onto the bottom of the pan, about 3 minutes. Just as the eggs are almost set but still a tiny bit runny, transfer to an ovenproof dish, sprinkle with the cheddar cheese, and place under the broiler for 30 to 45 seconds, or until the cheese begins to melt. Remove from the broiler and sprinkle with the green onion and parsley. Serve immediately.

ROASTED MUSHROOM SKILLET SCRAMBLE

SERVES 2

Mushrooms occupy a very weird space for me. There can be times that they are painfully forgettable, placed in a dish for little more than textural reasons. At other times, they are nothing short of resplendent, like when they are sautéed with way too much butter and spiked with barely warmed garlic and herbs. One of my favorite ways to prepare them is to give them a good hot roast and put a little bit of a crispy crust on them. It invariably brings a meaty taste to them, especially when they are tossed with a little Worcestershire sauce before roasting. This recipe is one of my favorite subtle, earthy, but totally luscious dishes.

5 eggs

¼ cup heavy cream

3 tablespoons chopped fresh herbs of your choosing

4 cups assorted whole mushrooms (such as oyster, chanterelle, enoki, shiitake), stemmed as needed (see Note)

¼ cup olive oil

1½ tablespoons Worcestershire sauce

1½ teaspoons minced garlic

1 teaspoon black pepper

½ teaspoon salt

3 tablespoons extra-virgin olive oil

⅓ cup slivered shallot

¼ cup grated fontina cheese

Preheat the oven to 400°F. Line a baking sheet with aluminum foil or parchment paper. Whisk together the eggs, cream, and 2 tablespoons of the herbs in a bowl until well combined. Set aside.

In another bowl, toss the mushrooms with the ¼ cup olive oil, Worcestershire sauce, garlic, pepper, and salt. Pour the mushroom mixture onto the prepared baking sheet. Bake for 10 minutes, then stir the mushrooms and bake until the mushrooms begin to brown and their edges get crispy, about 5 minutes more. Remove from the oven and allow to cool briefly. When cool enough to handle, slice into small bite-size pieces. Preheat the broiler.

Meanwhile, warm 1½ tablespoons of the extra-virgin olive oil in a 10-inch nonstick skillet over medium heat for 30 seconds. Add the shallot and cook, stirring, until it begins to turn transparent, 30 to 45 seconds. Stir in the mushrooms and cook until warmed thorough, about 45 seconds.

Pour in the egg mixture and allow to sit, without stirring, for 15 seconds. Stir from time to time gently with a silicone spatula, scraping up large curds from the bottom of the pan and tilting the skillet to let loose, uncooked egg run onto the bottom of the pan, about 3 minutes. Just as the eggs are almost set but still a tiny bit runny, transfer to a medium-size ovenproof dish and sprinkle with the cheese. Place under the broiler for 30 to 45 seconds, or until the cheese just melts. Remove from the broiler, drizzle with the remaining 1½ tablespoons extra-virgin olive oil, sprinkle with the remaining 1 table-spoon mixed fresh herbs, and serve immediately.

NOTE: Most mushrooms have edible stems. Certain varieties like shiitake, though, have tough inedible stems. Consult the Internet, should you have questions about a specific variety.

YARD WORK SKILLET SCRAMBLE

SERVES 2

Ladies and gentlemen, please meet one of the vegetarian menu items on the planet that actually sells. I say this because the dirty little secret is that as much as we get beaten up by people demanding vegetarian menu items, they are invariably the worst-selling dishes on the menu. As a result, we take great pride in rising to the challenge of creating things "off the menu" for our vegetarian guests.

This recipe is meant to be adjusted to wherever your tastes may run. Different vegetables are in season at different times of the year, but the ones here can be found in the grocery store at almost any time. Use the vegetables listed or be bold and select whatever's growing in your yard or available at your local farmers' market whenever you want to go all "hippie" and make this. Whatever you do, you'll end up happy.

5 eggs

¼ cup whole milk

Salt and black pepper

2 tablespoons water

2 cups fresh spinach, stems removed

1½ tablespoons clarified butter (page 30) or your preferred cooking fat

3 tablespoons diced yellow onion

2 teaspoons minced garlic

¼ cup chopped button mushrooms

¼ cup (¼ inch) diced zucchini

¼ cup (¼ inch) diced yellow squash

¼ cup chopped tomato

3 tablespoons diced red and green bell pepper

1½ tablespoons chopped fresh herbs of your choosing

½ cup Potato Hash (page 87)

¼ cup crumbled soft goat cheese

3 tablespoons grated Swiss cheese

Preheat the broiler.

Whisk together the eggs, milk, a pinch of salt, and 2 pinches of black pepper in a bowl until well combined. Set aside.

Warm the water in a large sauté pan over medium heat for 45 seconds. Place the spinach in the pan and turn the heat to low. Begin turning the spinach carefully. The spinach will wilt in a matter of a few minutes. As soon as it has completely wilted, remove to a strainer and press out as much of the water as you can. Set aside and keep warm.

Warm the clarified butter in a 10-inch, nonstick sauté pan over medium heat for 30 seconds. Add the onion and garlic and sauté, stirring constantly, until the onion begins to turn transparent, about 30 seconds. Add the mushrooms, zucchini, and yellow squash and cook, stirring constantly, until they begin to soften, 1 to 2 minutes. Stir in the tomato, bell pepper, and herbs, season lightly with salt and pepper, and sauté until the tomato begins to break down slightly, 1 minute more. Add the spinach and Potato Hash, stir until combined, and cook until warmed through, about 30 seconds.

Pour in the egg mixture and allow to sit, without stirring, for 15 seconds. Stir from time to time with a silicone spatula, scraping up large curds from the bottom of the pan, and tilting the skillet to let loose, uncooked egg run onto the bottom of the pan, about 3 minutes. Just as the eggs are almost set but still a tiny bit runny, transfer to an ovenproof dish, add the goat cheese and stir one last time. Sprinkle the Swiss cheese on top and put under the broiler for 30 to 45 seconds or until the Swiss cheese just begins to melt. Remove from the broiler and serve immediately.

PANCAKES, WAFFLES, CREPES,

AND OTHER THINGS "BREADY"

THIS CHAPTER SHOULD REALLY BE CALLED "THE BRUTALLY CRUEL Deception of Breakfast." Why? Well, the things contained herein are just that: a deception, a mirage, a scam, a lie. These bready goods *seem* like a good idea when you sit down to order them. "I should have something light and vaguely healthy," you tell yourself, foolishly ignoring the pathological pull of a plate of waffles or pancakes. Unable to avoid the urge, you order that giant stack of pecan pancakes, convinced that this time things will be different. This time they will not fill you up and you *will* go to the gym and work them off. Your first sugary, syrupy bite delivers an endorphin rush like a roller coaster, but after the second or third bite you begin to fade quickly. Bread and cake will beat you every time, but it is so freaking good.

CHAPTER
4

At Big Bad Breakfast, we offer a solution for reasonable diners who want to sate their sweet tooth without committing to a morning of overfull groaning: side orders of either a single pancake or a small serving of silver dollar pancakes. These smaller portions allow you to soothe the pancake beast within and still get a savory option.

For those of you who go down the waffle rabbit hole, well, you're on your own. I haven't figured out how to make a silver dollar waffle yet. Buck up, though—things could be a hell of a lot worse.

SILVER DOLLAR AND SHORT STACK BUTTERMILK PANCAKES

MAKES ABOUT 30 SILVER DOLLAR-SIZED PANCAKES OR 8 GIANT-SIZED ONES

I am not sure who the fool was who presented me and my brother with silver dollar pancakes when we were lads, but I am certain that my parents still want to do terrible things to him or her. Because the moment the first one crossed my lips, no other pancake size would ever again be acceptable. You see, there is something weirdly mystical about miniaturized food that makes kids go insane. Maybe it's that the scale of the food gives children a greater sense control. As a youngster, I imagined the little pancakes made me a giant. We loved that we could eat them in spades rather than in a mere stack of three.

This is the exact same recipe we use for our buttermilk short stack, which is something I find infinitely entertaining because there is *nothing* short about it and its girth . . . well, it's impressive. These are amazingly light and fluffy and the heavy hand of vanilla extract gives them a punch-in-the-mouth flavor. They are a good make-ahead-and-freeze breakfast to reheat for the kids. But make no mistake, they are never better than eaten straight out of the pan, no matter what size you make them.

2½ cups all-purpose flour

6 tablespoons sugar

2 tablespoons baking powder

1 teaspoon baking soda

¾ teaspoon salt

1½ cups buttermilk

¾ cup whole milk

3 eggs

2¼ teaspoons pure vanilla extract

6 tablespoons unsalted butter, melted

Clarified butter (page 30) or your preferred cooking fat

Unsalted butter, cane syrup, fresh fruit, peanut butter, or sausage, for topping (optional)

In a bowl, whisk together the flour, sugar, baking powder, baking soda, and salt. In a separate bowl, whisk together the buttermilk, milk, eggs, and vanilla. Pour the buttermilk mixture into the flour mixture and whisk together until the batter is smooth. Pour in the melted butter and stir with a spatula until fully incorporated.

Warm 1½ tablespoons of the clarified butter in a sauté pan over medium heat for 30 seconds. To make silver dollar pancakes, spoon heaping tablespoonfuls of batter into the pan. To make regular pancakes, spoon the batter into the pan a scant ½ cup at a time. Cook until the tops begin to bubble lightly, about 1½ minutes. Flip over and cook until the other side begins to brown lightly and the pancakes look good and fluffy, about 30 seconds more. Repeat with the remaining batter, adding more clarified butter between batches as needed. Consume immediately with butter and cane syrup and strawberries, and bananas, and peanut butter, and sausage.

BELGIAN WAFFLES

MAKES 3 TO 4 WAFFLES

I will not lie, waffles didn't play a huge part in our lives when I was growing up. And it wasn't for lack of equipment: we had a hulking, brittle plastic and tarnished metal "waffle bot" capable of producing said foodstuff, but using it fell within my dad's realm of responsibility. My brother and I loved waffles and the process of them being made, but for some reason our dad dug his heels in like a man on his way to the electric chair whenever we set our minds to waffles. Apparently the waffle bot was a gigantic pain in the ass to clean, so like many of the noisemaking things of our childhood toy collections, the waffle bot inexplicably disappeared one day. That just meant I became even more determined to order waffles every time we went out for breakfast or brunch. The experience, from the crispy edges to the little syrup-holding indentations naturally built into the waffle, was the stuff of dreams. I never once hesitated over whether or not to order a waffle, and if I had the chance to do it again, I'd make the same freaking choice every time.

    This origin of this recipe is the *Joy of Cooking*; however, I've tweaked it over and over. The thing that remains from the original is that I use whipped egg whites to leaven the waffle, making for an airy, crispy product, unlike its bicarbonate of soda–leavened counterpart. Take the time, do the work, and enjoy the fruits of your toil.

2 eggs, separated

2 pinches of cream of tartar

2¼ cups all-purpose flour

¼ cup granulated sugar

½ teaspoon salt

1½ cups whole milk

6 tablespoons unsalted butter, melted

1½ teaspoons pure vanilla extract

Softened butter, whipped cream, syrup, confectioners' sugar, sliced strawberries, or whatever garnish you prefer

---

Preheat the waffle maker. Preheat the oven to 175°F. Line a baking sheet with parchment paper.

In the bowl of a stand mixer fitted with the whip attachment, whisk the egg whites and cream of tartar to stiff peaks, being careful not to overwhip. It will take about 1½ minutes to whip until the whites just hold stiff peaks and are nice and matte looking. If they start to glisten, they will ultimately break down, go watery, and not rise very well. Set aside.

In a separate bowl, stir together the flour, granulated sugar, and salt and set aside. In a third bowl, whisk together the milk, yolks, melted butter, and vanilla. Pour the milk mixture into the flour mixture and whisk together until the batter is well combined. Gently fold in the whites until fully incorporated.

Spoon the batter ¾ cup at a time into the waffle iron (the batter expands dramatically, so be careful not to overfill the waffle iron or you will have a little bit of a mess). Cook until browned on both sides (the cooking time will vary based on your iron; check after 3 minutes and cook another minute or two if needed). Eat the waffle the very second you remove it from the iron. If you must, transfer the waffle to the baking sheet and keep warm in the oven while you cook more for your friends. Top with softened butter, whipped cream, syrup, confectioners' sugar, or fruit and serve immediately.

PEANUT BUTTER AND BANANA PANCAKES

SERVES 4

I've rarely seen a man as mad as my buddy Mike Gulotta was at an *Iron Chef*–style cook–off we did at a children's hospital in Memphis in the spring of 2014. We were asked to team up with a fellow chef, take a basket of mystery ingredients, and cook for a group of the hospital's patients. Consummate asshole that I am and knowing who I was cooking for, I brought a box full of stuff I knew kids would like. I cooked some crazy peanut butter and banana pancakes with marshmallow and chocolate chips and stole the trophy. I don't think Mike has forgiven me to this day. Sucker . . . These will make a hero out of you.

2¼ cups all-purpose flour

2 tablespoons granulated sugar

2 tablespoons baking powder

1½ teaspoons baking soda

¾ teaspoon salt

1¾ cups buttermilk

2 eggs

3 tablespoons unsalted butter, melted

2 teaspoons pure vanilla extract

½ cup crunchy peanut butter

1 ripe banana, sliced

⅓ cup semisweet chocolate chips

⅓ cup mini marshmallows, chopped

Clarified butter (page 30) or your preferred cooking fat

Whipped cream and confectioners' sugar, for topping

In a bowl, whisk together the flour, granulated sugar, baking powder, baking soda, and salt and set aside. In a separate bowl, whisk together the buttermilk, eggs, melted butter, and vanilla. In a microwavable bowl, microwave the peanut butter for 15 seconds, then blend the peanut butter with the banana, mashing together with the tines of a fork.

Pour the buttermilk mixture into the flour mixture and whisk together until the batter is well combined. Stir in the peanut butter–banana mixture, followed by the chocolate chips and marshmallows.

Warm 1½ tablespoons of the clarified butter in a sauté pan over medium heat for 30 seconds. Spoon the batter into the pan ¼ cup at a time. Cook until the tops begin to bubble lightly, about 1½ minutes. Flip and cook until the bottom browns slightly, 30 to 45 seconds more. Repeat with the remaining batter, adding more clarified butter between batches as needed. Serve immediately with whipped cream and confectioners' sugar.

SHRIMP AND PICKLED ONION CREPES WITH MORNAY

MAKES 8 CREPES; SERVES 4

Sunday brunch was a big deal when I was a kid. In the late 1960s and early 1970s, most folks didn't eat out very often. Sundays after church were the rare exception. Every few weeks, we would go downtown for a special brunch. The old-line French restaurants in the Quarter and a fistful of the big, old-school restaurants still did tableside presentations. Flaming desserts like crepes suzette were big, but savory crepes also made the occasional appearance. Spinach, chicken, and mushrooms were regulars in these dishes, but a sautéed shrimp crepe was my favorite. For this one, I've added some pickled red onion for some bite and sass.

BATTER

1¼ cups chicken stock

1 cup whole milk

6 eggs

¼ cup plus 2 tablespoons unsalted butter, melted

2 cups all-purpose flour

¼ cup finely chopped fresh herbs of your choosing

1 teaspoon black pepper

1½ teaspoons salt

FILLING

2 tablespoons olive oil

1 tablespoon bacon fat

1½ pounds medium shrimp, fully peeled

Salt and black pepper

¼ cup cooked bacon bits

1 tablespoon minced garlic

3 tablespoons sliced green onion, green part only

2 tablespoons chopped fresh parsley

Clarified butter (page 30) or your preferred cooking fat

2 cups Mornay Sauce (recipe follows), warmed

1 cup grated Gruyère cheese

½ cup Pickled Red Onions (recipe follows)

To make the batter, whisk together the stock, milk, eggs, and melted butter in a stainless steel bowl until fully combined. In a separate bowl, stir together the flour, herbs, pepper, and salt until combined. Pour the stock mixture into the flour mixture and whisk together until the batter is well combined. The batter should be thin and free of any clumps. Allow to stand for 1 hour at room temperature, allowing the glutens to relax.

To make the filling, warm the oil and bacon fat in a large sauté pan over medium heat for 45 seconds. Add the shrimp and spread them out in an even layer in the pan. Season immediately with salt and black pepper and cook, stirring constantly, until they just begin to turn opaque, about 1 minute. Add the bacon and garlic and cook, stirring, until warmed through, about 30 seconds. Remove from the heat and stir in the green onion and parsley.

Warm 1½ teaspoons of clarified butter in a 10-inch nonstick pan over medium heat for 30 seconds. Add 2 tablespoons of batter to the pan and swirl the pan to coat it with a thin layer of batter. The moment the batter appears to dry on top, about 30 seconds, flip over with a small spatula and cook for 10 seconds more. Slide the crepe onto a plate and cover with a paper towel. Repeat with the remaining batter, adding more clarified butter between batches as needed.

Crepes are best straight from the pan, but are still excellent for 30 minutes or so, if you must cook them in advance. (They don't need to be rewarmed; a warm filling will bring them right back to temperature because they are so thin.)

CONTINUED

To assemble the crepes, lay 2 crepes on each plate. Spoon 3 tablespoons of Mornay down the center of each crepe and sprinkle with a little Gruyère. Place 5 or 6 shrimp on top of the Mornay and sprinkle with the pickled onions. Fold the sides of the crepes to cover the filling and flip over the crepes so that the seam side is down. Spoon a little Mornay over the top. Garnish with a couple of shrimp and some pickled onion. Serve immediately.

If you are making these for a group, you can assemble the crepes with the filling but no topping and keep on a baking sheet in a 175°F oven for no longer than 20 minutes. To serve, place the crepes on a plate and finish with the Mornay, a couple of shrimp, and some pickled onion.

MORNAY SAUCE

MAKES ABOUT 2 CUPS

2 tablespoons unsalted butter

2 tablespoons all-purpose flour

2 cups whole milk

⅓ yellow onion, root intact

1 clove garlic

1 bay leaf

¼ cup grated Gruyère cheese

Pinch of ground nutmeg

¼ teaspoon salt

½ teaspoon white pepper

Melt the butter in a small saucepan over medium heat. Add the flour and whisk until a roux forms. Continue to cook, whisking constantly, until the roux turns a light gold and gives off a nutty aroma, about 5 minutes. Whisk in the milk, then stir in the onion, garlic, and bay leaf. Turn the heat to low and simmer, stirring often, until the sauce thickens, about 10 minutes. Discard the onion, garlic, and bay leaf. Add the cheese and nutmeg and cook, stirring, until the cheese melts, about 1 minute. Stir in the salt and white pepper. Serve warm. Refrigerate any remaining Mornay in a plastic container for up to 3 days.

PICKLED RED ONIONS

MAKES ABOUT 4 CUPS

2 cups apple cider vinegar

¾ cup sugar

½ cup white wine

10 cloves garlic, thinly sliced

2 tablespoons mustard seeds

1 tablespoon black peppercorns

4 whole cloves

3 bay leaves

3 red onions, thinly sliced

Combine the vinegar, sugar, wine, garlic, mustard seeds, peppercorns, cloves, and bay leaves in a nonreactive saucepan and bring to a boil over medium heat. Turn the heat to low and simmer for 5 minutes. Stir in the onions and bring to a boil again. As soon as the mixture comes to a boil, remove from the heat and allow to cool to room temperature. Pour the onions and their brine into a glass or plastic container. Refrigerate for up to 1 year.

MULTIGRAIN PANCAKES

MAKES 20 PANCAKES; SERVES 5

In an effort to be a respectable peddler of culinary sin, we try to put things out from time to time that really are good for the heart, mind, soul, and waistline, such as these multigrain pancakes. (And, as it turns out, a lot of what we serve at Big Bad Breakfast is just as healthy as this, I just can't control what you choose to slather on your food once I hand it to you, ya know?)

Here we substitute a significant portion of the processed white flour for whole wheat flour and add whole grains as well, all of which add layers of flavor. The quinoa and bulgur are both whole grains and extremely high in nutrients, fiber, and protein. Not only are they healthy, but they both also have a slightly nutty flavor when cooked, so they complement the pancake idea well.

These ingredients might not create as pillowy an offering as straight-up buttermilk pancakes, but your body will be a little happier after eating these and you might even sleep a little better that night. So here it is, hippie. Eat up and feel good. Now go make me a candle.

½ cup rolled oats

⅔ cup water

¼ cup quinoa

¾ cup boiling water

¼ cup cracked bulgur

1 cup all-purpose flour

½ cup whole wheat flour

¼ cup flaxseed meal

¼ cup cornmeal

3 tablespoons sugar

½ teaspoon baking soda

1 teaspoon baking powder

¾ teaspoon salt

1½ cups buttermilk

¼ cup unsalted butter, melted

2 eggs

3 tablespoons sour cream

2 teaspoon pure vanilla extract

Clarified butter (page 30) or your preferred cooking fat

Pats of cold unsalted butter, for serving

Honey, for drizzling

Preheat the oven to 350°F.

Place the rolled oats on a baking sheet and toast in the oven, stirring every several minutes, until they are fragrant and begin to brown just barely, 7 to 8 minutes. Remove from the oven and set aside.

Bring the ⅔ cup water to a simmer over medium heat and stir in the quinoa. Reduce the heat to low and stir constantly until the quinoa is tender, about 12 minutes. Remove from the heat, allow to cool to room temperature, and set aside.

Pour the ¾ cup boiling water over the cracked bulgur in a heatproof bowl and allow to stand for 10 minutes, or until all of the water has been absorbed. Set aside.

In a mixing bowl, stir together the toasted oats, flours, flaxseed meal, cornmeal, sugar, baking soda, baking powder, and salt. In another bowl, whisk together the buttermilk, melted butter, eggs, sour cream, and vanilla. Pour the buttermilk mixture into the flour mixture and whisk together until the batter is well combined. Stir in the quinoa and bulgur until well combined.

Warm 1½ tablespoons of the clarified butter in a sauté pan over medium heat for 30 seconds. Spoon the batter into the pan ¼ cup at a time. Cook until the tops begin to bubble lightly, about 1½ minutes. Flip and cook until the bottoms brown, about 30 seconds more. Repeat with the remaining batter, adding more clarified butter between batches as needed. Serve with pats of butter and drizzle with honey.

HOECAKES

There is significant debate over the origin of the word *hoecake*. The most pervasive theory is that it is called such because slaves would cook them on hoe blades on the edges of the fields in which they worked. This theory, however, has a few holes. It's hard to imagine that the slaves were given enough break time to build a fire, burn it down until it was a good cooking fire, mix up their batter, and cook their cakes. And second, after working a hot Mississippi morning in a field, building a fire is likely the last thing grown men and women would want to do—not to mention, these corn cakes are quite shelf-stable and don't need to be cooked and eaten on the spot.

Modern etymologists and scholars lean toward the theory that the *hoe* is actually a griddle-like surface for cooking that was used mostly for cooking bread on, or in front of, an open fire. These cakes are also known as johnnycakes or journeycakes and could be made with flour or corn—this recipe incorporates both. We like to dollop our hoecakes with a spoonful of sour whipped buttermilk and a sprinkle of salt. Call 'em what you will, I call them freaking delicious.

1 cup all-purpose flour

1 cup cornmeal

1 tablespoon sugar

1½ teaspoons baking powder

¾ teaspoon baking soda

1 teaspoon salt

½ teaspoon cayenne pepper

¾ cup buttermilk

½ cup whole milk

2 eggs plus 2 yolks, lightly beaten

3 tablespoons unsalted butter, melted

2 tablespoons melted lard or bacon fat

½ cup fresh corn kernels, chopped (or frozen corn, thawed)

¼ cup minced red onion

Clarified butter (page 30) or your preferred cooking fat

Buttermilk Crema (recipe follows), for serving

In a stainless steel bowl, stir together the flour, cornmeal, sugar, baking powder, baking soda, salt, and cayenne. In a separate bowl, whisk together the buttermilk, milk, eggs and yolks, melted butter, and lard and combine well. Pour the buttermilk mixture into the flour mixture and whisk together until the batter is well combined. Stir in the corn and onion and allow to sit for 30 minutes for the flavors and starches to develop.

Warm 1½ tablespoons of the clarified butter in a sauté pan over medium heat for 30 seconds. Spoon the batter into the pan 2 tablespoons at a time. Cook until the tops begin to bubble lightly, about 1½ minutes. Flip and cook until the bottoms brown, about 20 seconds more. Repeat with the remaining batter, adding more clarified butter between batches as needed.

Top with a dollop of Buttermilk Crema.

BUTTERMILK CREMA
MAKES ABOUT 1½ CUPS

1 cup heavy cream

1 teaspoon freshly squeezed lemon juice

¼ teaspoon salt

½ teaspoon black pepper

Pinch of cayenne pepper

¼ cup buttermilk

Place the cream in the bowl of a stand mixer and whip on high speed until medium peaks form, about 1½ minutes. Reduce the speed to low. Stir together the lemon juice, salt, black pepper, cayenne, and buttermilk in a measuring cup and slowly add to the whipped cream until fully incorporated. Store in a glass jar and refrigerate for up 2 days.

TOASTED OATMEAL PANCAKES

MAKES 12 TO 15 PANCAKES; SERVES 3

Despite my reputation as a bacon-and-eggs guy, I secretly believe in the magical healing power of oatmeal. At the restaurant, we make oatmeal and granola from steel-cut oats from Anson Mills in South Carolina.

Anson is the brainchild of Glenn Roberts, one of the smartest guys you could ever want to meet. While this may sound melodramatic, truly, there are few people on this planet I enjoy talking to as much as Glenn. His passion for excavating, studying, preserving, propagating, and celebrating heirloom grain is unparalleled. He has single-handedly rescued a couple dozen Southern heirloom plants from complete obscurity and perhaps even extinction. And if his passion were not enough, his generosity matches heartbeat for heartbeat. I can't tell you how many times we have discussed a particular corn, pea, or bean I wanted to grow when he didn't immediately gather the seed and ship it to me, with the only stipulation being that if my crop was successful, I return the seed to him. Anson supplies the absolute best of everything it sells. And Anson's oats are so good, I started testing other recipes so I could work this delicious ingredient into as many dishes as possible.

For these pancakes, we lightly toast and grind some steel-cut oats in a spice grinder and then sprinkle some unground steel-coat oats on top while the pancakes are cooking. These earthy pancakes are lightly sweet. They are a great crowd-pleaser and a total surprise because they are good for you and just plain good. You can substitute any whole rolled oats for this recipe, but they will be better if you use Anson Mills. Just sayin'.

1½ cups steel-cut oats

4 cups all-purpose flour

¾ cup sugar

¼ cup baking powder

2 teaspoons baking soda

1½ teaspoons salt

3 cups buttermilk

1½ cups whole milk

6 eggs

1½ teaspoons pure vanilla extract

¾ cup unsalted butter, melted

Clarified butter (page 30) or your preferred cooking fat

Pats of cold unsalted butter, sliced strawberries, and cane syrup, for serving

---

Preheat the oven to 350°F. Spread out the oats on a baking sheet and bake, stirring every few minutes, until toasted, about 12 minutes. Remove from the oven and allow to cool briefly. Place 1¼ cups of the toasted oats in a spice grinder or food processor and pulse until finely ground. Reserve the remaining ¼ cup of whole toasted oats.

In a bowl, whisk together the flour, ground toasted oats, sugar, baking powder, baking soda, and salt. In a separate bowl, whisk together the buttermilk, milk, eggs, and vanilla. Pour the buttermilk mixture into the flour mixture and whisk together until smooth. Stir in the melted butter until well combined.

Warm 1½ tablespoons of clarified butter in a sauté pan over medium heat for 30 seconds. Spoon the batter into the pan ¼ cup at a time and sprinkle the reserved toasted oats on top. Cook until the tops begin to bubble lightly, about 1½ minutes. Flip and cook until the bottoms begin to brown, about another 30 seconds. Repeat with the remaining batter, adding more clarified butter between batches as needed.

Serve immediately with the cold butter, strawberries, and cane syrup.

FRESH CORN AREPAS

MAKES ABOUT 24 AREPAS; SERVES 6

I was first exposed to these crazy delicious little cakes when I made my inaugural trip to Argentina in the early 1990s. I loved them for their utilitarian nature. They were used as a taco shell, burger bun, sandwich bread, and biscuit. They have an earthy corn flavor and adapt themselves nicely to any number of uses.

When I returned home and began playing with them, we added chopped fresh corn kernels, bell peppers, onions, and the like. The arepas only got better with the addition of fresh ingredients and really stood on their own. So much so that we would serve silver dollar–size arepas with a small cup of super garlicky chimichurri and call it a dish. I freely admit that these arepas bear little resemblance to the more English muffin–like versions you will see at street fairs or in parts of South America, but this is a fun interpretation.

These go great alongside runny-yolk fried eggs (page 30) with a touch of ketchup, and make a killer substitution for tortillas in Huevos Cocineros (page 144). These are also great with grilled meat or fish and your favorite chimichurri recipe, or with cream cheese and sliced ham.

½ cup fresh corn kernels or frozen corn kernels, thawed

1 ½ tablespoons olive oil

1½ cups cornmeal

½ cup all-purpose flour

1 teaspoon black pepper

½ teaspoon salt

¼ teaspoon cayenne pepper

¼ cup minced yellow onion

¼ cup chopped fresh cilantro

¼ cup grated sharp cheddar cheese

1½ cups whole milk

¾ cup buttermilk

¼ cup unsalted butter, melted

2 eggs

Clarified butter (page 30) or your preferred cooking fat

Preheat the oven to 350°F.

In a small bowl, toss the corn kernels and olive oil together and spread on a baking sheet. Roast for 7 to 8 minutes, or until the kernels begin to brown lightly. Remove, let cool to room temperature, and set aside.

In a stainless steel bowl, stir together the cornmeal, flour, black pepper, salt, and cayenne. Stir in the corn, onion, cilantro, and cheese until well combined. In a separate bowl, whisk together the milk, buttermilk, melted butter, and eggs until well combined. Pour the milk mixture into the cornmeal mixture and whisk together until smooth.

Warm 3 tablespoons of the clarified butter in a sauté pan over medium heat for 30 seconds. Spoon the batter into the pan ¼ cup at a time. Cook until the bottoms brown, about 2 minutes. Flip and cook until the second side browns, 1 minute more. Drain on paper towels. Repeat with the remaining batter, adding more clarified butter between batches as needed. Serve immediately.

MAMIE'S FAVORITE FRENCH TOAST

MAKES 8 PIECES; SERVES 4

I've learned late in life that everything you are told about little girls wrapping you around their fingers is totally fucking true. There is absolutely no goddamned reason according to natural law why anyone who's only thirty pounds should hold as much sway over a two hundred–pound man's emotions as my daughter does over me. It totally sucks. I do everything Mamie says when she says to do it. I seek her approval and her love *way* more than I ever went after my dad's, and I am absolutely crushed when I don't get it. My life is a constant emotional negotiation with a little midget terrorist. And every once in a while she tosses me a kiss or an "I love you" just to get what she wants. I am, by all measure, pathetic.

So when she has me run around the kitchen making her ten different things that she won't eat, it's nice to know there is a good fallback dish she'll always gobble up so I can feel like a hero. Or, at least, I win a very small emotional battle. And for those of you out there who understand my pain, that shit can mean *everything.*

(I've never shared this recipe with my wife, because it's the only weapon I have in my arsenal, and I am just insecure enough that I like to have a leg up on at least one thing. I am banking on the fact that she is unimpressed enough with me that she will never read this, so I'll thank you to keep this quiet.)

4 eggs

½ cup whole milk

2 tablespoons granulated sugar

1 teaspoon pure vanilla extract

½ teaspoon almond extract

¼ teaspoon salt

Clarified butter (page 30) or your preferred cooking fat

8 slices Pepperidge Farm Multigrain Bread (see Note) or any whole-grain bread

Confectioners' sugar, cane syrup, fresh berries, bananas, or whipped cream, for serving

In a mixing bowl, whisk together the eggs, milk, granulated sugar, vanilla, almond extract, and salt.

Warm 3 tablespoons of the clarified butter in a large skillet over medium heat for 45 seconds. Dip the bread, one slice at a time, into the batter, allowing it to fully soak into the bread, about 45 seconds. Place the soaked slice of bread, after allowing any excess egg mix to drip off, in the skillet and cook until browned on both sides, about 2 minutes per side. Repeat with the remaining bread and batter, adding more clarified butter between batches as needed.

Serve warm with confectioners' sugar, cane syrup, berries, bananas, whipped cream—whatever your little terrorist loves. You're welcome!

NOTE: Pepperidge Farm Multigrain makes a really nice French toast. I would have never thought so, as I usually react strongly to whole wheat breads, but this loaf is sturdy, flavorful, and sweet. If it gets a little stale, it's even better.

BRIOCHE FRENCH TOAST

SERVES 2

There are few bread products I have *not* tried to turn into bread pudding or French toast in the last thirty years. Brioche, it turns out, has magical properties in this arena. And that magical power, to be honest, derives from the copious amounts of butter it takes to make this exquisite French masterpiece. To be perfectly fair, doughnuts make a bread pudding that is nothing short of orgasmic, and French toast made with croissants are a close second, but brioche is truly the king. Buy a brioche loaf and let it get stale and hard for about 48 hours. Then prepare for as magnificent a breakfast as you have ever had since the morning after your wedding.

½ cup heavy cream

2½ tablespoons confectioners' sugar

3 teaspoons pure vanilla extract

½ cup half-and-half

3 eggs

3 tablespoons bourbon

1½ tablespoons granulated sugar

⅛ teaspoon ground cinnamon

⅛ teaspoon salt

Clarified butter (page 30) or your preferred cooking fat

4 thick slices stale brioche

1 cup assorted fresh berries (if strawberries, then sliced), for serving

In the bowl of a stand mixer, combine the heavy cream, confectioners' sugar, and 1 teaspoon of the vanilla. Whip on high speed until stiff peaks form, 1 to 1½ minutes.

In a medium-size mixing bowl, whisk together the half-and-half, eggs, bourbon, granulated sugar, cinnamon, salt, and remaining 2 teaspoons vanilla.

Warm 3 tablespoons of the clarified butter in a large skillet over medium heat for 30 seconds. Dip the brioche, one slice at a time, into the batter, allowing it to fully soak into the bread, about 30 seconds. Remove from the egg mix and allow any excess to run back off into the bowl. Place the soaked slices of bread in the skillet and cook until browned on both sides, about 2 minutes per side. Repeat with the remaining bread and batter, adding more clarified butter between batches if needed.

Serve warm with the berries and whipped cream.

GERMAN PANCAKE

SERVES 1 OR 2

Credit for this dish goes entirely to our corporate fixer, Rusty Boyd. You see, restaurants that survive very long all end up in cycles. Staffs change, leadership changes, and every so often, you find yourself in a rut. Morale turns poor, leadership is ineffective, quality suffers, things just need a shot in the arm. Rusty was a man who presented himself at a time when Big Bad Breakfast was struggling to find its way. He came in full of piss and vinegar and was hell-bent on fixing what was broken. He took the reins and in a couple of months had put us on the right path. We kept him there for a couple of years, and he made the restaurant a better place to work than it had ever been. His food was exceptional, and his spirit and enthusiasm were unparalleled.

One of the best recipes he developed was this German apple pancake. Unlike a griddled pancake, this is baked. It's as delicious as any breakfast dish I have ever tasted, and there is little better to eat on one of those cool fall mornings, particularly when apples are in season, fresh and crisp. Do not be surprised that when this comes out of the oven, it will be nicely puffed and then collapse almost immediately, so that it looks more like an ugly crepe than a pancake. That's what it's supposed to do.

Rusty has gone on to fix a couple of our other restaurants, and though he is no longer in the heat of the kitchen at Big Bad Breakfast, he is never far and he's certainly never a stranger. His spirit and leadership linger on.

1 cup all-purpose flour

1 tablespoon granulated sugar

1 teaspoon salt

½ cup whole milk

¼ cup buttermilk

6 eggs

1 teaspoon pure vanilla extract

¼ cup unsalted butter, melted

1 Granny Smith apple, cored, peeled, and sliced into thin wedges

¼ cup clarified butter (page 30) or your preferred cooking fat

⅓ cup firmly packed dark brown sugar

Confectioners' sugar and freshly squeezed lemon juice, for sprinkling

Preheat the oven to 425°F.

In a bowl, stir together the flour, granulated sugar, and salt. In a separate bowl, whisk together the milk, buttermilk, eggs, and vanilla. Pour the milk mixture into the flour mixture and whisk together until smooth. Whisk in the melted butter, then stir in half of the apple.

Warm an 8-inch cast-iron skillet (or nonstick skillet) over medium heat for 1 minute. Add the clarified butter, then place the remaining apple slices around the bottom of the skillet and sprinkle with the brown sugar. Pour the batter evenly over the top and slide the skillet into the oven. Bake until the top of the pancake is golden brown, puffy, and firm to the touch, 12 to 14 minutes. Remove from the oven, sprinkle with confectioners' sugar and lemon juice, and serve immediately, preferably directly from the pan.

BIG BAD BREAKFAST
PAIN PERDU

SERVES 4

Pain perdu roughly translates as "lost bread"—the bread "lost" to being stale, that is. This recipe is a way of rescuing bread that would otherwise be tossed. In a town where my people can tell to the hour how long Leidenheimer bakery's po'boy bread has been out of the oven, there is little forgiveness for remotely stale bread. And so pain perdu is a breakfast staple in New Orleans and occasionally even makes an appearance on a dessert menu.

While I am on the record saying that Southerners default to frying everything and should explore other cooking methods, I will say with no shame whatsoever that this deep-fried version of French toast is absolutely amazing.

Bill Neal, the legendary chef at Crook's Corner in North Carolina, was the first person I knew to fry his French toast. It was light, airy, and surprisingly not greasy. We expand on that same idea here, using super-light New Orleans–style French bread and lacing the eggy batter with Cognac. Doused with confectioners' sugar, there is little better for a breakfast sweet tooth.

½ cup plus 2 tablespoons heavy cream

2½ tablespoons confectioners' sugar, plus some for dusting

2½ teaspoons pure vanilla extract

Vegetable oil, for frying

5 eggs

½ cup whole milk

3 tablespoons brandy, preferably Cognac

1 tablespoon granulated sugar

¼ teaspoon ground nutmeg

⅛ teaspoon ground cinnamon

Pinch of salt

12 (¾-inch-thick) slices baguette

Sliced bananas, for serving

Rum Sauce (recipe follows), for serving

Preheat the oven to 200°F.

In the bowl of a stand mixer, combine ½ cup of the heavy cream, the confectioners' sugar, and 1 teaspoon of the vanilla. Whip on high speed until stiff peaks form, 1 to 1½ minutes. Set aside.

Pour 4 inches of oil into a deep skillet or countertop fryer and heat over medium heat to 375°F.

Whisk together the eggs, milk, brandy, granulated sugar, nutmeg, cinnamon, salt, remaining 2 tablespoons cream, and remaining 1½ teaspoons vanilla. Dip the baguette, one slice at a time, into the batter, allowing it to fully soak into the baguette, about 30 seconds. Remove from the egg mix and allow excess egg mix to run off back into the bowl. Gently place the soaked bread pieces into the hot oil (you can fry 4 or 5 pieces at a time) and fry, turning constantly with tongs, until golden brown, 2 to 3 minutes. Repeat with the remaining baguette and batter. Remove the fried bread to a baking sheet lined with paper towels. Hold in a warm oven on the baking sheet if you are cooking for a group.

Serve dusted with confectioners' sugar, slices of banana, a dollop of whipped cream, and a drizzle of Rum Sauce.

RUM SAUCE
MAKES ½ CUP

¼ cup firmly packed dark brown sugar

1 teaspoon water

2 tablespoons rum

2 tablespoons cold unsalted butter, cut into cubes

Combine the brown sugar and water in a small saucepan and bring to a boil over high heat. Lower the heat to medium and cook, swirling the pan constantly, until the sugar begins to thicken, 3 to 4 minutes. Carefully add the rum, simmer for an additional minute, and remove the pan from the heat. Swirl in the butter. If you want the sauce a little thicker, return the pan to a low flame and simmer until it reaches the thickness you like. Store chilled for up to 10 days.

HOMEMADE POP-TARTS

MAKES 10 TOASTER PASTRIES

Seriously, why the hell not? At the restaurant, we make fresh pie dough and we make our own preserves. That puts us a tablespoon or two of cornstarch away from the end zone. Making Pop-Tarts at home is easy and fun. It's one of those projects everyone can get in on. Uncooked Pop-Tarts can be frozen and the finished product is way better for you and your waistline than the processed, store-bought counterparts. Kids go nuts for them, and if you don't feel you are getting enough of a sugar rush from them, drizzle with Vanilla Glaze (page 10), you Tasmanian Sucrose Devil, you.

PASTRY

6 egg yolks

½ cup heavy cream

6 cups all-purpose flour, plus more for dusting

½ cup sugar

¼ teaspoon salt

1½ cups cold butter, cut into cubes

½ cup cold lard

FILLING

1½ tablespoons cornstarch

1 tablespoon water

1½ cups of your favorite jelly or jam

To make the pastry, in a mixing bowl, whisk together the egg yolks and cream. Cover and refrigerate for 15 minutes or so, until chilled. In a food processor, combine the flour, sugar, and salt and pulse several times to combine. Add the cold butter and lard and pulse several times again, just until a coarse meal forms. Drizzle in the cream mixture while pulsing, until the dough just begins to come together. (It will still be a little crumbly.)

Turn the dough out onto a floured surface, gather the dough, and shape it into a ball. Briefly knead the dough, pressing it out and folding it back over itself 4 or 6 times, until the dough just starts to look smooth. Divide into 3 equal balls and flatten into disks. Cover with plastic wrap and refrigerate until firm, at least 2 hours and up to 5 or 6 days.

To make the filling, in a small bowl, stir together the cornstarch and water with a fork. Warm the jelly in a small saucepan over low heat until it softens and liquefies. Pour the cornstarch mixture into the jelly and bring to a simmer, whisking constantly. Simmer for 30 seconds, then remove from the heat and pour into a glass container.

CONTINUED

HOMEMADE POP-TARTS, CONTINUED

To assemble, preheat the oven to 350°F.

Remove the dough from the refrigerator, unwrap the plastic, and allow to rest at room temperature for 5 minutes. Roll out the dough until it's about ⅛ thick. With a paring knife, cut into 5 by 4–inch rectangles. You should have about 6 rectangles from each disk, with trimming left that can be rerolled once and made into a couple more rectangles.

On each of 10 pastry rectangles, spread 1½ tablespoons of jelly to cover all but the edges of the pastry. Place a second rectangle of pastry on top and seal the edges with the tines of a fork. Cut a few small slits in the top of the pastry. Bake for 12 to 14 minutes, or until the pastries are golden brown. Uncooked pastries can be wrapped in plastic and kept frozen for up to 4 months, then baked for 14 minutes at 350°F.

BFD:
BREAKFAST FOR DINNER
(AND VICE VERSA)

THE THING THAT HAS ALWAYS TROUBLED ME ABOUT CHAIN BREAKFAST
places, other than that they usually smell like sour mop water and ashtrays, is that their menus all stop at the very basics. There are a pile of fried and scrambled egg plate options, omelets of all varieties, a steak offering, and then a burger and some sandwiches that make use of existing inventory. They are patently boring.

CHAPTER 5

When we conceived Big Bad Breakfast, the idea was to apply the same principles to breakfast as we did to lunch and dinner at our other restaurants, i.e., to be creative and not lazy. I'll admit, our first menu's offerings were on the more conservative and predictable side. We topped English muffins with any variety of egg preparations and slathered every one of them with hollandaise flavored with anything and everything under the sun. We put anything in a pancake that you could possibly think of and stuffed crepes with all manner of sea creatures or confiture.

But as time progressed, we started venturing further and further out of the breakfast box. We moved into more ethnic and nontraditional breakfasts, such as posole with a poached egg and piles of fresh cilantro, or lamb curry with a fried egg; even Monday's red beans and rice (made with smoked sausage instead of andouille) topped with a soft-boiled egg became an acceptable breakfast item that was worthy of excitement. The ultimate freedom came with the understanding that it was not *just okay* to take anything, put an egg on it, and call it breakfast, but people freaking loved it. And from that point forward, there has been little or nothing we haven't made into breakfast, which also means that any of these recipes makes a mighty tasty dinner as well, or lunch, or midnight snack . . .

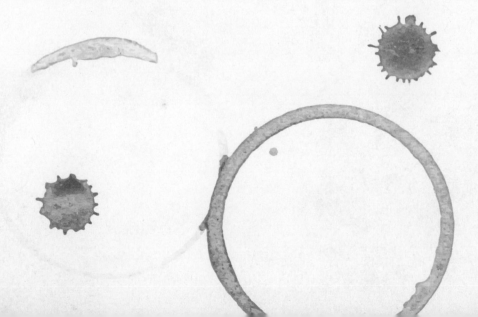

SHRIMP AND GRITS

SERVES 2

I started my professional cooking life at Crook's Corner in Chapel Hill, North Carolina, as I was trying to piece together the most ridiculous patchwork college career and play music simultaneously. Crook's was ground zero for restaurant-offered shrimp and grits. It was the only place I had ever heard of it being served, and until we opened our doors at City Grocery in 1992 (and unapologetically built our notoriety off our version of the same dish), I never knew it to be served anywhere else. You see, before Bill Neal, chef at Crook's, rolled it out on his menu, it was a Low Country brunch dish that fishermen and families cooked to make use of what was most abundant. It wasn't something you might expect to find at a fancy restaurant, nor was cornbread, collards, or country ham. It was the early 1980s, and folks weren't interested in exploring the food of the American South.

As the years moved forward, that dish became enormously popular in restaurants. For a while in the very late 1990s, you couldn't swing a dead cat without hitting a fucking menu with shrimp and grits on it. It was so prolific that John T. Edge, founder and director of the Southern Foodways Alliance (and more important, godfather to my baby girl), wrote a piece in *Gourmet* on its prevalence, questioning chefs for trying to improve on a classic and wondering if its proliferation might forever destroy the memory of the minimalist original.

As a result of its overexposure, most of my contemporary chefs avoided shrimp and grits like the plague. Few people wanted to look like bandwagon jumpers. I, however, was stuck with it. I had been on the leading edge of the shrimp and grits' revival, and the reputation of City Grocery was tied to it. The guys on my team, as a result, all wanted to outdo the next with their version. It was enormously difficult for me to swallow. I felt a little like a one-trick pony in a small town where all of my chefs wanted to create the next best version of the one thing that had already been done to death, but I didn't want to step on anyone's

autonomy or creativity by telling them they couldn't experiment with it.

We now have several versions at our restaurants, which are all tried and true, and we have customers who hotly debate which one is best. I will always be a fan of City Grocery's version, slightly more purist and simple, but this one from Big Bad Breakfast is a very close and extremely fun second.

1½ tablespoons clarified butter (page 30) or your preferred cooking fat

1½ tablespoons bacon fat

8 ounces medium, fully peeled, Gulf brown shrimp

Salt and black pepper

2 teaspoons minced garlic

¼ cup cooked bacon bits

¾ cup chopped tomato

2 teaspoons freshly squeezed lemon juice

2 cups Garlic Cheese Grits (page 187), warmed

2 Poached Eggs (page 31), warmed

¾ cup Red-Eye Gravy (page 198), warmed

¼ cup sliced green onion, green part only

Warm the clarified butter and bacon fat in a sauté pan over medium heat for 30 seconds. Add the shrimp and spread them out in an even layer in the pan. Season immediately with salt and black pepper and cook, stirring constantly, until they just begin to turn opaque, about 1 minute. Add the garlic and bacon and cook, stirring, until warmed through and the garlic becomes fragrant, about 30 seconds. Add the tomato, season lightly with salt and pepper, and cook, stirring, for 1 minute more. Add the lemon juice and stir to combine.

To serve, divide the grits between 2 plates, top with a poached egg, and spoon the shrimp over the egg. Ladle the gravy over the top and sprinkle with the green onion. Serve immediately.

BRULÉED GRAPEFRUIT

SERVES 2

Grapefruit exploded onto the breakfast scene (in our house) in the early 1970s. I found them disgusting. With the addition of a little salt, the bitterness was knocked down and they were slightly more palatable. With that, I could get through about a third of one. About the same time, many restaurants began offering a broiled grapefruit on their brunch menus. They were everywhere, alongside canned pineapple rings with fucking cottage cheese and a dyed cherry on top.

When we opened Big Bad Breakfast, I wanted to reference that moment in American culinary history for some reason I cannot explain. It just seemed like the perfectly weird thing to put on the menu. So we started taking grapefruit halves and bruleéing them. It was delightful, and I decided to name the dish Tender Hooks after the lovely and delightful author Beth Ann Fennelly's book of poems. It sells like crazy, but still takes a dash of salt to get me through one.

If you have a handheld blowtorch, you can bypass the broiler and caramelize the grapefruit on a baking sheet on the counter.

½ teaspoon salt

2 grapefruit, cut in half through the equator

¼ cup sugar

Preheat the broiler. Sprinkle the salt over the cut sides of the grapefruit, followed by the sugar, spreading them in an even layer. Place the grapefruits on a baking sheet. Slide under the broiler and broil, turning constantly, until the sugar caramelizes, 5 to 8 minutes depending on how hot your broiler is. Remove from the oven, cool briefly, and serve warm.

BREAKFAST "SUCCOT-HASH"

SERVES 4

Yes, that's spelled right. This is our hybrid succotash, the traditional Southern dish of fresh corn and lima beans with a hint of bacon and herbs, and potato hash, everyone's favorite way to use up leftover potatoes. We combine our cubed hash browns, sweet potatoes, and a blend of whatever peas and/or beans are currently in season and top it all with a couple of poached eggs. It's a winner and arguably healthy-ish. Spare not the hot sauce here.

1 cup (½-inch) diced Idaho baking potatoes

1 cup (½-inch) diced, peeled sweet potatoes

Salt and black pepper

1 tablespoon olive oil

½ cup chopped bacon

½ cup diced yellow onion

½ cup baby lima beans

½ cup fresh corn kernels

¾ cup chopped tomato

2 tablespoons chopped fresh tarragon or basil

3 tablespoons cold unsalted butter, cut into cubes

4 Poached Eggs (page 31), warmed

Place the potato and sweet potato in a medium saucepan with 8 cups of water and 2 tablespoons of salt. Bring to a boil over medium heat and cook until the potatoes and sweet potatoes can be easily pierced with a knife, 5 to 7 minutes. Set up an ice bath by adding ice and cold water to a large bowl. Remove the potatoes and plunge into the ice bath to stop the cooking process. Drain and set aside.

Warm the oil in a large skillet over medium heat for 45 seconds. Add the bacon and cook, stirring constantly, until almost crispy, 2 to 3 minutes. Turn the heat to high, add the onion, and sauté just until the onion begins to turn transparent, about 2 minutes. Add the potatoes and sweet potatoes, stirring to combine, and season lightly with salt and pepper. Continue to cook, slowly stirring, until the potatoes begin to lightly brown, about 4 minutes. Stir in the baby lima beans and corn until well combined and warmed through, about another 30 seconds. Add the tomato and tarragon, season lightly with salt and pepper, and cook, stirring, until the tomato begins to break down, about 30 seconds. Add the cold butter and cook, stirring, just until the butter melts. Spoon the Succot-hash evenly onto 4 plates and top each with a poached egg. Serve immediately.

SHRIMP GRAVY BISCUIT SUNDAE

SERVES 1

Years ago, I developed a habit of grabbing a 16-ounce Styrofoam cup, crumbling a biscuit into it, breaking a slice of patty sausage on top of that, and topping it with tomato gravy, mustard, pickles, and a poached egg. It was my Big Bad Breakfast on the run.

The Southern Foodways Alliance, an academic organization of chefs, food lovers, restaurant owners, writers, scholars, critics . . . and drunks, hosts its fall symposium in Oxford every year. It is four days of immersion into the world of Southern food, its history, lore, and preservation. It is an eating and drinking extravaganza that culminates with a hugely entertaining artistic performance on Sunday morning and a final brunch, at which a significant number of the participants are blisteringly hungover.

For that closing program a couple of years ago, we decided to tune up my cup idea (because it is fucking awesome) and offer it as a snack on Sunday morning to hold folks over before the final farewell brunch. So we amped up the tomato gravy, added shrimp, and topped it with a little fresh cilantro, green onion, and crushed pumpkin seeds. We then loaded it all into Chinese to-go containers and created this little smash hit. It's another one of those things that is equally as great at midnight as it is for breakfast.

1½ tablespoons clarified butter (page 30) or your preferred cooking fat

6 to 8 large shrimp, chopped

Salt and pepper

2 tablespoons cooked bacon bits

3 tablespoons sliced green onion, green part only

1 Black Pepper Buttermilk Biscuit (page 183)

¾ cup Tomato Gravy (page 201)

3 tablespoons Buttermilk Crema (page 104)

2 tablespoons chopped fresh cilantro

3 tablespoons toasted pumpkin seeds

Warm the clarified butter in a sauté pan over medium heat for 30 seconds. Add the shrimp, season with salt and pepper, and cook just until the shrimp are opaque, about 1½ minutes. Stir briefly and add the bacon. Stir again and add the green onion. Stir very briefly. You want the green onion to retain most of its crunch and bright green color. Remove from the heat and set aside while you assemble the sundae.

Crumble the biscuit into a bowl (or Styrofoam cup) and ladle the gravy over the top. Spoon the shrimp over the gravy and top with the crema, cilantro, and pumpkin seeds. Trying to refrain from eating at this point will be as futile as driving more than 30 feet from the Burger King drive-thru without eating one of those fucking fries.

CRAWFISH CAKES

SERVES 4

3 tablespoons olive oil

½ cup diced yellow onion

¼ cup diced red bell pepper

¼ cup diced green bell pepper

2 tablespoons minced garlic

12 ounces chopped frozen cooked crawfish tail meat, thawed

3 tablespoons Creole mustard or whole-grain Dijon mustard

2 tablespoons mayonnaise

2 tablespoons Louisiana hot sauce

1 tablespoon Worcestershire sauce

1 tablespoon Creole seasoning

2 eggs plus 1 yolk, lightly beaten

¾ cup panko bread crumbs, plus extra for coating

2 tablespoons clarified butter (page 30) or your preferred cooking fat

Sliced tomatoes, bitter greens, and Hollandaise (page 56), for garnish

There is no way to describe the ingenious culinary process I went through to mutate a crab cake into a crawfish cake. If I tried to explain it to you, your brain would probably implode due to the intricacies of the process. Just kidding. I simply swapped in slightly more affordable but equally delicious crawfish meat for the oh-so-common crab. End of story. This sort of simple ingredient switch is exactly the kind of misdirection chefs use to look like some sort of genius.

Please, take the time and energy to find domestic (preferably Louisiana) crawfish for this recipe. The tails are frequently a little smaller than their imported Asian counterparts, but there is less water content to them, and the 1-pound bags they come sealed in are loaded with delicious fat (yes, crawfish have fat), which is where their flavor comes from. Whatever variety you find, they will be frozen. The best practice with these is to slowly thaw them overnight in your refrigerator. Keep this in mind when preparing to make this dish. The tenacious among you might wait until crawfish season and harvest tails by hand. You will be rewarded with more delicious crawfish cakes and in heaven by a choir of angels. Cajun angels, of course.

For the record, it's CRAW-fish, not CRAY-fish and, while we're at it, pah-CAWN, not PEE-can (as my grandmother used to say, "That's what we keep under the bed!").

Warm the oil in a sauté pan over medium heat for 30 seconds. Add the onion, bell peppers, and garlic and sauté until barely softened, about 1 minute. Remove from the heat and cool to room temperature.

In a stainless steel bowl, stir together the crawfish, mustard, mayonnaise, hot sauce, Worcestershire sauce, Creole seasoning, eggs, and ¾ cup panko. Stir in the cooled onion and pepper mixture and blend until completely combined. Cover and refrigerate for 30 minutes.

Divide into 8 equal portions. Form each portion into 2-inch cakes that are about ¾ inch thick. Roll in extra panko to coat each cake fully.

Preheat the oven to 200°F.

Warm the clarified butter in a 10-inch sauté pan over medium heat for 30 seconds. Place the crawfish cakes in the pan 4 at a time and cook until lightly brown on both sides, 2 to 3 minutes per side. Remove to a baking sheet lined with paper towels and place in a warm oven while cooking the remaining 4 cakes.

Place the hot cakes over the sliced tomatoes on each of 4 plates and garnish with bitter greens and a simple vinaigrette and topped with hollandaise. Serve immediately.

THE PYLON

SERVES 1

Dinglewood Pharmacy in Columbus, Georgia, makes a thing called the Scramble Dog. It's a hot dog car wreck on a plate—a couple of open-faced hot dogs with all of a chili dog's fixings piled on top and dusted with crushed oyster crackers. We married that idea with Roscoe's House of Chicken and Waffles famous dish—sweet waffle topped with fried chicken and drizzled with honey—and this was the bastard child. We call it The Pylon because everything is "piled on" the waffle.

I am proud to say I actually watched it single-handedly bring Dave Chang back from the grave the morning after his first book party, and I've seen it breathe life into hundreds of hungover college students, postgraduate students, and post-postgrads. Yes, people, this is miracle food. Or at least on that particularly rough morning, you will fall to your knees and thank God I brought it to you.

1½ tablespoons clarified butter (page 30) or your preferred cooking fat

2 hot dogs, split lengthwise

¾ cup Breakfast Chili (page 72)

½ cup Sweet Slaw (recipe follows)

¼ cup chopped bread-and-butter pickles

¼ cup grated cheddar cheese

¼ cup crumbled oyster crackers

2 tablespoons minced pickled jalapeño

2 tablespoons mayonnaise

2 tablespoons yellow mustard

1 Belgian Waffle (page 98), warmed

Heat a skillet over medium heat with the clarified butter for 1 minute. Place the hot dogs in the pan, cut side down, and cook for 2 to 3 minutes, or until the bottom side begins to blacken slightly. Pile the hot dogs and all the remaining ingredients on top of the warm waffle in whatever order you see fit. Eat. Shower and nap. You can thank me later.

SWEET SLAW
MAKES ABOUT 3 CUPS

2 cups shredded green cabbage

¼ cup minced yellow onion

¼ cup shredded carrot

⅓ cup mayonnaise

¼ cup sweet pickle relish

2½ tablespoons sugar

2 tablespoons white vinegar

1 tablespoon vegetable oil

1 tablespoon Texas Pete hot sauce or your preferred vinegar hot sauce

½ teaspoon celery seed

½ teaspoon salt

In a stainless steel bowl, toss together the cabbage, onion, and carrot. In a separate bowl, whisk together the mayonnaise, relish, sugar, vinegar, oil, hot sauce, celery seed, and salt. Pour the mayonnaise mixture over the cabbage mixture and stir together until well combined. Allow to stand, refrigerated, for several hours before serving so the flavors can develop. Stir well before serving. This recipe makes more than you will need for a single Pylon, but it keeps well in the refrigerator for about 4 or 5 days and it goes great with sandwiches and burgers, and *really* well with barbecue.

ROASTED TOMATO COBBLER

SERVES 6 TO 8

This was a dish born of necessity. During the height of tomato season, we are constantly trying to figure out how to use the bounty of local tomatoes we come into. We also always have piles of biscuit dough around. And so this tomato cobbler is a result of the savory collision of those two things. A scoop of tomato cobbler sprinkled with freshly grated Parmesan cheese and topped with a runny poached egg is as good a way as any to start the day This recipe is obviously best with vine-ripened heirloom tomatoes, but in a pinch (or if the craving hits you) you can make a reasonable facsimile of it with good-quality hothouse tomatoes.

6 ripe slicing tomatoes

Salt and black pepper

3 teaspoons fresh thyme leaves

3 tablespoons minced garlic

Olive oil, for roasting tomatoes

¼ cup extra-virgin olive oil

¾ cup diced yellow onion

4 cups diced fresh Roma tomato

1½ teaspoons chopped fresh rosemary

1½ teaspoons chopped fresh oregano

Unsalted butter, for the pan

4 tablespoons all-purpose flour

¾ cup crumbled goat cheese

1 recipe Black Pepper Buttermilk Biscuit dough (page 183)

Clarified butter (page 30), for brushing biscuits

Preheat the oven to 275°F. Line a baking sheet with parchment paper.

Core the slicing tomatoes and cut in half across the equator. Squeeze out the seeds and place the halves, cut side up, on the prepared baking sheet. Season the tomatoes with salt and pepper and sprinkle with 1½ teaspoons of the thyme and 1½ tablespoons of the minced garlic. Drizzle with olive oil. Bake, rotating the baking sheet every 30 minutes, until the tomatoes are golden and very soft, about 3 hours. Allow to cool to room temperature.

Turn the oven to 350°F.

Warm the extra-virgin olive oil in a large sauté pan over medium heat for 30 seconds. Add the onion and remaining 1½ tablespoons garlic and sauté until the onion begins to turn transparent, about 2 minutes. Stir in the diced tomato, season lightly with salt and pepper, and combine well. Stir in the rosemary, oregano, and remaining 1½ teaspoons thyme, and bring to a simmer for 4 minutes, stirring constantly. Remove from the heat and set aside.

Rub a 9 by 9-inch casserole dish with butter. Spread out half of the tomato mixture in the bottom of the prepared dish, then sprinkle with 2 tablespoons of the flour followed by half of the goat cheese. Place 6 of the roasted tomato halves on top of the goat cheese. Repeat the layers one more time, using the remaining tomato mixture, flour, goat cheese, and roasted tomatoes. Cover the dish with aluminum foil and bake until the cobbler begins to thicken, about 35 minutes.

Meanwhile, roll out the biscuit dough to ½ inch thick and cut into 3-inch rounds. Remove the cobbler from the oven, peel back the foil, place the biscuits on top, covering as much of the surface as possible without overlapping, and brush with clarified butter. Bake until the biscuits turn golden brown, about 15 minutes. Serve immediately.

CRAWFISH ÉTOUFFÉE

SERVES 4

When I worked cooking on a tugboat in the Gulf of Mexico after my senior year in high school, I found it hard to believe that most of the guys wanted nothing more than a scoop of rice, a piece or two of fried tasso, and a couple of fried eggs for breakfast. A few dashes of Tabasco and a cup of really bad black coffee set these guys off to work every morning. I was surprised. I guess I expected them to all eat shrimp Creole, jambalaya, gumbo, boudin, and the like, the things I associated with Cajuns, so the eggs and rice thing just blew me away.

Thirty years later, this particular étouffée is kind of a revisitating of that fascination. It is a dressed-up rice that we slap an egg on and all of a sudden it is breakfast.

Étouffée is, after all, little more than tomato gravy, heavy on the bell peppers and onion, that's splashed with Creole seasoning, a hint of white wine, and crawfish tails. A slice or two of crispy, soft white toast and a runny egg with this and you will never look at étouffée the same way ever again . . . guaranteed.

Frozen crawfish should be thawed overnight in the refrigerator.

1 cup chopped yellow onion

¾ cup chopped celery

¾ cup chopped green bell pepper

3½ tablespoons unsalted butter

2½ tablespoons all-purpose flour

2 teaspoons minced garlic

1 (1-pound) bag frozen cooked Louisiana crawfish tail meat, thawed, fat drained and reserved

2 teaspoons freshly squeezed lemon juice

2 teaspoons black pepper, plus more for the eggs

1½ teaspoons Creole seasoning

1¼ teaspoons Worcestershire sauce

¾ teaspoon dried oregano

¾ teaspoon salt, plus more for the eggs

½ teaspoon MSG (see Note)

1 bay leaf

1 cup chicken stock or water

Tabasco pepper sauce, for seasoning

2 tablespoons sliced green onion, green part only

2 tablespoons clarified butter (page 30) or your preferred cooking fat

4 eggs

4 cups cooked long-grain white rice, for serving

2 tablespoons chopped fresh parsley

4 slices sourdough bread, toasted and buttered

Combine the onion, celery, and bell pepper in a food processor and pulse several times until finely chopped but not pureed.

Melt the butter in a cast-iron skillet over medium heat. Add the flour and whisk until a roux forms. Continue to cook, whisking constantly, until the roux turns a light gold and gives off a nutty aroma, 5 to 7 minutes. Stir in the finely chopped vegetables and minced garlic and sauté, stirring constantly, until the vegetables soften, 5 to 7 minutes. Whisk in the reserved crawfish fat and simmer for 2 minutes. Add the crawfish, lemon juice, black pepper, Creole seasoning, Worcestershire, oregano, salt, MSG, and bay leaf, followed by the chicken stock. Bring to a boil, then turn the heat to low and simmer, covered, until the sauce thickens, about 20 minutes. Remove from heat. Season with Tabasco and stir in the green onion. Remove the bay leaf.

Preheat the broiler.

In an ovenproof skillet, pour in the clarified butter, swirl to coat the pan, and warm for 1 minute more. Crack the eggs into a small bowl and check to make sure there is no shell. Slowly and carefully pour the eggs from the bowl into the pan and allow to sit, undisturbed, for 1 minute. As the whites begin to set, agitate the pan gently in a circular motion. Sprinkle with salt and pepper and continue to agitate the pan. After about 2 minutes, when the whites are cooked almost through (they will still be slightly clear and runny on the top), place the pan directly under the broiler for 20 to 30 seconds to finish cooking the tops of the whites.

To serve, divide the rice among 4 bowls, ladle the étouffée on top, and sprinkle with the parsley. Serve with toasted sourdough the side and a fried egg dropped on top.

ADD A LITTLE MSG TO YOUR LIFE

So let's talk about MSG for a second. There is a magnificent and almost universal misconception in the United States that monosodium glutamate (MSG) is somehow bad for you. Here's the very simple news: it isn't. MSG is a naturally occurring sodium component of an amino acid. It was originally isolated for use in re-creating the savory taste of a particular kind of seaweed used prolifically in Japanese cooking. On its own, it delivers a sensation on the palate similar to that of table or kosher salt, but it has an amazing flavor that I can only describe as akin to the most delicious potato chip you've ever eaten.

American researchers tried to make a case that MSG caused headaches and sore muscles in the mid-1970s, when ingested in the right quantities. This was never proven, but the bad rap still hangs around MSG's neck. Like that of lard, MSG's unhealthy reputation is totally undeserved. We use it in most of our kitchens because it allows us to boost flavor without adding salt, which, as we all know, *does* affect us adversely. So there it is. MSG myth: busted. Pick some up next time you're at the store; it's in the spice aisle.

SAUTÉED TROUT, SOFT SCRAMBLED EGGS, CHANTERELLE MUSHROOMS

SERVES 2

At first, this may not sound like a quick go-to breakfast, but I promise you, it's one of the best combinations of textures and flavors you can imagine. The soft scrambled eggs, the crispy skin and creamy flesh of the trout, and the tender chanterelle mushrooms make for an amazing bite. The layers of garlic, lemon, and a touch of white wine make it transcendent. Once you've had it, your life will feel oddly empty until you can have it again.

You can substitute shiitakes or morels for the chanterelles, but there is something about the sweet taste and meaty texture of chanterelles that makes this dish sing. If you can get your hands on fresh speckled trout, do so; a good brook trout or farm-raised rainbow trout works nicely, too.

2 (4- to 5-ounce) skin-on trout fillets, scaled

Salt and black pepper

2 tablespoons bacon fat

2 tablespoons clarified butter (page 30) or your preferred cooking fat

2 tablespoons minced shallot

1 teaspoon minced garlic

1½ cups chanterelle mushrooms, cut into large bite-size slices

2 teaspoons fresh thyme leaves

1 tablespoon white wine

2 teaspoons freshly squeezed lemon juice

1 tablespoon chopped fresh parsley

SCRAMBLED EGGS

5 eggs

5 tablespoons whole milk

Salt and pepper

2 tablespoons clarified butter (page 30) or your preferred cooking fat

Preheat the oven to 200°F.

Season the trout fillets with salt and pepper. Warm the bacon fat in a 10-inch sauté pan over high heat for 30 seconds. Carefully place the fillets, skin side down, in the pan and allow to sit, undisturbed, for 1 minute. Loosen the fillets with a spatula and flip them over to cook the flesh side. Lower the heat to medium and cook, shaking the pan gently to keep the flesh from sticking, until the skin begins to brown slightly around the edges, about 2 minutes. Flip the fillets over again and cook the skin side until the trout is firm to the touch, about 1½ minutes more. Remove the trout and drain on a paper towel–lined baking sheet and place in the warm oven.

In the same pan, warm the clarified butter over medium heat for 30 seconds. Add the shallot and garlic and cook, stirring, just until warmed through, about 30 seconds. Add the mushrooms and thyme and sauté, stirring gently, until the mushrooms begin to soften and their edges begin to get crispy, about 1½ minutes. Stir in the wine, lemon juice, and parsley. Remove from the heat but keep the pan on the stove top to stay warm.

To make the scrambled eggs, stir together the eggs, milk, and a sprinkling of salt and pepper with a fork in a large bowl; set aside.

Warm the clarified butter in a 10-inch nonstick skillet over low heat for 1 minute. Pour in the eggs and allow to sit, without stirring, for 15 seconds. With a silicone spatula, push the eggs from one side of the pan gently toward the other side, then tilt the pan and allow the uncooked eggs to fill the void. Allow the eggs to sit again, without stirring, for 15 seconds, then push the eggs to the opposite side and tilt the pan again. Run your spatula around the edge of the pan, tilting and allowing the last of the uncooked egg to move to the bottom of the pan. Just as the eggs are almost set but still a tiny bit runny, give them a gentle stir and remove from the heat.

To assemble, divide the scrambled eggs between 2 plates, top with a trout fillet (flesh side up), and spoon the mushrooms over the top. Serve immediately.

OYSTER "POTPIE"

SERVES 6

Little says "comfort" like potpie. Whether it's a traditional American version, like chicken potpie in a flaky piecrust, a lamb shepherd's pie under a blanket of creamy mashed potatoes, or Greek kreatopita covered in flaky phyllo, there is something undeniably alluring about richly stewed meats topped with pastry or dough.

This one veers in another direction, with oysters in place of the traditional meat and the addition of fennel for an anise-tinged bite. The best thing about it, though, is that all of the components can be made in advance. So the pie can be assembled in a heartbeat just before baking—or even be completely baked and then rewarmed in the oven just before serving.

Find a good source for shucked oysters. Boutique grocery stores frequently have a good line on local oysters, you can befriend a local restaurant owner, or the ambitious among you can certainly shuck your own.

PIE DOUGH

5 cups all-purpose flour

4 teaspoons fresh thyme leaves

2½ teaspoons salt

1 cup cold unsalted butter, cut into cubes

¾ cup cold lard

¼ cup cold whole milk

FILLING

¾ cup chopped bacon

3½ tablespoons unsalted butter

¼ cup plus 3 tablespoons all-purpose flour

1 cup diced yellow onion

¾ cup diced fennel bulb

½ cup diced celery

½ cup (½-inch) diced baking potato

2 teaspoons minced garlic

4 cups shucked oysters, drained and oyster liquor reserved (add enough water to make ½ cup)

½ cup heavy cream

¼ cup white wine

1½ tablespoons Creole seasoning

1½ teaspoons salt

2 teaspoons chopped fresh oregano

2 teaspoons fresh thyme leaves

Zest and juice of 1 lemon

½ cup sliced green onion, green part only

⅓ cup chopped fresh parsley

Freshly ground pepper

1 egg, lightly beaten

1 tablespoon whole milk

To make the dough, combine the flour, thyme, and salt in a food processor and pulse several times to combine. Add the cold butter and lard and pulse several times again, just until a coarse meal forms. Drizzle in the milk, pulsing all the while, until the dough begins to come together. Transfer the dough to a floured surface. Briefly knead the dough until smooth, about 2 minutes. Divide into 2 balls (one slightly larger than the other) and flatten into disks. Cover with plastic wrap and refrigerate until firm, at least 1 hour and up to 6 days.

To make the filling, heat a large sauté pan over medium heat for 1 minute. Add the bacon and cook until brown and just about crispy, 3 to 4 minutes. Remove from the pan with a slotted spoon and drain on paper towels. In the same pan, add the butter, allow it to melt, and whisk in flour. Whisk for 4 minutes. Add the onion, fennel, celery, potato, and garlic and cook, stirring, until the onion begins to soften, about 3 minutes. Stir in the reserved oyster liquor, cream, and wine and cook until the liquid begins to thicken, 2 to 3 minutes. Whisk in the Creole seasoning, salt, oregano, thyme, and lemon zest and juice and stir until well combined. Stir in the oysters, reserved bacon, green onion, and parsley and season with pepper. Remove from the heat and set aside or allow to cool to room temperature and refrigerate in plastic, covered, for up to 2 days.

Preheat the oven to 350°F.

Whisk together the egg and whole milk in a small bowl and set aside.

To assemble the potpie, turn out the larger disk of dough onto a floured surface and roll it into a 10-inch round that's about ⅛ inch thick. Lay into a 9-inch round pie dish, trimming the dough to ¼ inch of the dish's edge. Spoon the filling to cover the dough and smooth the top. Roll the second disk of dough into a 10-inch round that's about ⅛ inch thick. Lay the dough over the filling, trimming the dough to ¼ inch of the dish's edge. Using the tines of a fork, work your way around the edge of the pie dish, pressing the top and bottom pieces of dough together, but not cutting through the dough. Cut 8 or 10 (½-inch) vents in the top of the pie and brush the dough with the egg wash. Bake until the top is golden brown, about 35 minutes. Remove from the oven, allow to cool for 5 to 7 minutes, and serve piping hot.

PORK TENDERLOIN 662 WITH CRABMEAT AND PECAN BUTTER

SERVES 2

I am not embarrassed to admit that I have comforting, nostalgic memories of many dishes I ate growing up, even though many of them are often painfully dated. This recipe was inspired by my longing for a French Quarter stalwart, La Louisiane, a restaurant my dad used to take me to as a kid. We would have these occasional midweek father-and-son lunches. The waiters wore tuxes, and alcohol-bloated mobsters literally occupied tables in the darkest corners. Their particular presence was very clear and strongly suggested that you kept your head down and your mouth shut.

La Louisiane served a chicken dish that was like a piccata and, like a big shot, I'd order it with sautéed crabmeat. You see, in the New Orleans of my childhood, those old-line French joints just gave out menus as a guideline. The server's job, it seemed, was to give you suggestions on how you could modify a menu item and customize it to your liking. Nothing was out of the realm of possibility, as far as they were concerned. It was basically a chef's worst nightmare.

This recipe is a nod to my crazy, awesome dad who taught me how to order like a New Orleans gentleman. Pork and pecans are my northern Mississippi additions (hence "662," the area code of Oxford) to the piccata and crabmeat of that childhood dish in NOLA I loved so much.

½ cup all-purpose flour

1 tablespoon plus ½ teaspoon salt, plus more as needed

½ teaspoon black pepper, plus more as needed

Pinch of cayenne pepper

¼ teaspoon paprika

½ cup asparagus tips, trimmed to 1 inch

4 (1-ounce) pork tenderloin medallions (see Note)

4 tablespoons unsalted butter

2 tablespoons minced shallot

1 teaspoon minced garlic

1½ tablespoons capers, rinsed, chopped roughly

1 cup fresh jumbo lump Gulf blue crabmeat (you can substitute another inferior quality crabmeat, but understand the final product will suffer accordingly)

Zest and juice of 1 large lemon

1½ tablespoons chopped fresh tarragon

¼ cup toasted pecan pieces

1 cup Hollandaise (page 56), warmed

3 tablespoons fresh chervil leaves

Preheat the oven to 200°F. Prepare an ice bath.

In a small mixing bowl, combine the flour, ½ teaspoon salt, pepper, cayenne, and paprika. Stir with a fork until well combined and set aside.

Bring 8 cups of water and remaining 1 tablespoon salt to a boil in a small saucepan over medium heat and blanch the asparagus tips for 1 minute, until bright green. Remove and submerge in the bowl of ice water to stop the cooking process. Drain and set aside.

Lay the pork medallions flat on a piece of plastic wrap and cover with a second piece. Gently pound the pork with a meat mallet until they're about ⅛ inch thick. Remove from the plastic and season lightly with salt and pepper. Place the seasoned flour on a plate and dredge the medallions in the seasoned flour. Set aside.

Melt 2 tablespoons of the butter in a large sauté pan over medium heat. Add the pork medallions 2 at a time and cook until browned on both sides, about 1½ minutes on each side. Remove to a baking sheet covered with paper towels to drain and put in the warm oven. Repeat with the remaining 2 medallions.

In the same pan, melt the remaining 2 tablespoons butter. Add the shallot and garlic and sauté until the shallot begins to turn transparent and the garlic is noticeably fragrant, about 30 seconds. Add the asparagus and capers, season lightly with salt and pepper, and sauté, stirring constantly, until warmed through, about another 30 seconds. Add the crabmeat, lemon zest, and tarragon and season with salt and pepper. Sauté, stirring constantly, until warmed through, about 1 minute. Stir in the pecans and lemon juice until well combined. Remove from the heat.

To serve, place the pork medallions on 2 plates and divide the crabmeat mixture over the top. Drizzle with the hollandaise and sprinkle with the chervil. Serve immediately.

NOTE: Buy a whole pork loin, unwrap it, and lay it on a cutting board. Slice the end off where the loin is most consistently round and the taper is the least dramatic. From that piece, cut four 1-inch-thick medallions. Wrap the remaining loin and trimmed piece in plastic for another time and refrigerate or freeze.

CREAMED "CHIPPED" MUSHROOMS ON TOAST

SERVES 2

Creamed chipped beef on toast is the first thing I remember my dad cooking me for breakfast, quite probably because he confided to me that they called it shit on a shingle in the military. That's really good stuff for a six- or seven-year-old. Despite the nickname, Dad's chipped beef was delicious.

So when we got ready to open Big Bad Breakfast, it was one of the weird dishes I wanted on the menu, but no matter how hard we scoured the Internet, the Armour brand of chipped beef I remembered from childhood just didn't exist anymore in bulk, nor did any reference to how to make it.

Turns out chipped beef was a product of World War II–era rationing, and apparently, I am the last of a generation to enjoy the licentious delicacy of yore. Perhaps it's for the best. It was probably made from very cheap cuts of beef that were slivered and salt-cured. This enhanced the flavor and made for an almost eternal shelf life, both of which were good for battlefield gourmands. And maybe its disappearance is a testament to that. This version with dried mushrooms, however, is an excellent substitute and a killer vegetarian offering, while still achieving the "shit on a shingle" excitement.

1½ cups dried mixed wild mushrooms

2 teaspoons salt, plus more as needed

5 tablespoons unsalted butter

½ cup diced yellow onion

2 teaspoons minced garlic

2½ teaspoons fresh thyme leaves

Freshly ground black pepper

2 teaspoons white wine

3 tablespoons all-purpose flour

1½ cups whole milk

Pinch of cayenne pepper

Pinch of ground nutmeg

2 tablespoons chopped fresh parsley

2 slices whole wheat bread, toasted and buttered

Place the mushrooms in a small saucepan and add enough water to cover plus the 2 teaspoons salt. Bring to a boil, then simmer for 7 to 10 minutes. Remove from the heat and allow the mushrooms and cooking liquid to cool to room temperature in the pan. Drain the mushrooms, reserving the cooking liquid. Chop the mushrooms and set aside.

In a separate small saucepan, melt 2 tablespoons of the butter over medium heat. Add the onion and garlic and cook, stirring, until the onions begin to turn transparent, about 1 minute. Add the chopped mushrooms and thyme, season with salt and pepper, and sauté until warmed through and fragrant, about 3 minutes. Add the white wine and stir until well combined. Remove from the heat and set aside.

In a small sauté pan, melt the remaining 3 tablespoons butter over medium heat. Add the flour and whisk until a roux forms. Continue to cook, whisking constantly, until the roux turns a light gold and gives off a nutty aroma, 5 to 7 minutes. Stir in the milk, ¾ cup of the reserved mushroom stock, the cayenne, and nutmeg and cook, whisking, until the sauce begins to thicken, about 3 minutes. Stir in the chopped mushrooms and parsley and simmer until thickened and velvety, 3 to 4 minutes. Season with salt and pepper.

Spoon over the toast and serve immediately.

THE EGG BOWL

SERVES 1

Named in honor of the football game played annually between Ole Miss and Mississippi State (a series that started in 1901 and which Ole Miss currently leads 62–43–6), the Egg Bowl is frequently an inconsequential, cold, terrible train wreck of a game. But it is always heated, and like most good in-state rivalries, it sees the occasional weird upset.

This is sort of an homage to that rivalry, in that it is a total mess of a dish. We toss everything at it, and in spite of the mess it may seem to be, it's always awesome. If you want to do it right, eat it on a crisp fall morning, then pour yourself a giant Solo cup full of bourbon and Coke and take a stroll (to a football game, if you can).

1 tablespoon clarified butter (page 30)

3 cups fresh spinach

¼ cup white wine

1 teaspoon olive oil

1 tablespoon minced shallot

½ teaspoon minced garlic

½ cup diced tomato

Salt and black pepper

¾ cup Garlic Cheese Grits (page 187)

½ cup Potato Hash (page 87)

¼ cup cooked chopped bacon

3 tablespoons Tomato Gravy (page 201), warmed

2 Poached Eggs (page 31), warmed

¼ cup Hollandaise (page 56), warmed

Crystal hot sauce (optional)

Warm a large sauté pan over medium heat for 30 seconds with the clarified butter. Add the spinach and cover for 30 seconds. Remove the lid, add the wine, and begin turning the spinach with tongs as it wilts. As soon as all of the spinach has wilted, remove it to a strainer and press as much liquid out as you can.

Warm the oil in a small sauté pan over medium heat for 30 seconds. Add the shallot and garlic and sauté until the shallot begins to turn transparent, about 1½ minutes. Stir in the tomato, season lightly with salt and black pepper, and cook until the tomatoes begin to soften slightly, about 1 minute more. Remove from the heat and set aside.

Layer the grits, hash, spinach, bacon, tomatoes, gravy, eggs, and hollandaise in a bowl. Splash with hot sauce. Dig in immediately.

HUEVOS COCINEROS

SERVES 2

I love the flavors of Mexico. Corn, cumin, cilantro, and jalapeño are a classic combination and as comforting as anything the French ever dreamed up. Well, that or these are the international flavors of hangover relief. Whatever the case, the flavors of huevos rancheros all work really well together, but more often than not, the dish leaves me wanting more. So here's our version, huevos cocineros, or "cook's eggs"—it's just rancheros with a little more "huevos."

4 tablespoons clarified butter (page 30) or your preferred cooking fat

4 eggs

Salt and black pepper

4 Fresh Corn Arepas (page 108)

1½ cups cooked long-grain rice

2 cups Saucy Black Beans (page 202)

¾ cup crumbled Cotija cheese

⅔ cup Roasted Jalapeño Salsa (recipe follows), for serving

3 tablespoons sour cream

2 tablespoons chopped fresh cilantro

Preheat the broiler.

Warm an ovenproof nonstick skillet over low heat for 1 minute. Pour in the butter, swirl to coat the pan, and warm for 1 minute more. Meanwhile, crack the eggs into a small bowl and check to make sure there is no shell. Slowly and carefully pour the eggs from the bowl into the pan and allow them to sit, undisturbed, for 1 minute. As the whites begin to set, agitate the pan gently in a circular motion. Sprinkle with salt and pepper and continue to agitate the pan. After about 2 minutes, when the whites are cooked almost through (they will still be slightly clear and runny on the top), place the pan directly under the broiler for 20 to 30 seconds to finish cooking the tops of the whites.

Lay 2 arepas on each of 2 plates and top with the rice followed by the beans. Sprinkle with the Cotija. Top with the eggs, salsa, sour cream, and cilantro.

ROASTED JALAPEÑO SALSA
MAKES ABOUT 3 CUPS

2 jalapeños

3 large tomatoes, chopped

¾ cup diced yellow onion

2 tablespoons extra-virgin olive oil

Zest and juice of 2 limes

2 teaspoons black pepper

1½ teaspoons salt

1 teaspoon minced garlic

1 teaspoon ground coriander

½ teaspoon ground cumin

2 pinches of ground cinnamon

Place the jalapeños over an open flame, such as on a charcoal grill or on a wire cooling rack placed over a gas burner turned on high. Cook for 4 to 5 minutes, turning them regularly, until the skin is blackened and/or blistered all over. Remove the jalapeños to a small stainless steel bowl, cover with plastic wrap, and allow to stand for 30 minutes at room temperature. Peel the jalapeños and remove the seeds.

Combine the roasted jalapeños, tomatoes, onion, olive oil, lime zest and juice, black pepper, salt, garlic, coriander, cumin, and cinnamon in a food processor and pulse several times until well combined but not pureed. Season with salt, if needed. Store in a plastic container and refrigerate for up to 1 week.

MISSISSIPPI

ASK FOR SAMPLE

SLIGHTLY HOT!

Salsa!

FRESH! GOOD!

CEREALS, GRAINS, AND OTHER PSEUDO-VIRTUOUS THINGS

I CAN'T ARGUE WITH THE FACT THAT A BREAKFAST BOOK WOULD be incomplete without cereal. Yet that food group is largely made up of terrible, processed, extruded nonsense—not anything I feel particularly excited writing about. Listen, I love and have been known to eat garbage can–size containers full of Frosted Flakes, Sugar-O's, Cap'n Crunch, Fruity Pebbles, Cocoa Puffs, Cinnamon Toast Crunch, Boo Berry, Franken Berry, and Count Chocula. But I have a daughter now, and like any good "hippie mom," I have decreed that she will not be eating that shit in our house. (News flash: No matter how hard you try, concentrate on it, pray, make deals with the fucking devil, you *do* turn into your parents.)

CHAPTER 6

As a means of compromise (and to make sure that Mamie doesn't become the bane of her sleepover group's existence come breakfast time), I have come up with a couple of homemade cereals. Admittedly, they vary wildly from their store-bought counterparts; they have very interesting and fun flavors and textures (just don't think for a second you are about to fool anyone). They make a killer Saturday afternoon experiment, and you end up with cereal that tastes great and you can feel good about putting in you.

Because grains are what make these cereals (which may help legitimize this chapter actually existing), we will examine cooked grains along with some cereal offerings. Truthfully, the South of my childhood was not a place where oatmeal played a huge role. Cream of Wheat was a curiosity to me that never existed beyond TV commercials during *The Honeymooners*. On very rare occasion, we had creamy rice with sugar or sweetened cornmeal mush at my grandmother's house, but that was about as close to Cream of Wheat as we ever got.

Lots of folks assume that grits might be eaten with sugar (since they are so similar to cornmeal mush), but in the South, grits and sugar are like oil and vinegar . . . they just don't mix. But no matter what you grew up with, the things that make getting out of bed on cold winter mornings worthwhile are largely members of the grain family. Oatmeal, Cream of Wheat, and grits are three of those things patently capable of pulling those of us who hate a cold morning back from the brink. I am not sure what it is about a bowl of steaming oatmeal with raisins, a splash of cream, and three times as much brown sugar as my mom wanted me to eat that is so miraculous, but its magical powers are many and undeniable, even in the South.

HOMEMADE VANILLA AND DOUBLE ALMOND GRANOLA

MAKES ABOUT 8 CUPS

This seemed like the friendliest place to start this chapter since it lays out a lot of the basic techniques of homemade cereal: cooking, drying, and recooking grains in order to achieve the desired texture (usually crispy).

Granola is fun because you can put pretty much anything in the world you want into it (within reason, for those of you out there who are jumping on the Interweb to crap all over that statement). It takes well to dried fruit, nuts, and different flavored syrups. The combinations are endless, but one of my favorites is a very classic French flavor combination inspired by wedding cake, of all things. The blending of almonds, vanilla, and a hint of lemon is a winner. Spoon a little yogurt over it and top with some fresh berries, and it's a knockout punch.

P.S. I think the greatest thing ever in the world would be if this granola included the dried strawberries I ate in the Carmel Market in Tel Aviv with my buddies Alon Shaya and Michael Solomonov. Holy Mary, mother of God, those things were some of the most delicious morsels I have ever put in my mouth. Unfortunately, I got so caught up eating lunch in the market, I ended up getting dragged out of there without buying any. So if anyone happens to be over there and wants to start their smuggling career with an entirely innocuous bit of contraband, I'll pay top dollar. Hook a brother up.

1 cup sliced almonds

1 cup pecan pieces

1 cup crushed peanuts

7 cups rolled oats

1 cup wheat germ

¾ cup honey

¾ cup firmly packed dark brown sugar

½ cup canola oil or other vegetable oil

½ cup unsalted butter, melted

1 tablespoon pure vanilla extract

1 teaspoon almond extract

¼ teaspoon ground nutmeg

Preheat the oven to 350°F. Line a baking sheet with parchment paper and coat with cooking spray.

Spread the almonds, pecans, and peanuts evenly over a second baking sheet and place in the oven. Toast, stirring every 3 minutes, for 12 minutes or until the almonds begin to color lightly. Remove from the oven and allow to cool to room temperature.

Combine all of the ingredients in a large mixing bowl and stir together until well combined. Pour the granola onto the prepared baking sheet and bake until lightly browned, 25 to 30 minutes. Stir every 10 minutes or so to help even browning. If at the end of 30 minutes, the granola isn't completely browned, continue in 5-minute intervals of baking and stirring until you reach your desired degree of doneness. Remove from the oven and allow to cool to room temperature. Store in an airtight plastic container in a cool, dry place for up to 1 month.

CINNAMON AND CITRUS OATMEAL WITH DRIED BLACK MISSION FIGS

SERVES 4

Much like steel-cut grits, quality steel-cut oats take a little more patience than you normally need for your run-of-the-mill Quaker cereal, but reveal a far superior end product.

Cinnamon just lights up a dish, but there's something about the earthy, creamy comfort of a good bowl of oatmeal that just reins it in and drives it straight to your deepest pleasure center. The citrus is a little surprising, but the figs add a toothy sweetness. These are ingredients normally not seen together on one stage, but they crush it here.

1¼ cups steel-cut oats

3 tablespoons unsalted butter

3 cups water

2 cups whole milk

½ cup diced dried Black Mission figs

4½ tablespoons firmly packed dark brown sugar

⅛ teaspoon salt

⅛ teaspoon ground cinnamon

¼ cup heavy cream

12 to 16 orange supremes (see Note)

12 to 16 grapefruit supremes (see Note)

Preheat the oven to 350°F.

Place the oats on a baking sheet and spread out into a single layer. Toast in the oven for 12 minutes, stirring every several minutes to cook evenly. Remove and cool briefly.

Melt the butter in a saucepan over medium heat. Add the oats and coat with the butter, stirring for 30 seconds. Meanwhile, combine the water and milk in a separate saucepan and warm over medium heat. Just before the milk and water reach the scalding point (the edges will begin to gently bubble), pour it over the toasted oats. Stir in the figs, 2½ tablespoons of the brown sugar, the salt, and cinnamon. Turn down the heat to low and cook, stirring constantly, until the oats are toothsome and soft, about 20 minutes.

To serve, divide among 4 bowls and top with the cream, the remaining 2 tablespoons brown sugar, and the orange and grapefruit. Serve immediately.

NOTE: To cut supremes of citrus, slice off the top and bottom of the fruit. Place a flat side of your fruit on a cutting board and cut the skin and pith off of the citrus all the way around the fruit. Pick up the fruit and, holding it in the palm of your hand over a bowl, slice between the separations in the fruit segments and the meat of the fruit itself, working your way around the fruit, releasing a perfectly clean citrus segment with no pith or skin on every second cut.

HOMEMADE FROSTED CORNFLAKES

SERVES 3

Let's face it, frosted flakes kick the shit out of regular cornflakes. So we aren't going to fool around with the crystal deodorant version of these guys. For the patchouli pirates out there who are still anti-sugar, feel free to eliminate the frosting part of the process. The rest of us will be having fun and bouncing off the walls.

2½ cups cornmeal

½ cup masa (see Note)

6 tablespoons sugar

1 tablespoon pure vanilla extract

¼ teaspoon salt

2 cups boiling water

Preheat the oven to 250°F. Line a large baking sheet with parchment paper and coat with cooking spray.

In a large bowl, stir together the cornmeal, masa, 3 tablespoons of the sugar, the vanilla, and salt. Add the boiling water and stir until the batter is well blended. It should be a little thinner than pancake batter. Pour the batter onto the prepared baking sheet and spread out into a layer that's about ⅛ inch thick.

Sprinkle the remaining 3 tablespoons sugar over the top of the batter and bake, turning the baking sheet every few minutes, until the batter begins to dry out and cracks, about 45 minutes. Remove from the oven and allow to cool briefly.

When cool enough to handle, crack the cornflakes into small bite-size pieces. Return to the oven and bake until fully dried, about 1 hour more. Remove from the oven and allow to cool completely. Store in an airtight plastic container in a cool, dry place for up to 1 month.

NOTE: Masa is wet ground cornmeal available at most grocery stores near the flour and cornmeal.

HOMEMADE GRAPE-NUTS AND FRUIT PARFAIT

SERVES 4

There was something I absolutely loved about Grape-Nuts when I was a kid. I knew it ran entirely counter to the sugary cereals I was supposed to love, but I adored them anyway. They were crunchy, they had a pile of really weird flavors, and I lived in deathly fear that I would bust a tooth wide open eating them. I also loved the terrifyingly dangerous and falling-apart roller coaster at Pontchartrain Beach (NOLA's own version of a Six Flags park) called the Wild Maus, so maybe that's just it. I love things that can potentially hurt me, which is exactly how I ended up in this profession, what with the fire, knives, substance abuse, shitty hours, and being constantly on your feet.

In this recipe we take those Grape-Nuts (for the many out there who are not fans) and layer them with fresh fruit, tangy yogurt, and some sweetened whipped cream for a fun and (arguably) healthy one-two punch.

For the record, these Grape-Nuts are a little more cinnamony and a little sweeter than store-bought, but my kid loves them, so who cares? If you feel strongly about thanking me for this, we are accepting donations for the "Mamie needs a pony" fund at a crowd-sourcing website near you.

3¼ cups Homemade Grape-Nuts (recipe follows)

1 cup sliced banana

1 cup diced peaches

1 cup quartered fresh strawberries

1 cup Greek yogurt

2 cups Whipped Buttermilk (recipe follows)

In 4 tall glasses, layer ¼ cup Grape-Nuts, followed by a few pieces of fruit and ¼ cup yogurt. Repeat the layers 2 more times, but substituting the Whipped Buttermilk for the yogurt. Sprinkle the remaining ¼ cup Grape-Nuts over the top (1 tablespoon per glass). Serve immediately.

HOMEMADE GRAPE-NUTS

MAKES ABOUT 4 CUPS

2¾ cups whole wheat flour

1 cup buttermilk

¾ cup graham cracker crumbs

⅓ cup plus 1 tablespoon molasses

6 tablespoons whole milk

½ teaspoon salt

⅛ teaspoon ground cinnamon

Preheat the oven to 300°F. Line a large baking sheet with parchment paper and coat with cooking spray.

Combine all of the ingredients in a large bowl and stir together until well combined. Pour the Grape-Nuts onto the prepared baking sheet and spread out into a layer that's about ¾ inch thick. Bake until the edges begin to pull away from the baking sheet and start to brown, 15 to 20 minutes. Remove from the oven and allow to cool to room temperature.

Turn down the oven to 250°F. Break the cake into 4 pieces, then crumble the pieces, one at a time, into the food processor and pulse several times until crumbled about the size of large BB pellets. Return the crumbles to the baking sheet and bake until fully dried, about 1 hour more. Rotate the baking sheet and stir every 10 minutes or so to help even browning. Remove from the oven and allow to cool to room temperature. Store in an airtight plastic container in a cool, dry place for up to 1 month.

WHIPPED BUTTERMILK

MAKES ABOUT 2 CUPS

¾ cup plus 2 tablespoons whipping cream

2 tablespoons confectioners' sugar

1 teaspoon pure vanilla extract

¼ cup buttermilk

In the bowl of a stand mixer fitted with the whisk attachment, whip the cream, confectioners' sugar, and vanilla to stiff peaks, about 1½ minutes. Slowly stir in the buttermilk until well combined. Store in a glass container and refrigerate for up to 2 days.

GRITS AND COLLARD SOUFFLÉ

SERVES 8

A grits soufflé frequently made an appearance on the holiday table around the Currence household when I was a kid. Grits were never something I had to be sold on, like loads of you out there, because I grew up eating good grits. That's not to say I was raised on heirloom corn, stone-ground, virgin-harvested, native corn grits that nobody will ever again experience, but my people knew how to cook store-bought grits and make them taste good. Mom was deft with salt and Dad was a monster with the butter. Mom's soufflé, coincidentally, was the first time I remember having cheese with grits. And the magic that happened with the addition of whipped egg whites and a little more dairy was my own personal, delicious monolith that arose from that giant soufflé dish.

A recent romance with the Appalachian combination of grits and greens has led me to this dish. Use any leftover greens from the night before to make this delight. The acidic bite along with the minerally goodness of the greens makes for a killer addition to the brunch table.

GREENS

¼ cup chopped bacon

⅓ cup diced yellow onion

2 teaspoons minced garlic

4 cups cleaned, hand-torn fresh collard, mustard, or turnip greens

½ teaspoon red pepper flakes

⅓ cup apple cider vinegar

¼ cup water

Salt and pepper

SOUFFLÉ

6 eggs, separated

Pinch of cream of tartar

¾ cup unsalted butter, cut into cubes, plus more for the pan

Flour, for dusting

3 cups whole milk

3 cups chicken stock

1½ cups stone-ground grits

2 teaspoons minced garlic

2 teaspoons black pepper

1½ teaspoons salt

½ teaspoon cayenne pepper

¾ cup grated sharp cheddar cheese

½ cup grated Parmesan cheese

Preheat the oven to 350°F.

To make the greens, warm a saucepan over medium heat for 30 seconds. Add the bacon and cook, stirring constantly, until the bacon is almost crispy, about 3 minutes. Stir in the onion and continue stirring until the onion begins to turn transparent, about another 1½ minutes. Add the garlic and combine well, then stir in the greens and combine fully. Cover the pot and allow the greens to begin wilting for 2 or 3 minutes. Remove the lid and stir in the red pepper flakes and vinegar. Stir the greens until they are completely wilted. Add the water, cover the pot, and allow the greens to simmer for 10 minutes. Season lightly with salt and black pepper. Turn off the heat and allow the greens to cool to room temperature. Remove from the pan and mince. Place the greens in a bowl and set aside.

To make the soufflé, in the bowl of a stand mixer fitted with the whisk attachment, whip the egg whites and cream of tartar to stiff peaks on high speed, 2 to 2½ minutes. Rub a 2-quart soufflé dish with butter and dust with flour.

In a large saucepan, bring the milk and stock to a boil over medium heat. Whisk in the grits in a steady stream. Turn down the heat to low and simmer, stirring constantly, until the grits are tender, about 15 minutes. Remove from the heat. Stir in the butter, garlic, black pepper, salt, and cayenne, followed by the cheeses and greens. Allow to cool for 5 minutes.

Stir in the egg yolks, then carefully fold in one-third of the egg whites until well combined. Fold in the remaining egg whites until fully incorporated. Pour into the prepared soufflé dish. Bake until the soufflé rises and is golden brown on top, about 25 minutes. Serve immediately.

ITALIAN SAUSAGE, SPINACH, HOMINY "RISOTTO"

SERVES 2

2 tablespoons olive oil

¾ cup sliced spicy raw Italian sausage

½ cup sliced yellow onion

¼ cup diced fennel bulb

½ cup chopped tomato

Salt and black pepper

¾ cup firmly packed fresh spinach

1 tablespoon sliced fresh sage

½ teaspoon red pepper flakes

3 tablespoons brandy

½ cup chicken stock

1½ cups fresh cooked hominy (or canned if necessary, but rinse well; see Note)

¼ cup cold butter, cut into cubes

5 tablespoons grated Parmesan cheese

When I was a contestant on the TV show *Top Chef Masters*, a couple of know-it-all clowns (i.e., the judges) kicked me off for making what they admitted was a perfectly cooked risotto. What's more, during the judging, they expressed how difficult cooking quality risotto actually was, much less for a hundred people, which was my task. They then turned around, called it unambitious, and told me to "pack my knives." So maybe I carry a bit of a chip on my shoulder.

As a result, I make risotto out of everything I can now. I learned my technique from my mentor Fernando Saracchi, native of Reggio Emilia, who told me, "This is how my grandmother taught me to cook the risotto. From now on, you will cook it like this, or you don't cook it at all!" I slow cook all sorts of grains to extract the creamy starches from them and finish with a generous amount of cold butter and Parmesan cheese to emulate the porridge-like delicacy of middle Italy. Bulgur, pearled barley, millet, and buckwheat have all seen this treatment at my hands.

Hominy is also particularly good and just kills it for brunch. The meaty bite of slow-cooked hominy and all of the wonderful starch that can be coaxed from it is as luxurious as you could want. It takes a little bit of concentration and you really have to tend to the pan, but persevere and you too can be humiliated on national TV for making something "perfect."

Warm the oil in a large sauté pan over medium heat for 45 seconds. Add the sausage and cook until lightly browned on both sides, about 3 minutes. Remove from the pan and drain on paper towels.

In the same pan, add the onion and fennel and sauté until the onion begins to turn transparent, about 1 minute. Add the tomato, season with salt and black pepper, and sauté until the tomato begins to soften, about 1 minute. Add the spinach and cook, stirring, until the spinach begins to wilt, about 1 minute. Stir in the sage and red pepper flakes.

Return the sausage to the pan, turn the heat to high, and deglaze with the brandy. (If you are cooking over a flame, the brandy will likely ignite. Just swirl the pan and allow the flame to burn out.) Add the stock and bring to a simmer. Toss in the hominy and allow to simmer until the cooking liquid almost evaporates, about 2 minutes. Add the cold butter, turn the heat to low and swirl it around the pan until it's fully absorbed by the "risotto." Remove the pan from the heat. Stir in the Parmesan and season with salt and black pepper. Spoon into 2 bowls and serve immediately.

NOTE: To cook fresh hominy, combine 1 cup of dried hominy, 4 cups of water, and 2 tablespoons of culinary lime in a nonreactive bowl and allow it to stand overnight and soak. Drain the water and lime and place the soaked hominy in a nonreactive saucepan. Add 6 cups of water and 1 tablespoon of culinary lime and bring to a simmer over a low flame. Simmer the hominy for 4 hours, adding water to keep the hominy well covered with liquid and skimming loosened hulls from the hominy. When it appears that no more hulls are floating to the surface, drain the hominy and cool to room temperature.

PORK POSOLE

SERVES 12 TO 14

Make this dish. That's all I really have to say. It's cheap. It's easy. It's so freaking good, I crave it constantly.

As much as I will advocate for the use of fresh ingredients, this comes out extremely well with canned hominy, which I call for here.

My hero, Josh Keeler, chef of at Two Boroughs Larder in Charleston, South Carolina, makes a goat posole for breakfast at his joint. Years after I tasted it, I still can't stop thinking about it. Plop a soft poached egg down in it, and holy Christ, have you got a brunch dish your friends will hoist you skyward over.

If you can't find pork rib tips, you can substitute pork butt or shoulder, but the gelatin in the bones of the rib tips adds a silkiness to the final dish that the butt and shoulder do not. Home-cooked hominy, rather than canned, makes a great posole as well (see Note, page 156).

1½ tablespoons cumin seeds, plus more if needed

3 cups fresh corn kernels

6 tablespoons olive oil

4 cups all-purpose flour

1 tablespoon black pepper, plus more as needed

¾ tablespoon salt, plus more as needed

2 teaspoons ground cumin

5 pounds pork rib tips

6 tablespoons lard

1½ cups diced yellow onion

¼ cup minced garlic

3 tablespoons chopped fresh oregano

3 bay leaves

5 cups chopped tomatillos

4½ cups Mexican canned hominy, rinsed thoroughly

2½ cups diced pimento

¼ cup diced fresh jalapeño

12 to 14 Poached Eggs (page 31)

Crumbled Cotija cheese (optional), for topping

Fresh cilantro leaves (not optional), for topping

Preheat the oven to 350°F.

Warm a small sauté pan over medium heat with the cumin seeds. Swirling constantly, toast the seeds for about 45 seconds, until they begin to brown and give off a strong, toasty cumin aroma. Remove from the heat and pour the seeds into a room-temperature bowl.

In a mixing bowl, toss the corn and 2 tablespoons of the olive oil together. Spread the kernels on a nonstick baking sheet and place in the oven for 12 minutes, or until the corn begins to brown lightly. Set aside.

Whisk together the flour, pepper, salt, and ground cumin in a shallow bowl. Pat the rib tips dry and dredge one by one in the seasoned flour, then set aside. Warm 3 tablespoons of the lard and the remaining 4 tablespoons oil in a large Dutch oven over medium heat for 1 minute.

Working in batches, add a few rib tip pieces to the pot at a time without crowding and cook until lightly browned on both sides, 3 to 4 minutes per side. Be careful not to burn the residual flour at the bottom of the Dutch oven. Remove the rib tips to a plate covered with paper towels and reserve. Dredge and brown the remaining rib tips and repeat until all rib tips are cooked.

Heat the remaining 3 tablespoons lard in the same pot, allow it to melt, and stir in the onion and garlic until the onion begins to turn transparent, about 1 minute. Return the rib tips to the pot and add enough water to cover. Add the oregano, toasted cumin seeds, and bay leaves and turn the heat to low. Cover and simmer until the rib tips are receding from the bone, about 2 hours. Add water as needed to keep the ribs covered.

Stir in the tomatillos, hominy, roasted corn, pimento, and jalapeño and simmer until the rib tips are falling apart, about 1½ hours. Season with salt and pepper, and more toasted cumin seeds, if needed. Remove and discard the bay leaves.

To serve, spoon into bowls and top with a poached egg. Sprinkle Cotija and cilantro over the top. Serve immediately.

CREAMED TOASTED BARLEY WITH NUTS AND DRIED FRUIT

SERVES 4

This dish falls in the gray area between oatmeal and risotto, because it has to be cooked slowly like a risotto, but it's not finished with butter to enhance its creaminess. It's a recipe you can do almost anything in the world you want with, as far as which nuts and fruits you add; I use chopped pine nuts, pecans, dried apricot, and pineapple. I also go heavy on the vanilla and top with some sweetened, softly whipped cream to just stir in for extra richness.

¼ cup pine nuts

¼ cup pecans

2 tablespoons unsalted butter

1 cup pearl barley

2 cups whole milk

½ cup water

1 teaspoon pure vanilla extract

⅓ cup diced dried apricot

3 tablespoons brown sugar, plus more for sprinkling

¼ teaspoon ground cinnamon

¼ teaspoon salt

⅓ cup diced fresh or canned pineapple

¼ cup heavy cream

Preheat the oven to 350°F.

Place the pine nuts and pecans on a baking sheet and toast in the oven for 10 to 12 minutes, or until the nuts begin to brown lightly. Remove, cool to room temperature, and chop roughly.

Melt the butter in a saucepan over medium heat. Add the barley and cook, stirring constantly, until the grains begin to toast, 4 to 5 minutes. Stir in the milk and water, turn the heat to low, and simmer until the barley is tender, about 30 minutes. Stir every few minutes and add more water, as needed, if the barley looks too dry.

Stir in the vanilla, apricot, brown sugar, cinnamon, and salt. Cover and simmer until the barley is soft and creamy, about 30 minutes more. Stir in the pineapple, cream, pine nuts, and pecans. Sprinkle the top with brown sugar and serve immediately.

HOMEMADE CRISPY RICE "ELVIS" TREATS

MAKES 10 TO 12 TREATS

This exercise is really about making puffed rice, and if you make puffed rice, why not turn it into treats, right? And if we are going to make a treat, why not make one that threatens to stop your heart? I'm not suggesting the addition of 1970s-strength barbiturates to the peanut butter, banana, bacon, and marshmallow, but if you do go that route, let me know how it works out. That being said, please don't die on the toilet from eating puffed rice treats, thanks. (My lawyer and my publisher hate me, if you haven't guessed. Fortunately, my editor thinks I am kind of amusing.)

PUFFED RICE

3 cups long-grain white rice

6 tablespoons sugar

¼ cup unsalted butter, cubed

2 teaspoons salt

4½ cups water

Vegetable oil, for frying

TREATS

¼ cup unsalted butter

5 cups mini marshmallows

½ cup peanut butter

Pinch of salt

1½ cups diced banana

½ cup cooked bacon bits

Melted butter, for the pan

6 ounces good-quality semisweet chocolate, finely chopped

2 tablespoons heavy cream

To make the puffed rice, preheat the oven to 175°F. Line 2 large baking sheets with parchment paper.

Combine the rice, sugar, butter, and salt in a saucepan and add the water. Bring to a boil over medium heat, swirling gently to melt the butter. Cover, turn the heat to low, and simmer until the rice is completely cooked, about 20 minutes. Remove from the heat and immediately spread the cooked rice into a single layer on the prepared baking sheets. Bake the rice, stirring every 30 minutes, until the grains are dry and transparent, about 2½ hours.

Pour 4 inches of oil into a large Dutch oven and heat to 375°F over medium heat. Working in batches, place ¾ to 1 cup of dried rice into a basket strainer, place in the hot oil, and agitate gently until the rice puffs, 15 to 20 seconds. Remove the strainer from the oil and dump the puffed rice onto a baking sheet lined with paper towels to drain. Set aside.

To make the treats, melt the butter in a saucepan over low heat. Add the marshmallows and stir until completely dissolved, about 3 minutes. Stir in the peanut butter and salt until well combined.

Place the puffed rice in a large bowl, add the marshmallow mixture, and stir until well combined. Stir in the banana and bacon. Brush a 12 by 9-inch glass baking dish with melted butter and pour the puffed rice mixture into the pan, spreading it out evenly. Allow to cool or sit while you melt the chocolate.

Combine the chocolate and the cream in a small nonreactive saucepan and melt over low heat, stirring constantly for 4 to 5 minutes. Drizzle the melted chocolate over the rice treats. Cool the treats to room temperature, cut into squares, and serve.

Because of the addition of the banana, these treats should be stored in the refrigerator, where they will keep for up to 4 days. They can be made without the banana, wrapped individually, and stored at room temperature for up to a week.

BREAKFAST SANDWICHES

LET'S FACE IT, SOMETIMES A SANDWICH IS THE ONLY THING BETWEEN
you and taking a plunge into the abyss. Whether it's the numbing pain resulting from those last libations the night before, the building hangry that can come with a slowly approaching lunch hour, or a simple debilitating craving, the sandwich contains mystical healing powers.

I am pretty sure I'm not the only person ever to suffer any, if not all, of these callings to the altar of bread and protein. (And, yes, a sandwich needs both of these base ingredients. Minus the protein, and you are eating a fucking salad on bread.) And though these little masterpieces are frequently relegated to lunch and dinner, there is a small mountain of breakfast ingredients that lend themselves to a sandwich. More to the point, there are plenty of sandwiches in existence that can be made more "breakfast-y" with the simple addition of an egg, including the anchor of lunch menus, the all-American hamburger.

This fact first came to my attention at the age of eight, as I boarded the school bus with egg yolk running down my arms from my egg sandwich. I grinned ear to ear with delight as I climbed aboard. Our bus driver, perhaps the crustiest, Irish Channel—born alcoholic to ever helm a bus full of grammar school kids, was named Skeeter and was missing a good 30 percent of his teeth. He was terrifying.

As I climbed on, covered in liquid egg yolk, he frowned at me and said, "If you get that shit on my bus, I'll use you to mop it up!" He slammed the door to the garbage truck we rode to school on and shoved me toward the back. Meanwhile, all I could think was of how crazy good this mayonnaise, egg, bacon, and toast concoction was and how it might even be worth the wrath of Skeeter. I never suffered the yolk-wiping fate and I never brought another sandwich on the bus, but that morning was the moment my love affair with the breakfast sandwich saw its genesis.

FRIED CHICKEN CATHEAD

SERVES 4

I am not sure what draws me uncontrollably to the chicken and cheese biscuit, but it is my Kryptonite. If I am anywhere near a Bojangles' and feel I can do it without being seen, I will buy as many chicken and cheese biscuits as I have money in my pocket. In college, I lived off chicken and cheese biscuits from Hardee's, Time Out, and Sunrise Biscuit Kitchen. My preference is to have them with a slice of cheddar and doused in a hot sauce with a high vinegar content, like Texas Pete or Crystal, but I will eat a good one any way I can get it.

For this sandwich, we take boneless thighs, give them a crispy fry, top them with cheese, and load them onto a buttery biscuit roughly the size of an average cat's head. The addition of an egg never broke anyone's heart, but this is a near-perfect symphony on its own. At home, cooking it is a commitment, but the end product will be your legacy. Go forth and build an empire, my friend.

CHICKEN

2½ cups buttermilk

1 cup whole milk

¼ cup dill pickle juice

2 teaspoons crushed dried dill

2 teaspoons cayenne pepper

1 teaspoon salt

4 boneless chicken thighs

Vegetable oil, for frying

1 egg

SEASONED FLOUR

3 cups all-purpose flour

2 teaspoons salt

2 teaspoons black pepper

2 teaspoons paprika

1½ teaspoons garlic powder

1½ teaspoons onion powder

½ teaspoon cayenne pepper

EGGS

3 eggs

4 tablespoons whole milk

½ teaspoon salt

½ teaspoon black pepper

2 tablespoons unsalted butter

4 Black Pepper Buttermilk Biscuits (page 183)

4 slices cheddar cheese

Cayenne Pepper Sauce (page 188) or your preferred hot sauce, for serving

To make the chicken, whisk together the buttermilk, milk, pickle juice, dill, cayenne, and salt and set aside. Lay the chicken thighs flat on a piece of plastic wrap and cover with a second piece. Gently pound the thighs with a meat mallet until they are about one-third larger than original size. Remove from the plastic, transfer to a stainless steel bowl, and cover with the buttermilk mixture. Refrigerate for 2 hours.

Preheat the oven to 200°F.

For the seasoned flour, stir together all the ingredients in a separate shallow bowl.

When the thighs are marinated, pour 4 to 5 inches of vegetable oil into a Dutch oven and heat to 375°F. Drain the thighs, reserving all of the marinade. Pat the thighs dry. Whisk together the egg with the reserved marinade in a shallow bowl.

One at a time, dredge the thighs in the seasoned flour, then dip into the egg wash, and finally dredge them again in the seasoned flour. Carefully drop the things into the oil and fry until deep golden brown, about 4 minutes. Remove from the oil with a slotted spoon and place on a baking sheet lined with paper towels. Place in the oven to keep warm.

To make the eggs, in a mixing bowl, whisk together the eggs, milk, salt, and pepper. Warm the butter in a large nonstick skillet for 30 seconds and swirl to coat. Add the eggs and tilt to cover the whole bottom of the pan. Turn the heat to low and cook, tilting the pan continuously to evenly distribute and cook the egg in a thin layer. As the egg begins to dry, flip it over with a spatula and remove from the heat. Remove the egg from the pan, slice it into 4 pieces, cover with a damp paper towel, and place in the warm oven with the chicken.

To assemble, split the biscuits and place 1 piece of chicken on the bottom halves. Top with the cheese and egg and as many dashes of hot sauce as you can handle. Put the tops on those biscuits, hand them out to the lucky recipients, and go to town, baby.

WITH SIGNS FOLLOWING

SERVES 1

I thought I was tragically clever when the idea struck me to name every dish on the Big Bad Breakfast menu after a different piece of Mississippi literature. But it wasn't long after we opened that I began to forget them, and it was about the same time that I began to notice people wrinkling their brows as they read through the menu selections.

With Signs Following is basically a BLT with a fried egg. It can be ordered with cheese in any number of varieties and with patty sausage, andouille, chicken sausage, or country ham. It is named for a book of photographs taken by one of my oldest friends, Joe York, who just by coincidence can't stand several of the things that come standard on the sandwich that bears his book's name, so he has a more difficult time ordering his own sandwich than most people ever dream of. Sorry, Joe.

Considering all the bread, condiment, egg, meat, and cheese choices available, there are probably about 8,400 different combinations for this sandwich, as we offer it. This combination is my favorite and what I have eaten most of at Big Bad Breakfast since the day we opened.

1 tablespoon clarified butter (page 30) or your preferred cooking fat

1 large egg

Salt and black pepper

2 tablespoons mayonnaise

½ teaspoon Tabasco pepper sauce (optional)

2 slices whole wheat bread, toasted

3 slices pan-fried bacon

3 thin slices heirloom tomato

½ cup loosely packed arugula or 2 large leaves of crispy iceberg lettuce

Warm an 8-inch nonstick skillet over low heat for 1 minute. Pour in the butter, swirl to coat the pan, and warm for 1 minute more. Meanwhile, crack the egg into a small bowl and check to make sure there is no shell. Slowly and carefully pour the egg from the bowl into the pan and allow it to sit, undisturbed, for 1 minute. As the whites begin to set, agitate the pan gently in a circular motion. Sprinkle with salt and pepper and continue to agitate the pan. After about 2 minutes, when the whites are cooked almost through (they will still be slightly clear and runny on the top), flip the egg and continue to cook for 10 to 15 seconds more. The yolk should be very soft to the touch if poked with your finger.

Stir together the mayo and Tabasco in a small bowl and spread evenly on each slice of bread. On the "bottom" slice, place the bacon followed by the egg and tomato. Season the tomato well with salt and black pepper (this step makes the sandwich . . . seriously, it saves lives), then top with the arugula and the second slice of bread. Slice in half and eat immediately. Thinking about making a second one while eating the first is all part of the umami/endorphin rush and completely normal. Follow your instincts.

MONTE CRISTO

SERVES 1

There is a ton of debate over the origins of and technique for assembling this little gem. I am not here to argue who did what when. What isn't up for debate is the decadence this sandwich implies. It's a club sandwich made on French toast, dusted with confectioners' sugar, and served with a touch of jelly. In ours we use a little pepper jelly, a Southern staple. We also add a little crunch with some sliced pear. This is the goddamned Frank Sinatra of sandwiches, in my book, no intro needed. So without further ado, I give you, remarkable . . .

3 eggs

¼ cup whole milk

1 tablespoon heavy cream

2 pinches of black pepper

Pinch of cayenne pepper

Pinch of salt

¼ cup unsalted butter, plus 4 teaspoons, at room temperature

2 slices brioche

3 thin slices smoked turkey

2 slices soft-cooked bacon (cooked, but not crispy)

8 slices ripe pear

2 slices Swiss cheese

Confectioners' sugar, for dusting

2 tablespoons pepper jelly

Whisk together the eggs, milk, cream, black pepper, cayenne, and salt in a bowl. Set aside.

Spread the 4 teaspoons of room-temperature butter on both sides of the brioche slices. On the "bottom" slice, place the turkey, followed by the bacon, pear, and Swiss cheese. Top with the second slice of brioche, secure the sandwich with toothpicks, and slice off the crusts.

Melt 2 tablespoons of the remaining butter in a nonstick skillet over medium heat until it begins to bubble. Dip the sandwich into the egg mixture, allowing it to soak into the bottom piece of brioche, about 30 seconds. Flip over the sandwich and allow the egg mixture to soak into the second piece of brioche, about 30 seconds more. Remove the sandwich from the egg wash and allow excess egg mixture to drip off back into the bowl. Place the sandwich in the skillet and cook until the bottom is browned, 2 to 3 minutes. Add the remaining 2 tablespoons butter, then flip the sandwich and cook until the second side is lightly browned, about 2 minutes more. Remove the sandwich from the pan, cut into quarters, and dust with confectioners' sugar. Serve with a side of pepper jelly.

MOUNTEY CRISCO

SERVES 1

Please meet the redneck cousin of Monte Cristo, Mountey Crisco (a pronunciation offered by a colorful local gentleman who used to eat with us back when we first opened). This version takes a little more conviction. Finding smoked bologna outside of the South is likely as tough a chore as cutting the yard with fingernail clippers, but you can stove top–smoke slices or just panfry the bologna without smoking it and have a great sandwich. Make no mistake about it, the cheapest pickles and cheapest yellow mustard you can find will make the best sandwich. Also, don't skimp on the confectioners' sugar. Bama apple jelly makes a lovely addition. This one is for my wife, Bess, who will put jelly on toast no matter what else is on it . . .

3 eggs

¼ cup whole milk

1 tablespoon heavy cream

2 pinches of black pepper

Pinch of cayenne pepper

Pinch of salt

1 teaspoon bacon fat

2 slices smoked bologna

1 tablespoon mayonnaise

1 tablespoon yellow mustard

2 thick slices sourdough or white bread

3 thin slices chicken breast

5 or 6 slices dill pickle

2 slices American cheese

¼ cup unsalted butter

Confectioners' sugar, for dusting

2 tablespoons apple jelly

Whisk together the eggs, milk, cream, black pepper, cayenne, and salt and set aside. Warm the bacon fat in a sauté pan over medium heat for 30 seconds. Make small cuts in the edge of the bologna all the way around to keep it from curling when it cooks. Place the bologna in the pan and cook until both sides are browned, about 2 minutes per side. Remove from the pan and drain on paper towels. Set aside.

Stir together the mayonnaise and mustard in a small bowl and spread evenly on the bread slices. On the "bottom" slice, place the bologna followed by the chicken, pickles, and cheese. Top with the second slice of bread, secure the sandwich with toothpicks, and slice off the crusts.

Melt 2 tablespoons of the butter in a nonstick skillet over medium heat until it begins to bubble. Dip the sandwich into the egg mixture, allowing it to soak into the bottom piece of bread, about 30 seconds. Flip over the sandwich and allow the egg mixture to soak into the second piece of bread, about another 30 seconds. Place the sandwich in the skillet and cook until the bottom is lightly browned, about 2 minutes. Add the remaining 2 tablespoons butter, then flip the sandwich and cook until the second side is lightly browned, about 2 minutes more. Remove the sandwich from the pan, cut into quarters, and dust with confectioners' sugar. Serve with a side of apple jelly.

EGG AND RICE BURRITO

SERVES 2

My mom went on these jags when we were kids—maybe it was because she would buy the ingredients and try to cook through them or maybe it was just routine—when we would have the same thing, pretty regularly, for breakfast every day. For a while she was stuck on Carnation Instant Breakfast drinks, for a while it was waffles, for a while it was egg sandwiches, for a while it was poached eggs, for a while it was grapefruit, and so on. One of her phases came after a weekend in Texas, when she made a connection with someone who started shipping the first decent-quality jarred salsa ever to hit NOLA. As a result, breakfast burritos crash-landed into our kitchen around the same time *Star Wars* did. It was a glorious time that I have never forgotten.

Get on the Latino bus, kids. This is as good a way to start the day as any. *Viva el burrito!*

2 (10-inch) flour tortillas

¼ cup roughly mashed ripe avocado

1 teaspoon freshly squeezed lime juice

½ teaspoon black pepper

¼ teaspoon ground cumin

2 shakes of Tabasco pepper sauce

Pinch of salt

SCRAMBLED EGGS

2 eggs

2 tablespoons whole milk

Pinch of salt

Pinch of black pepper

1 tablespoon clarified butter (page 30) or your preferred cooking fat

½ cup cooked long-grain white rice, warmed

¾ cup Saucy Black Beans (page 202), warmed

⅓ cup grated cheddar cheese

3 tablespoons minced pickled jalapeño

3 tablespoons chopped fresh cilantro

3 tablespoons olive oil

Preheat the oven to 250°F. Wrap the tortillas in a damp kitchen towel and place in the oven until warm, 12 to 15 minutes.

Meanwhile, stir together the avocado, lime juice, pepper, cumin, Tabasco, and salt in a bowl and set aside.

To make the scrambled eggs, crack the eggs into a small bowl and beat well with the tines of a fork. You want to thoroughly mix the yolk and white to get an even color to your eggs. Once done, beat in the milk, salt, and pepper. Warm the clarified butter in an 8-inch nonstick skillet over low heat for 1 minute. Pour in the eggs and allow to sit, without stirring, for 15 seconds. With a silicone spatula, push the eggs from one side of the pan gently toward the other side, then tilt the pan and allow the uncooked eggs to fill the void. Allow the eggs to sit again, without stirring, for 15 seconds, then push the eggs to the opposite side and tilt the pan again. You want large fluffy curds to form as you scrape the pan. Run your spatula around the edge of the pan, and just as the eggs are almost set but still a tiny bit runny, another 10 to 15 seconds, remove them to a plate.

Remove the tortillas from the oven and lay on a flat surface. Spread half of the avocado mixture in a horizontal line across the center of each of the tortillas. Spoon the rice down the center of the tortilla over the avocado, followed by the beans and the eggs. Sprinkle the cheese, jalapeño, and cilantro on top. Take the two sides of the tortilla and fold toward the center. Fold the bottom up and over the filling, and pull the wrapped part back toward you so the filling is nice and tight. Roll the wrapped part up toward the top of the tortilla to finish sealing it. Let the burrito rest with the top edge of the tortilla underneath, so that the burrito holds itself closed with its own weight. Secure with a toothpick.

Warm the oil in a large nonstick skillet over medium heat for 1½ minutes. Place the burritos in the skillet and cook until lightly browned on all sides, about 1½ minutes per side. Place in the oven until warm, about 5 minutes. Wrap in aluminum foil and serve immediately.

CHICKEN SAUSAGE PANCAKE SANDWICH

SERVES 8

This drives directly to the heart of the sweet and salty thing. I fell for this combination the very first time it accidentally crossed my lips when I was maybe three. The "corn dog" process (skewering the sausage link and dipping it into pancake batter before deep frying) is preferred—you'll need 8 (6-inch) wood skewers to do so. But if you are opposed to that, just cook pancakes traditionally, wrap them around sausage links, and secure with a toothpick. As far as a definition of this dish as a "sandwich" goes, I consider the combination of anything bready with protein a sandwich. Corn dogs occupy a weird place as far as semantics go, but if you don't like my recipe placement, well, write your own damn book.

The liberal use of syrup is the only part of this experience that isn't up for negotiation. I call for real maple syrup here. This is very important. If the label suggests anything artificial, throw it in the garbage. You won't get that shitty battery acid taste out of your mouth for the rest of the day. I'll be expecting a giant pat on the back whenever I get back to Vermont.

PANCAKE BATTER

1½ cups all-purpose flour

3 tablespoons sugar

1 tablespoon baking powder

½ teaspoon baking soda

¼ teaspoon salt

¾ cup buttermilk

5 tablespoons whole milk

1 egg plus 1 egg yolk, lightly beaten

½ tablespoon pure vanilla extract

4 tablespoons unsalted butter, melted

8 skinny chicken sausage links or any skinny breakfast link

Vegetable oil, for frying

2 tablespoons all-purpose flour

Real maple syrup, for serving

Preheat the oven to 350°F.

To make the pancake batter, in a bowl, whisk together the flour, sugar, baking powder, baking soda, and salt. In a separate bowl, whisk together the buttermilk, milk, eggs, and vanilla. Pour the buttermilk mixture into the flour mixture and whisk together until the batter is smooth. Pour in the melted butter and stir with a spatula until fully incorporated.

Skewer the sausages on 6-inch bamboo or wood skewers. Place on a baking sheet and bake for 12 minutes, rolling them occasionally, so they don't stick. Set aside.

Pour 4 inches of oil into a large Dutch oven and heat to 375°F over medium heat.

Stir together the pancake batter and flour. One at a time, pat a sausage dry, dip into the batter, and gently place into the oil. Fry until browned, 3 to 4 minutes. Remove from the oil with a slotted spoon and drain on paper towels. Allow to cool for several minutes. Serve with a side of maple syrup.

BREAKFAST CROQUE MONSIEUR

This is a traditional croque with bacon as well as pit-smoked ham and a dollop of sweet slaw to cut the saltiness. A spoonful of Comeback Sauce makes it the poor man's Reuben. An egg over the top makes it the Jerry Lawler (YES, that's the second pro wrestling reference of the book), or "king" of breakfast sandwiches.

3 tablespoons Comeback Sauce (page 211)

4 thick slices sourdough bread

4 to 6 slices pit-smoked ham

4 slices cooked bacon

⅓ cup Sweet Slaw (page 129)

½ cup grated Gruyère cheese

¼ cup unsalted butter

¼ cup Mornay Sauce (page 102)

1 Fried Egg (page 30; optional)

Preheat the broiler.

Spread the Comeback Sauce evenly on the bread slices. On the 2 "bottom" bread slices, place the ham, followed by the bacon, slaw, and cheese. Top with the remaining 2 slices of bread.

Melt 2 tablespoons of the butter in a large nonstick skillet over medium heat until it begins to bubble. Place the sandwiches in the skillet and cook until the bottom sides are browned, about 2 minutes. Add the remaining 2 tablespoons butter, then flip the sandwiches and firmly press the tops with a spatula. Cook until the second side is browned, about 2 minutes more.

Transfer the sandwiches to a baking sheet and spoon the Mornay over the top. Slide under the broiler and broil, watching constantly, until the sauce bubbles and browns, about 1 minute. Add a fried egg to the top for a trip into the stratosphere. Serve immediately.

GRILLED HAM AND PIMENTO CHEESE SANDWICH

SERVES 2

Inspired by my friends John T. Edge and Mary Beth Lasseter, this little gem is named the Southern Belly on the Big Bad Breakfast, Oxford, menu. It is the stark antithesis of what the traditional, minimalist grilled cheese ought to be, which, frankly, is nothing more than butter, bread, and cheese. And while I hold pretty steadfastly to the conviction that simple things should be left exactly *that*, I bend the rules here.

This works only with a pimento cheese that has a low mayonnaise content, and I suppose the reason I give in on my normally rigid and unwavering opinion about "leaving simple things simple" is because it just works so well. This is one of the crowd favorites at Big Bad Breakfast. I guess there is a reason for that and maybe I just don't know everything.

⅔ cup Pimento Cheese (page 204)

4 thick slices sourdough or whole wheat bread

4 thin slices pit-smoked ham

4 slices cooked bacon

10 to 12 dill pickle slices

4 thin slices heirloom or hot house tomato

½ cup Sweet Slaw (page 129)

¼ cup unsalted butter

Spread the Pimento Cheese evenly on the bread slices. On the 2 "bottom" bread slices, place the ham, followed by the bacon, pickles, tomato, and slaw. Top with the remaining 2 slices of bread.

Melt 2 tablespoons of the butter in a large nonstick skillet over medium heat until it begins to bubble. Place the sandwiches in the skillet and cook, firmly pressing the tops with a spatula a couple of times, until the bottoms are browned, about 2 minutes. Add the remaining 2 tablespoons butter, then flip the sandwiches and cook, firmly pressing the tops with a spatula a couple of times again, until the second sides are browned, about 2 minutes more. Remove the sandwiches from the pan, cut in half, and serve immediately.

COUNTRY HAM
EGG MUFFIN

SERVES 4

Dear McDonald's,

You make shit for food. I'm not sure what your high-paid marketing analysts are telling you, but that is the simple fact of the matter. Granted, it is cheap, but that is the only "positive" thing you can say about it. (My little consulting tidbit is absolutely free, by the way.) Here we go: crappy muffin + flavorless ham + rubbery egg + plastic non-cheese = SHIT. Quality sourdough muffin + pit-smoked ham + freshly cooked farm egg + real American cheese = delicious. Please stop offering garbage for our stomachs, if you'd like your business to survive; otherwise, I will enjoy watching your continued downward spiral. I am happy to meet in person to continue this discussion.
Sincerely,
John

This recipe calls for English muffin rings. These are simply 4-inch metal rings that are used to hold the shape of an English muffin's runny batter while it cooks. They just happen to help hold an egg in the same shape, too, which makes for a nice presentation. You can just as easily scramble and flat cook an egg; it's entirely up to you. The secret here is that I add a little mayonnaise, well, because it goes insanely well on this sandwich. That said, I know some of us will differ in opinion on that point. But whatever, after the above letter, I am sure McDonald's will be more pissed off than you are.

4 homemade Sourdough English Muffins (page 14) or your preferred store-bought English muffins

½ cup unsalted butter, at room temperature

8 thin slices country ham or smoked ham

4 eggs

1 teaspoon fresh thyme

Salt and black pepper

¼ cup mayonnaise

Tabasco pepper sauce, for serving

4 slices real American cheese (see Note, page 73)

Preheat the oven to 375°F.

Split the muffins and spread with ¼ cup of the butter. Place the buttered muffins on a baking sheet and bake until lightly toasted, about 3 minutes.

Melt 2 tablespoons of the remaining butter in a large nonstick skillet over medium heat. Place the ham in the skillet, a couple of slices at a time, and cook until browned on both sides, about 1½ minutes per side. Remove from the pan and set aside. In the same skillet, melt the remaining 2 tablespoons butter, then place the 4 egg rings in the skillet. Crack an egg into each ring, then sprinkle with the thyme, salt, and pepper. Turn the heat to low and cook until the egg whites look almost completely cooked, about 2 minutes. Transfer the skillet to the oven and cook until the whites are just set, about 1½ minutes. Remove from the oven and set aside.

To assemble the sandwich, spread the mayonnaise evenly on the muffin halves. On the "bottom" muffin halves, place the ham, followed by the eggs and a couple of shakes of Tabasco. Top with the cheese slice and the remaining muffin tops. Eat immediately, then write me a letter and tell me how cool I am.

EGG SALAD

SERVES 4

About a year ago, I woke up on a Sunday morning with a craving for egg salad that was so bad that I told my wife she couldn't talk to me until I had gone to the store, gotten the ingredients, made the egg salad, and eaten it on toasted white bread. Ask her. That is not a lie. My cravings are just that bad. It was a high of my insane cravings. As I was about to put the final sandwich together, I noticed some leftover hanger steak from dinner the night before in the fridge and realized I could totally trump my psycho craving with an extra-special ingredient. We sliced the cold pink-centered steak and had the best steak and eggs I had ever dreamed of.

Homemade mayonnaise is by no means an absolute, but if you want the gift that keeps on giving, make your own mayonnaise once and see how good it is.

8 eggs

¼ cup plus 2 tablespoons mayonnaise, homemade (page 205) or store-bought

⅓ cup minced celery

¼ cup grated yellow onion and its juice (see Note)

2 tablespoons toasted sesame seeds

1 tablespoon minced cornichons or gherkins

2 teaspoons Dijon mustard

1 teaspoon freshly squeezed lemon juice

¼ teaspoon cayenne pepper

Zest of 1 lemon

Salt and black pepper

4 slices sourdough bread, toasted and buttered

12 ounces cold, sliced cooked steak, for serving (optional)

Valentina hot sauce, for serving

Place the eggs in a saucepan and cover with water by 1 inch. Bring to a boil over high heat and boil for precisely 8 minutes after the water comes to a boil. Remove from the heat and allow to cool for 3 minutes. Place the pan in the sink and run cold water over the eggs until they are cool enough to handle. Crack, peel, and chop the eggs.

Combine the eggs, mayonnaise, celery, onion and its juice, sesame seeds, cornichons, mustard, lemon juice, cayenne, and lemon zest in a large bowl. Season with salt and black pepper. Cover and refrigerate for at least 1 hour and up to 3 days. Taste and season with salt and pepper, if needed, before serving.

Serve with toast, steak, and a splash of hot sauce.

NOTE: When I was a kid, recipes used to call for grated onion and/or onion juice all the time. I watched my grandmother rub onions over a box grater for what seemed like hours, with tears gushing from her eyes the whole time. It was terribly perplexing, because every time she made potato salad, egg salad, slaw, or any number of other things, she was constantly bawling. It's something you rarely ever see in a recipe anymore, but it very much serves a purpose. Grating an onion creates tiny little flecks of goodness and a load of juice that distributes the onion flavor without any giant chunks. Plus, it provides a use for that forlorn box grater in the corner.

SIDES, CONDIMENTS, MEATS, AND EXTRAS

WELCOME TO THE CHARM BRACELET OF THE BREAKFAST MENU!

These are the jars, bottles, bags, and boxes that clutter the pantry and refrigerator, but also make breakfast shine like a brand-new penny. If that weren't enough, these are the things that also happen to make great gifts for friends and family.

This is where I turn the intro into a statement of vendetta. You see, the good folks at White Lily flour used to be extremely generous benefactors to the Southern Foodways Alliance. In exchange, every fall at our annual symposium, we staged a Sunday brunch that featured White Lily products front and center. Every year, our friends would show up at City Grocery early on that Sunday morning and decorate the tables with linen flour sacks, White Lily propaganda, and other various bits of swag.

In 1998, though, magic happened. It was the year of the unsurpassed biscuit cutter. The White Lily representative came loaded with these beautiful stainless steel works of art. They were buffed, they were etched, they were adorned, they were beveled to a cutting edge on one side. They were beautiful works of art that looked more like something designed for NASA than for a commercial kitchen. I gladly accepted mine, had it engraved with my initials, took it home, and never made a batch of biscuits without using it from that day forward.

When we opened Big Bad Breakfast in 2008, I brought it in as it was the perfect size cutter for our biscuits. I told the story, I made it clear that it was simply "on loan from my collection." I was categorically stupid in my nobility. I visited my buddy, the most perfect biscuit cutter ever, every once in a while. He cut perfect biscuits. About eighteen months into the life of Big Bad Breakfast, I noticed the biscuits looked different. The layering wasn't as clear and the edges were not as crisp and sharp. After a brief investigation, I determined that someone had made off with my most prized possession. Nobody, but nobody, wanted to tell me.

So here it is: I know you are out there, and *I will find you*. I will find my baby. We will be reunited and it will be the most glorious, Popeyes-tasting batch of biscuits ever made when it happens. There is no way you can love my biscuit cutter like I do, and it will ultimately be unfaithful to you because of that. Buff off my initials, bury it deep in a drawer full of other shit you don't care about, neglect it like you do your very soul, you shitbird, but I will find you and then I will reclaim what is rightfully mine, but I will *never* forgive you, for when you took my biscuit cutter, you took part of my heart. Sleep on that.

BLACK PEPPER BUTTERMILK BISCUITS

MAKES 6 TO 8 LARGE BISCUITS

When we were working on the original menu for Big Bad Breakfast in the winter and spring of 2008, biscuits were at the top of the list of things we knew had to stand way apart from the crowd. We experimented with various ratios of butter to lard, we weighed flour and measured it by the cup, we raised and lowered the amounts of sugar and salt, and played around with the ratios of baking soda to baking powder. After testing about 40 different recipes, we arrived at the very biscuit we wanted. And then, at the very last second, we added a touch of black pepper, which created the earthy, slightly spicy edge I was looking for. That was it, the Big Bad Breakfast biscuit was born and it has remained exactly the same for about a half million biscuits (by my count today, around 572,400, and I am likely conservative). We cut a generous 3½-inch-diameter biscuit at Big Bad Breakfast. Feel free to cut whatever size or shape you like. Time Out Chicken and Biscuits in Chapel Hill, North Carolina, runs a purist program—they make square biscuits so they never reroll their dough (one of the reasons it is one of my favorite places on the planet, but that's a story for another time). That said, cut your biscuits however makes you happy.

2 cups all-purpose flour

1 tablespoon baking powder

½ tablespoon sugar

1 teaspoon baking soda

1 teaspoon salt

½ teaspoon black pepper

6 tablespoons unsalted butter, cut into cubes and frozen

3 tablespoons lard, frozen

1 cup buttermilk

2 tablespoons melted unsalted butter, for brushing

Preheat the oven to 400°F.

Line a baking sheet with parchment paper.

In a food processor, combine the flour, baking powder, sugar, baking soda, salt, and pepper and pulse several times to combine. Add the frozen butter and lard and pulse several times again, just until the mixture resembles a coarse meal. Turn out the flour mixture into a stainless steel bowl, add the buttermilk (see photos on the following page), and stir with a dinner fork until combined. (It will be crumbly, but still very wet in places.) Dust your hands generously with flour, gather the dough while it's still in the bowl, and work it with your hands until it barely holds together.

Turn the dough out onto a floured surface and knead, folding and turning the dough, until it becomes slightly smooth and homogenous, about 4 or 5 turns of the dough. Roll out the dough until it's ¾ inch thick. Cut the biscuits with a 3-inch biscuit cutter (or whatever size you like). Gather the scraps, knead gently just until the dough comes back together, reroll, and cut. Discard the scraps. Place on the prepared baking sheet and brush with the melted butter. Bake until golden brown, about 12 minutes. Serve warm.

CONTINUED

GARLIC CHEESE GRITS

SERVES 4 TO 6 (ABOUT 4 CUPS)

There are few people on the planet who can claim to have cooked as many different kinds of grits as I have. When we opened City Grocery in 1992, stone-ground grits were nowhere to be found. I knew a few specialty spots that carried them to bolster family-owned mills, but most of those places operated more for passing tourists than for food lovers seeking out quality grits. Our challenge was to take something as simple and flavorless as Quaker quick grits and make something delicious out of them.

It wasn't until I met Glenn Roberts from Anson Mills that I woke up to the remarkable difference between store-bought grits and the otherworldly flavors of stone-ground heirloom grits. I remember standing over a pot of Glenn's antebellum coarse grits while he cooked for a full three hours, coaxing smells and flavors I never dreamed of coming from a pot of unseasoned grits. From that moment on (it must have been 1997), we were done with Quaker.

Our grits at Big Bad Breakfast are ground for us by Georgeanne Ross, "the Original Grit Girl," and she is one of the people in the world who, no matter what is going on, brings a smile to my heart. She is a joy and she also makes beautiful grits. This is the recipe we developed for Big Bad Breakfast. A spot of garlic really wakes them up and a fistful of Parmesan gives a rich, earthy flavor. I'll eat anything in the world over the top of these grits.

2 cups whole milk

2 cups chicken stock

1 cup stone-ground grits

1 teaspoon salt, plus more as needed

6 tablespoons unsalted butter, cut into small pieces

½ cup grated Parmesan cheese

1 teaspoon minced garlic

Freshly ground black pepper

Combine the milk and stock in a saucepan and bring to a boil over high heat. Stir in the grits and salt. Turn the heat to low and simmer, stirring constantly, until the grits are tender and cooked all the way through, about 15 minutes. Remove from the heat and immediately stir in the butter, Parmesan, and garlic until fully combined. Season with salt and pepper. Serve immediately or hold warm for up to 30 minutes and serve (see Note).

NOTE: If the grits sit for very long (longer than about 30 minutes), they will get stiff. Just add a little warm milk, water, or stock and stir until well blended. Taste for seasoning each time you add more liquid. By following this method, you can bring grits back to life hours after cooking them without compromising their integrity.

CAYENNE PEPPER SAUCE

MAKES 8 CUPS

I am fascinated with both process and science . . . well, and hot sauce. Fortunately for my little science experiment–fixated mind, making hot sauce involves both, and it is a great way to deal with the bounty of peppers you will invariably end up with if you ever plant your first seed. Make no mistake, this takes a little bit of commitment, equipment, and patience, but the end result is way better than most hot sauces you grab off the store shelf. If you find that the recipe is too hot, dial down the cayenne peppers and increase the red bell peppers (or vice versa, if you want it hotter). This recipe is meant to give you a quick medium–hot sauce. The pepper flavor will still be very fresh. The longer you allow the base pepper mix to ferment, the more nuanced a flavor you will end up with. Play with the amounts of garlic and sugar and fiddle with the fermentation time to get what you want. Feel free to experiment with different peppers and different vinegars. Whatever the case, you've just found another use for your meat grinder.

3 pounds fresh cayenne peppers

1 pound red bell peppers, stemmed, seeded, and deribbed

25 cloves garlic, peeled

¼ cup salt

3 tablespoons sugar

2½ cups white vinegar

2 cups apple cider vinegar

2 teaspoons xanthan gum

Set up your meat grinder with the smallest die, or get out your food processor. Trim the stems from the top of the cayenne peppers, but leave the little green stem caps intact. Run the cayenne and red bell peppers and garlic through the meat grinder, if you have one, or process in a food processor until very finely chopped.

Transfer the pepper mixture to a large nonreactive bowl and stir together with the salt and sugar. Cover with cheesecloth. Give the pepper mixture a stir every day and let stand at room temperature until it starts to bubble, 2 or 3 days. This means the mixture is beginning to ferment. The yeast from the seed caps and the yeast that naturally occurs in the air cause the fermentation to happen.

Once it begins to bubble noticeably, place in the refrigerator in the same bowl (or divide it into smaller jars, if that's more convenient) and allow to sit for at least 2 weeks and up to 3 months. The longer the pepper mixture sits, the more its flavors will mellow.

To finish the sauce, blend the pepper mixture and vinegars in a blender until smooth, about 2 minutes. Add the xanthan gum and blend until well combined. Store in a glass container and refrigerate for up to a year.

LOUISIANA SATSUMA JELLY

MAKES 4 CUPS

A little-known fact about south Louisiana is that it produces a tremendous amount of citrus every year. I am not talking Florida production, but there are a significant number of producers who are growing a variety of different citrus plants. Meyer lemons, satsumas, mandarins, tangerines, tangelos, grapefruits, and kumquats of dozens of varieties blanket the fertile southern growing region of the state and is ever expanding. Little of the fruit is on the national market, so for now, you have to hit the area during the season or know someone who will ship stuff to you. Some of the most delicious oranges I have had come from Louisiana every year. One of my wife's greatest joys is my family's visit at Thanksgiving and my dad's morning ritual of squeezing fresh juice for everyone. Bottom line is, there's just never enough of it. Its high sugar content makes for a delicious jelly.

4 cups freshly squeezed satsuma juice

¼ cup freshly squeezed lemon juice

6 large sprigs thyme, wrapped in cheesecloth

4 cups sugar

1 (1¾-ounce) package pectin

Pinch of salt

Line a fine-mesh strainer with several layers of cheesecloth or a coffee filter and set over a bowl. Strain the satsuma and lemon juices for a clearer jelly. Warm the strained juices and thyme in a saucepan over medium heat until bubbles begin to form around the edge of the pan, about 3 minutes. Turn off the heat and allow to stand for 10 minutes.

Remove the thyme and discard. Stir in 1 cup of the sugar, the pectin, and the salt and bring to a simmer over medium heat, about 3 minutes. Stir in the remaining 3 cups sugar and bring to a boil, stirring constantly. After about 2 minutes, the jelly should begin to bubble up with thick bubbles that don't go away when you stir. Turn the heat to low and continue to simmer for 10 minutes, skimming off foam as it rises to the top. Pour the hot jelly into jars and refrigerate for up to 2 weeks, or process according to the USDA's guidelines for home canning and store in a cool, dry place for up to 1 year.

BLACK PEPPER HONEY

MAKES 2 CUPS

I love honey. It doesn't ever get its fair due considering how magnificent it is and how deep its story runs. Its history dates back as far as historians have been able to gather information. A well-preserved cave painting from Valencia, Spain, dated around 8000 BCE depicts people raiding a beehive. As far as we know, it was the first sweetening agent used by people other than readily available fruits and berries. It was, at times, traded as currency and has seen uses in most all facets of life. It is a fascinating foodstuff.

What I love most, though, is how distinctly the terroir of individual wild honeys reveal themselves across the palate. Sulfur, tree bark, herb, and so on all jump directly to the senses when you taste honey. So while it is all sweet, primarily, it does have extremely distinct flavor depending on where is comes from. It has inspired poets, writers, and songwriters as long as written history has existed. And as much as it has inspired metaphor, it has also inspired myth. Cupid, according to legend, would dip his arrow tips in honey before shooting them, and it has had aphrodisiac powers attributed to it. All in all, it's a magical little part of our diets that simply doesn't get the attention it truly deserves.

This simple Black Pepper Honey is delicious drizzled over biscuits. It is equally good on pancakes, grilled pork, roasted duck, or my favorite, fried chicken. Dip your arrow tips and get busy.

2 cups local honey

2 teaspoons black pepper

Pinch of salt

Warm the honey in a small saucepan over medium heat until bubbles begin to form around the edges, about 3 minutes. Stir in the pepper and salt. Bring to a very gentle simmer, then immediately remove from the heat and cool to room temperature. Store in an airtight glass container at room temperature for up to 6 months. If the honey crystallizes, place the jar in a pan of water over medium heat and simmer, stirring, until the honey returns to its original state.

SPICY BACON ONION JAM

MAKES ABOUT 4 CUPS

My old chef Larkin Selman from Gautreau's was the most talented person I ever worked for. It was under Larkin that I came to understand that a finished dish is only as good as the sum of its parts and how critical it is to ensure that every component of a dish be as good as it could possibly be, down to the flour you dredged the fish in before it was battered and fried. Chef created dishes that exploded with flavor and challenged the senses. Gautreau's was an incredible place to work, and in thirty years, it has launched dozens of careers, including mine. I will remember my first bite of Larkin's red onion marmalade on his perfectly salty and crispy duck confit for the rest of my life. It inspired this recipe, which is a little more minimalist than his and adds a punch of bacon. Patience and diligence are the keys to making it work, and like so many things in this chapter, it goes just as well on grilled meat as it does on a biscuit.

2 cups diced bacon

1 gallon thinly sliced sweet yellow onions

¾ cup thinly sliced garlic cloves

4 cups white wine

1 cup apple cider vinegar

½ cup bourbon

½ cup firmly packed dark brown sugar

5 bay leaves

½ tablespoon black mustard seeds

1 teaspoon red pepper flakes

2 teaspoons dried thyme

In a large skillet, cook the bacon over medium heat until soft and lightly browned, about 5 minutes. Add the onions and garlic and cook, stirring, until the onions are soft and transparent, about 7 minutes. Stir in the wine and simmer until reduced by half, about 15 minutes. Add the vinegar, bourbon, brown sugar, bay leaves, black mustard seeds, red pepper flakes, and thyme, stirring to combine. Turn the heat to low and simmer until almost all of the liquid has evaporated, 15 to 20 minutes. Remove from the heat and cool to room temperature. Remove and discard the bay leaves. Pour the jam into jars and refrigerate for up to 8 weeks.

On top toast: Spicy Bacon Onion Jam; on bottom toast: Apple Butter (page 207)

FIG PRESERVES

MAKES 8 CUPS

The fig is a native of Southeast Asia, and some six thousand years ago, it was transported to Egypt, where it was prized for its sugar content. In Greece, figs were so sought after, and smuggling them became so highly prevalent, that informants, trying to curry favor with authorities, inspired the label *sycophant* (revealer of figs), a less than flattering moniker still used today.

I had the blessing several years ago to visit one of the UC Davis extension farms during the middle of fig season. The thirty-five-acre plot had hundreds of different varieties, each of them more complex and delicious than the next. I spent hours tasting through them with a local botanist who explained the complex structure of the fruit (the fruit begins to develop with the flower on the inside) and the even more daunting process of fertilizing, or caprification (a single tiny wasp crawls inside the fig and fertilizes the flower. As the wasp crawls out of the fig, its wings are pulled off and the wasp perishes. All I could think in that moment was why a bad restaurant in California shouldn't be punishable by death . . .

Figs are as versatile a fruit as there is. They are as easily paired with savory dishes as they are with sweet. They are earthy and complex, but never better than when pulled from the branch and bitten into straightaway. This preserves recipe is one of the first I wrote after we opened City Grocery, and it goes just as well on grilled meat as it does on toast. Get to know the fig. A perfectly nice wasp died for your enjoyment.

8 cups washed, stemmed, and quartered figs

6½ cups sugar

1¼ cups bourbon

¼ cup freshly squeezed lemon juice

4 teaspoons fresh thyme leaves

⅛ teaspoon salt

Combine the figs and sugar in a nonreactive saucepan. Cover the pan and allow to stand in the refrigerator for at least 2 hours and up to overnight. Stir in the bourbon, lemon juice, thyme, and salt and bring to a boil, stirring constantly, over medium heat. Turn the heat to low and simmer until the syrup is thick, about 1½ hours. Pour the hot preserves into jars and refrigerate for up to a year, or process according to the USDA's guidelines for home canning and store in a cool, dry place for up to 2 years.

PONTCHATOULA STRAWBERRY JAM

MAKES 8 CUPS

Louisiana strawberries come early, so much so that a single year's crop (which is usually an early winter crop) is starting to come in as early as Thanksgiving, before the next year even begins. The varieties grown are many, and a majority of them are plump, meaty, and sweet.

The most famous of the Louisiana crop come from a little town on the northwest corner of Lake Pontchartrain called Ponchatoula. In the spring of each year, the town hosts a festival to celebrate its crop. When I went in my senior year of high school, it was one of the most fun Saturday afternoons of my entire life. My best friend and I snuck off to this little town, drank beer, played carnival games, wrestled a greased pig, and laughed as hard as we ever did.

As a result, some thirty years later, I still have a soft spot for those nice folks and their berries. I grab as many as I can every season, and they make the best strawberry jam we preserve. For imported strawberries, up your sugar by about ½ cup. And if you are ever in the neighborhood, stop in for the festival. Totally worth the trip.

8 cups fresh strawberries, hulled and quartered

2 (1¾-ounce) packages pectin

2 tablespoons freshly squeezed lemon juice

6 cups sugar

Working in 2 batches, place the strawberries in a food processor and pulse several times until coarsely chopped. Combine the chopped strawberries, pectin, and lemon juice in a nonreactive saucepan and bring to a boil over medium heat. Stir in the sugar, turn the heat to low, and simmer, skimming off foam as it rises to the top, for about 20 minutes. The jam should be thickened and forming nice, thick bubbles. Pour the hot jam into jars and refrigerate for up to 1 year, or process according to the USDA's guidelines for home canning and store in a cool, dry place for up to 2 years.

RED-EYE GRAVY

MAKES ABOUT 3 CUPS

My friend, the late John Egerton, on the subject of red-eye gravy, wrote, "Cookbooks are strangely muted on this divine elixir; it is only the fortunate consumers of it who wax eloquent." There is little more than speculation on the origins of this recipe, and though I am certain sticklers may claim there is nothing to it, early recipes all suggest that they likely came into being out of necessity. Traditional recipes call for nothing more than ham drippings and black coffee.

My theory is this: Pioneers on the trail would carry country ham or maybe bacon for its stability. Since it was salt-cured, there was limited risk of spoilage. For breakfast on the trail, biscuits or grits could be cooked in cast iron, removed, and ham or bacon cooked in the same skillet. When the cooking was done, the skillet would need to be washed and put away and a quick deglaze of a hot pan would be the easiest cleaning technique. On the trail, water would be at a premium, so perhaps leftover coffee would be used to deglaze the pan and loosen all of the stuck-on ham and rinse out the residual fat. Somewhere along the trail, somebody thinks, "Holy shit, I bet that would be good on a biscuit." And the rest is history. I'm no scholar, but I'd bet money on that.

While ours is a little bit of a departure from the traditional (we knock some of the bitterness of the coffee off with sugar, use the viscosity of the veal stock to help it cling a little more, and—most heinous of all—thicken it slightly with a touch of cornstarch), it still plays. Strip it down if you want to be a true Southerner.

2 tablespoons bacon fat

4 ounces country ham, diced very small

¾ cup coffee

½ cup veal or beef stock

2 tablespoons sugar

½ teaspoon red pepper flakes

½ tablespoon cornstarch

1½ tablespoons cool water

Warm the bacon fat in a large sauté pan over medium heat for 45 seconds. Add the country ham and cook until browned, stirring, about 2 minutes. Deglaze the pan with the coffee, scraping any crusty bits of ham stuck to the bottom of the pan loose with a wooden spoon. Add the stock, sugar, and red pepper flakes, and bring to a simmer over medium heat. Mix the cornstarch with the cool water in a small cup and then stir into the simmering gravy. Simmer until bubbles thicken slightly, about 5 minutes. Serve hot.

SAUSAGE GRAVY

MAKES ABOUT 4 CUPS

You'd never know it by looking at me, but there may well be gravy running in my veins. I'm kind of kidding, but right before I was checked into the hospital for pancreatitis in 2009, my blood was almost half fat. My triglyceride count was so high (4,000–plus) that they couldn't accurately identify its level. I blame my first chicken-fried steak for this. From the first bite I had at about seven years old, on the way to duck hunt with my dad, I was sunk. Milk gravy became my very best friend, and we've been going steady ever since. Sausage gravy is a simple milk gravy with the addition of sausage. In our case, *really* awesome sausage and a little added spice. You guys are destined to become friends as well. I can feel it. (Pictured on page 201.)

4 ounces breakfast sausage, homemade (page 213) or store-bought

¼ cup unsalted butter

¼ cup all–purpose flour

3 cups whole milk

½ teaspoon red pepper flakes (optional, suggested if not using BBB sausage)

Salt and black pepper

In a nonstick skillet over medium heat, cook the sausage, stirring, until browned and cooked through, about 4 minutes. Let cool to room temperature, then crumble by hand until the pieces are the size of peas. Reserve.

Melt the butter in a saucepan over medium heat. Add the flour and whisk until a roux forms. Continue to cook, whisking constantly, until the roux turns a light gold and gives off a nutty aroma, 3 to 4 minutes. Remove from the heat and set aside.

Warm the milk in a medium saucepan over medium heat for about 2 minutes. Add the milk to the roux and cook over medium heat, whisking often, until thickened, about 5 minutes. Add the cooked sausage and stir until fully combined, followed by the red pepper flakes. Season with salt and black pepper. Keep warm on the stove top for up to an hour. Serve warm.

TOMATO GRAVY

MAKES ABOUT 5 CUPS

The definition of tomato gravy is the subject of a certain amount of confusion . . . or maybe "debate" is a better word. Italians, particularly in the American South, have adopted the name for basic pasta red sauce. For Cajuns, "tomato gravy" is a roux-based tomato and pepper sauce. Appalachians, on the other hand, use the same moniker to refer to a roux-based, tomato-centric breakfast gravy indigenous to the mountains of North Carolina and Virginia. The origin of tomato "gravy" or what "it" actually is remains a mystery. Roux has little or no place in most Appalachian cooking, and gravy, as I understand it, has little place in Italian cooking. Tomato and roux both play a central part in the food of south Louisiana, but rarely in breakfast cooking. Like most deeply rooted Southernisms, archeological supposition and speculation are as close to fact as you will get about things created by survivalist pioneers. Ultimately, I think, there is little sense in trying to pull these things apart. Tomato gravy is to different people what they want it to be. For me, however, it is entirely perplexing. I was a boy whose family had Appalachian roots, but I lived in south Louisiana and often ate at little mom-and-pop Italian restaurants. There was fucking tomato gravy everywhere, and it meant different things depending on the context it was being used in.

This tomato gravy is akin to the ones I remember eating as a child in the mountains of North Carolina with my family. It most definitely was born among the Scottish settlers in Appalachia and is a delicious mixture of tomatoes and herbs, spiked with bacon fat and tightened with a little roux. We finish with a hint of heavy cream for richness, and it is excellent over biscuits, rice, pork, and even fried fish. A hint of lemon juice spikes the acid in the tomatoes and makes it a particularly good addition to hard protein. Here's your utility breakfast sauce. If you aren't familiar with it, trust me—make this and then be prepared for people to pledge undying loyalty to you . . . like the Godfather of breakfast. If you end up with stalkers, talk to my lawyer; you make this recipe at your own risk.

3 tablespoons unsalted butter	1 cup canned crushed tomatoes
½ cup diced yellow onion	1½ teaspoons dried thyme
1 tablespoon bacon fat	½ teaspoon cayenne pepper
¼ cup all-purpose flour	½ cup heavy cream
2 cups cored, seeded, and diced fresh tomatoes	1½ teaspoons freshly squeezed lemon juice
Salt and black pepper	¾ cup chopped green onions, green part only

Melt the butter in a saucepan over medium heat. Add the onion and cook until tender and transparent, about 3 minutes. Add the bacon fat and cook until it melts. Add the flour and whisk until a roux forms. Continue to cook, whisking constantly, until the roux turns a light gold and gives off a nutty aroma, 2 to 3 minutes. Stir in the fresh tomatoes and season lightly with salt and black pepper. Once the tomatoes begin to soften and break down, about 4 minutes, add the canned tomatoes, thyme, and cayenne. Simmer, stirring, until the gravy begins to tighten up slightly, about 5 minutes. Add the heavy cream and lemon juice and bring back to a simmer, stirring often, until the gravy thickens and coats the back of a spoon, about 2 minutes. Remove from the heat and stir in the green onions. Serve warm.

This can be served immediately or held warm over a double-boiler for up to a couple of hours.

On top biscuit: Tomato Gravy; on bottom biscuit:
Sausage Gravy (page 209)

SAUCY BLACK BEANS

MAKES ABOUT 4 CUPS

I get insane cravings. I mean, they are just fucking ridiculous. I turn into a Mr. Hyde–type demon and cannot be talked to or looked directly in the eye when they hit. Having been subject to this affliction for decades and having had the opportunity to deeply analyze this condition, I have concluded that they are entirely mineral–based and are a direct result of my body telling me how poor a fucking job I do of taking care of myself.

My worst cravings are for home–cooked dried beans and for cooked greens, though cravings for fried chicken, ice cream, fish sandwiches, pasta with red sauce, and bourbon are not entirely uncommon. Red beans are unquestionably at the top of my craving list; black beans, cooked with a heavy hand of cumin, run an extremely close second. These are great with rice, in burritos, with tortillas and eggs, or just cold out of the refrigerator with a good dousing of Valentina hot sauce.

2 cups dried black beans

½ cup chopped bacon

¼ cup unsalted butter

½ cup diced yellow onion

¼ cup diced green bell pepper

1 tablespoon minced garlic

2 teaspoons toasted cumin seeds, crushed

4 cups chicken stock

1 bay leaf

¼ cup sherry

¼ cup apple cider vinegar

2 tablespoons olive oil

Salt

Place the beans in a saucepan and add enough water to cover by 4 inches. Cover loosely with a kitchen towel, plastic wrap, or aluminum foil, and allow to soak for at least 5 hours or up to overnight. Once soaked, drain the beans, discarding all but ½ cup of the soaking water.

In a large saucepan, cook the bacon over medium heat until the fat renders, but the bacon is not crispy, about 3 minutes. Remove the bacon with a slotted spoon and drain on paper towels. Discard all but 1 tablespoon of the bacon fat from the pan. (Reserve the remaining bacon fat to cook with later.) Add the butter to the pan and warm over medium heat for 30 seconds. Add the onion, bell pepper, and garlic and sauté until tender, about 3 minutes. Stir in the cumin.

Add the soaked beans, chicken stock, and bay leaf and cook over low heat until tender, about 1½ hours.

In another saucepan, combine the sherry and vinegar and cook over medium heat until reduced by half, 3 to 4 minutes. Add ½ cup of the reserved bean soaking liquid and cook until reduced by a third, 2 to 3 minutes. Pour the sherry reduction into the bean pot, add the olive oil, stir to combine, and simmer for an additional 2 minutes.

Transfer ½ cup cooked beans to a blender and puree until smooth. Return the pureed beans to the pot and stir until well blended. Simmer for 5 minutes more. Season with salt. Remove and discard the bay leaf.

Serve immediately. Allow the remaining beans to cool to room temperature. Store in a plastic or glass container and refrigerate for up to 1 week.

A NOTE ON CUMIN

Chefs go through cycles of fascination. Whether it be a texture, dish, ingredient, ethnic cuisine, herb, spice, style of service, and so on, it matters not. We all have our moments with food. For a very long time now, my obsession has been cumin. And while it may strike some as an odd fascination (and don't get me wrong, it isn't like I'm working it into nooks and crannies where it has no place), my fascination is more with cumin's history. Cumin pops up as a central player in cuisines all around the world. From Mexico and India to the Middle and Far East, it is a common player in the spice cabinets of all of these regions.

Cumin can quite literally be traced to the beginning of written history. A pair of inscribed stone tablets of recipes from Babylon, dated circa 1750 BC, referred to as the Yale culinary tablets, references the use of cumin. Egyptians used it as a cooking spice and in the mummification process. Numerous civilizations have employed it for medicinal purposes, while also using it as a flavoring agent. To this day, cumin is a table spice in a number of countries, including several on the western coast of Africa, just as salt and pepper are in the United States.

And this is where my deepest fascination lies: why doesn't this spice play a bigger role in the food of the South? A significant number of the ingredients we take for granted as being indigenous to the United States, and that make up the core of ingredients that you think of when considering Southern food, are actually only really here as a result of the West African slave trade. When slaves were loaded in the ships, so too was food to feed them. A significant amount of that was foodstuffs indigenous to their homeland. Okra, lima beans, black-eyed peas, peanuts, sorghum, watermelon, and sweet potatoes, to name a few, are things only on this continent (originally, at least) as a result of the African slave trade.

Many of the dishes we consider our own, too, stem from Liberian and Senegalese traditions. Okra gumbo, hopping John, cala, hoecakes, and many others have their origin there. The cumin that spiced so many of those dishes, however, did not make the crossing with them.

Instead, Caribbean spices (such as cayenne and paprika) and western European herbs took center stage in the seasoning and flavoring of New World food. Cumin, which admittedly some people find a little distasteful, took not just a backseat, but a totally different ride in getting to the American palate. It is a latecomer, but definitely working its way into vogue. And while I don't think we will see a mutiny in the way gumbo is seasoned in south Louisiana, and neither do I see cumin shakers becoming common on family tables, my favorite spice is definitely elbowing its way to the front of the crowd.

PIMENTO CHEESE

MAKES ABOUT 2½ CUPS

There is little that can be considered more pedestrian in the canon of Southern food than pimento cheese. Now, please try to understand, there is actually nothing pedestrian about this particular manna; it has just suffered, like so many other things in the "mayonnaise salad" family, a blanket dismissal due to perceived health issues. It was, in my mother's hands, something sublimely special, like so many other things. During the time of the Great American Culinary Shame (better known as the 1970s), it was, for the most part, buried and relegated to processed, cheap, flavorless, prepackaged, supermarket crap. We began to reexamine it in the 1980s and 1990s, as Southern food gained traction in our nation's consciousness, and it has once again become an item that a good Southern cook is measured by. This one is a throwback to the pimento cheese I remember from Crook's Corner. It is simple, tasty, and versatile. It in no way represents what we used to make there, though it references the message of minimalism and quality ingredients.

⅓ cup cream cheese, at room temperature

1 cup grated cheddar cheese

1 cup grated Havarti cheese

¼ cup minced pimentos

¼ cup minced bread-and-butter pickles

3 tablespoons bread-and-butter pickle juice

3 tablespoons mayonnaise, homemade (page 205) or your preferred brand

1 teaspoon Tabasco pepper sauce

¼ teaspoon cayenne pepper

Salt and black pepper

Your favorite crackers, for serving

In the bowl of a stand mixer fitted with the paddle attachment, mix the cream cheese at medium speed until soft and creamy, about 3 minutes. Add the cheddar, Havarti, pimentos, pickles and pickle juice, mayonnaise, Tabasco, and cayenne and mix at low speed until smooth and well combined, about 2 minutes. Season with salt and black pepper. Store in a plastic or glass container and refrigerate for up to 10 days.

Serve immediately or chilled, with crackers.

MAYONNAISE

MAKES 3 CUPS

Mayonnaise is another of those things that gets an unnecessarily bad rap. Granted, it is higher in calories than most condiments, at about 90 calories per tablespoon (ketchup is about 20 calories and mustard clocks in at 3 to 5). The mayonnaise you get in the store in no way resembles the sublime texture and flavor of homemade mayonnaise. You see, mayonnaise is little more than the emulsification of egg yolks and oil with a little lemon juice, salt, and seasonings. It is a famously stable emulsion, when prepared properly, but any amount of heat will destabilize and break the mayonnaise. Homemade mayonnaise will never be shelf-stable as a result of its instability and low acid levels. Ratios in commercially produced products are tinkered with and flavorings and stabilizers are added, but the resulting product always has an institutional flavor and texture compared with homemade.

I was gifted a crazy cool 1950s–era Wesson mayonnaise maker and it makes the best mayo I have ever had, though a stand mixer also does a wonderful job. Make this a little at a time and keep it on hand. This should not be kept for more than about a week or 10 days. This will change the landscape of your condiment appreciation immensely.

5 egg yolks

1½ tablespoons Dijon mustard

2½ cups peanut oil

½ cup olive oil

2½ tablespoons red wine vinegar

1 tablespoon freshly squeezed lemon juice

¼ teaspoon cayenne pepper

Salt and black pepper

In the bowl of a stand mixer fitted with the whisk attachment, combine the egg yolks and mustard and whisk at high speed until creamy, about 1 minute. While the mixer is running, combine the oils and drizzle in very slowly, whisking until fully incorporated, about 2 minutes.

Turn the mixer speed to low and add the vinegar, lemon juice, and cayenne and whisk until well combined, about 30 seconds. Season with salt and black pepper. Store in a plastic or glass container and refrigerate for up to 10 days.

STRAWBERRY CREAM CHEESE

MAKES 2 CUPS

When I was a kid, the skirt of our Christmas tree was filled every year with presents from our neighbors. Back then, to be gifted with whatever a neighbor's "thing" was, well, it was the highest form of flattery. My mom spent weeks making dozens of containers of her chicken liver pâté. Mrs. McCall made this crazy delicious chocolate fudge sauce, Mrs. Devlin made these sick chocolate peanut butter balls, Mrs. Monstead made her famous English muffins, Mrs. Baldwin made delicious spiced pecans, another neighbor made hot cider spice, and even our bus driver made mulled wine in filthy mason jars, which I am entirely sure he medicated himself with while driving to drown out the sounds a pile of shithead kids could make in the confines of his rolling death trap.

My godmother, Nell Lanier, though, made the best of the best. She made this strawberry cream cheese that was fucking lights-out. I am not sure my parents ever tasted it again after the first time my brother and I got our hands on it, because we attacked like banshees when it hit our door. This is a great spread for toast and bagels, and is even killer on pancakes and waffles. And it is remarkably easy to make.

¾ cup hulled and quartered fresh strawberries

2 tablespoons sugar

1 tablespoon water

Zest and juice of 1 lemon

1 (1-pound) block cream cheese, at room temperature

Pinch of salt

Combine the strawberries, sugar, water, and lemon zest and juice in a nonreactive saucepan and bring to a boil over medium heat. Turn down the heat to low and gently simmer, stirring constantly, until the strawberries are extremely tender, about 5 minutes. Remove from the heat and cool completely.

Place the cream cheese in the bowl of a stand mixer fitted with the paddle attachment and beat on medium speed until soft and creamy, about 1 minute. Add the strawberry mixture and the salt and beat on low speed until just combined. Transfer to an airtight plastic or glass container and refrigerate for up to 10 days.

APPLE BUTTER

MAKES 10 CUPS

There was one fruit for me when I was a child, and it was apples. I loved fried apple pies, applesauce, apple juice, apple jelly, and when I first tasted a spoonful of this slow-cooked masterpiece, I was simply sunk. Be warned that this recipe is a bit tricky in that it needs constant tending, and the cooking time and flavor will vary depending on the apple you use, because of the differing water contents of various apples. This is one of those projects to undertake when you have a Saturday free to stick around the house so you can return to the pot to give an occasional stir and add a pinch of this or that to get it just how you like it. (Pictured on page 193.)

12 Granny Smith apples, cored, peeled, and sliced

2 cups firmly packed dark brown sugar

1½ cups apple cider

1 tablespoon freshly squeezed lemon juice

1½ teaspoons ground cinnamon

1 teaspoon ground allspice

1 teaspoon ground nutmeg

2 pinches ground cloves

Working in batches, place the apples in a food processor and pulse several times until finely chopped. Combine the chopped apples, brown sugar, cider, lemon juice, cinnamon, allspice, nutmeg, and cloves in a large nonreactive saucepan or slow cooker.

If using a saucepan, bring to a boil over medium heat, then turn the heat to very low. Cover and simmer, stirring constantly (every 10 minutes or so), until the apple butter is deep brown and appears about the thickness of applesauce, 4 to 5 hours. When the apple butter reaches this consistency, uncover the pan, and continue to cook until it reaches your desired texture, an additional 15 to 25 minutes.

If using a slow cooker, cook on the medium setting until the apple butter is deep brown and appears about the thickness of applesauce, 6 to 8 hours. When the apple butter reaches this consistency, uncover the slow cooker, and continue to cook for an additional 45 minutes or so, until the apple butter reaches your desired consistency.

Place the hot apple butter into jars and refrigerate for up to 3 months, or process according to the USDA's guidelines for home canning and store in a cool, dry place for up to 1 year.

RASPBERRY BUTTER

MAKES 1¼ CUPS

I made this for my daughter, Mamie. When we renovated our house in Oxford right after she was born, I built raised beds outside her window and planted figs and blueberries all over the yard. The first year blueberries came in, she would get impossibly excited to go outside with Dada to pick berries, but she steadfastly refused to eat them. It was something patently baffling to me. How could anyone, especially a little one, not like blueberries. She didn't like them in her oatmeal, cereal, or muffins. I just couldn't get them in her, and frankly, it pissed me off.

My last-ditch effort was to make a creamy butter blueberry spread that I thought I could completely disguise them in. #FAIL. The butter was really good, but her otherworldly palate was not to be fooled. I retooled the butter with raspberries and she couldn't get enough. I am still totally perplexed at her weirdness about the blueberries, but after doing some deep reflection over it, I guess it's just one fewer person I will have to fight with for the summer's bounty of blueberries.

1 cup unsalted butter, at room temperature

1½ tablespoons sugar

¼ cup heavy cream

⅛ teaspoon salt

½ cup fresh raspberries

Place the butter in the bowl of a stand mixer fitted with the paddle attachment and beat on medium speed until smooth and creamy, about 1 minute. Add the sugar, cream, and salt and beat until just combined. Add the berries and beat until just barely combined.

Lay a 1-foot piece of plastic wrap on a flat surface. With a silicone spatula, transfer the raspberry butter to the center of the plastic wrap. Fold the plastic wrap over the butter and roll into a log. Refrigerate for at least 2 hours and up to 3 weeks. Alternatively, scoop the raspberry butter into a bowl and serve immediately.

Top: Blackberry Mascarpone (page 210); bottom: Raspberry Butter

BLACKBERRY MASCARPONE

MAKES 2 CUPS

It is amazing to think how twenty-five years ago, things that are now as commonplace as mascarpone, chipotle peppers, sun-dried tomatoes, and nori were entirely exotic. I use the Kroger in Oxford as my measuring stick. If it is available on the shelf there, it is available almost anywhere. I was introduced to the beautiful versatility of mascarpone cheese by my Italian mentor, Chef Fernando Saracchi. Fernando was one of my favorite people to ever work for. He was as passionate about the food of his home as anyone I have ever known. His food was entirely without pretense and it spoke to exactly who he was and where he came from. It was unapologetically honest, simple, and delicious.

When Fernando moved to New Orleans as head chef of Bacco, which we would open together, he had never worked in a restaurant of its size or scope. We were literally thrown into a battle that we would have to try and figure out as a team. One of the challenges was breakfast service. The concept of the restaurant was rustic country Italian, and since the Italians have cigarettes and espresso for breakfast mostly, the breakfast menu was a little bit of a challenge to create.

One of the dishes we offered was chestnut flour crepes with berry mascarpone filling. It was a smash and it was one of the first menu items I ever wrote. This berry mascarpone spread is wonderfully adaptable and can be used on just about anything. The sweet, velvety creaminess of the mascarpone will just take you out at the knees. (Pictured on page 209.)

¾ cup fresh blackberries
2½ tablespoons sugar
2 tablespoons water
Zest of 2 lemons

1 pound mascarpone cheese
Pinch of ground cinnamon
Pinch of salt

Combine the blackberries, sugar, water, and lemon zest in a nonreactive saucepan and bring to a boil over medium heat. Turn down the heat to low and gently simmer, stirring constantly, until the blackberries have broken down almost completely, about 3 minutes. Remove from the heat and cool completely.

Place the mascarpone in the bowl of a stand mixer fitted with the paddle attachment and beat on medium speed until soft and creamy, about 1 minute. Add the blackberry mixture, cinnamon, and salt and beat on low speed until just combined. Transfer to an airtight plastic or glass container and refrigerate for up to 10 days.

COMEBACK SAUCE

MAKES 2 CUPS

All hail the Greeks of the Deep South. One of the larger groups of Greek immigrants to hit the South settled in north central Alabama to work in the mining and steel industries that fueled the local economy in the early and middle parts of the twentieth century. As the steel market softened and/or folks started to migrate out of it, Greek families began setting up restaurants in and around Birmingham. Bright Star, Johnny's, and Niki's were all stalwarts in that community. As families grew, movement became inevitable, and a number of those families ended up moving west to Jackson, Mississippi. The Mayflower, Primos, Dennery's, and Crechale's were all part of those families' legacies. Out of them sprang comeback sauce. From a culinary standpoint, comeback sauce is one of the very few things that Mississippians can claim as their own, and it is remarkable. It goes great on fried pickles, fish, shrimp, and chicken or drizzled over a salad. We use it on our Reuben and as a sandwich dressing regularly. It is also great for french fries. So just make a little and keep it in the fridge. It's kinda good for everything.

¾ cup mayonnaise, homemade (page 205) or your preferred brand

¾ cup ketchup

¼ cup Heinz chili sauce

2 tablespoons grated yellow onion and its juice (see Note, page 179)

1 tablespoon Worcestershire sauce

1 tablespoon freshly squeezed lemon juice

¾ tablespoon minced garlic

1 teaspoon paprika

1 teaspoon mustard powder

½ teaspoon salt

½ teaspoon black pepper

2 tablespoons olive oil

In a food processor, combine the mayonnaise, ketchup, chili sauce, onion and its juice, Worcestershire, lemon juice, garlic, paprika, mustard powder, salt, and black pepper and process until combined, about 20 seconds. With the food processor running, drizzle in the oil and process until fully combined, about 20 seconds more. Store in a plastic or glass container and refrigerate for up to 10 days.

BREAKFAST SAUSAGE

MAKES ABOUT 5 POUNDS, ENOUGH FOR 40 PATTIES OR 5 (1-POUND) LOGS

5 pounds pork shoulder, cut into 1½-inch cubes with fat intact

8 ounces pork fat, cut into 1½-inch cubes (see Note)

7 tablespoons rubbed sage

6 tablespoons dark brown sugar

5 tablespoons minced fresh garlic

¼ cup salt

3 tablespoons black pepper

2 tablespoons red pepper flakes

1½ tablespoons toasted fennel seeds, crushed

2 teaspoons cayenne pepper

My grandfather and his friends made a breakfast sausage that he sold from the meat counter of his country store, and I loved it as a kid. Like hundreds of communities around the South, friends and relatives had community hog-killing parties in the early winter during which they killed, cut up, preserved, and cooked their hogs en masse. Every single ounce of the pig was used, from bones and blood to ears and tails. They cured hams; they cut chops and spareribs. They made blood sausage, headcheese, and livermush. They boiled the skin and dried it for cracklings; they salted lard and packed chitterlings; and they made bacon and ground breakfast sausage—lots of breakfast sausage.

These communitywide events were a significant bonding experience for everyone who participated. The slaughter was typically held just before Christmas, when farm work was done for the year and when temperatures were good for storing meat. Sadly, I never participated, but as a little one, I was treated to all the gruesome stories of hog guts and warm pig blood.

My grandparents had long since passed when we started developing recipes for Big Bad Breakfast, but I knew right from the start that one of the things I wanted to re-create was the flavor of my granddad's sausage. I suppose that my granddad took his secret with him to the grave. Sadly, there was no recipe to follow. And so we developed the recipe based on my memory alone. We made precisely seven test batches of sausage before we hit it. I remember exactly where I was standing and how quickly that taste brought me to tears. The flavors carried me right back to my grandparents' table, with a plateful of fluffy pancakes and a sticky bottle of clear Karo syrup. I have rarely been happier than I was in that exact moment.

This recipe calls for a meat grinder, but if you don't have one, use fatty ground pork from a friendly butcher and mix your sausage by hand. If you try to blend it in a mixer, you will emulsify the fat and meat proteins and end up with a very strangely textured sausage.

Stir together all of the ingredients in a stainless steel bowl until well combined. Cover and refrigerate for 2 hours. Meanwhile, set up your meat grinder with the smallest die, according to the manufacturer's directions. Working in batches, feed the meat mixture into the grinding tube and grind the sausage mixture into a separate bowl.

At this point you can form the sausage into 2-ounce patties or 1-pound logs.

To form into patties, weigh 2 ounces of sausage and press into a 2-inch patty that that's about ½ inch thick. Repeat, forming patties, until all of the sausage has been used. These will keep chilled for 3 or 4 days or for 6 months frozen.

To form into logs, lay a 1-foot piece of plastic wrap on a flat surface. Lay 1 pound of sausage down the center of the plastic, then fold the plastic to cover the top and roll the sausage into an 8-inch-long log about 2 inches in diameter. Grab the end of the plastic and begin to roll the sausage like a hard candy, holding onto the ends of the plastic, so the log gets tighter as you roll. Fold the plastic ends under the log, so its weight will hold the ends in place when it is frozen. Repeat, forming logs, until all of the sausage has been used. The logs will keep for 3 or 4 days chilled or for 6 months frozen.

To cook the patties, warm a sauté pan over medium heat for 1 minute. Add the patties and cook, turning every couple of minutes, until browned on both sides and the center is firm to the touch, about 10 minutes.

To cook the logs, slice them into patties and follow the above cooking instructions.

NOTE: You can omit the pork fat, but the finished product will not be quite as rich. If you add salted fat (like a salted fatback), cut the salt in the recipe in half.

CHICKEN SAUSAGE

**MAKES ABOUT 6 POUNDS, ENOUGH FOR
60 LINKS OR PATTIES**

The idea for chicken sausage was actually kind of a laugh at first. Other than fried chicken, I don't give the bird much thought. Chickens are, for the most part, raised in abominable conditions, fed a terrible diet, and end up tasting about like you'd think something raised under those circumstances would. That said, I admit there are some large operations trying to operate differently and there are hundreds of boutique chicken ranchers out there raising delicious birds.

Whatever the case, I never really considered it a protein suitable for consideration as a sausage. As we got feedback from customers saying they would love a lighter meat offering, I jokingly said, "Let's give 'em chicken sausage."

At the time, our menu didn't have a small breakfast link, which is one of my secret pleasures. You see, when I was a kid we lived in Scotland for several years, and I've loved little British breakfast sausages ever since. We went to work on a recipe, and in short order, our sausage man, Kirk Lovejoy, hit on this. It's spicy and earthy with a touch of sweetness. Folks love it, maybe because of the pork we use as a binder.

This recipe calls for a meat grinder. If you don't have one, try substituting ground turkey (available almost everywhere these days). Chop your bacon in a food processor and blend your sausage by hand. I also call for a sausage stuffer. If you don't have one of these contraptions, then just form your sausage into 1½-ounce patties and panfry them.

5 pounds boneless, skinless chicken thighs

1 pound pork fat, cut into 1-inch cubes, or fatty smokeless bacon, chopped

5 tablespoons dark brown sugar

2½ tablespoons black pepper

2 tablespoons salt

1½ tablespoons crushed mustard seeds

1½ tablespoons roasted garlic powder

1 tablespoon ground thyme

2 teaspoons rubbed sage

1½ teaspoons red pepper flakes

1 teaspoon cayenne pepper

4 ounces (1-inch) lamb casings, for stuffing (optional)

Rinse the chicken several times, then pat dry. Cut into 1-inch cubes and place in a large mixing bowl. Add the pork fat or bacon, brown sugar, black pepper, salt, mustard seeds, garlic powder, thyme, sage, red pepper flakes, and cayenne and stir together with a large spoon until well combined, 2 or 3 minutes. Cover with plastic wrap and refrigerate for 2 hours.

Meanwhile, set up your meat grinder with the medium die. Grind the chilled chicken mixture into a second mixing bowl, working in batches. Cover and refrigerate again for 1 hour.

Either form the sausage into 1½-ounce patties (about 2 inches in diameter) or stuff them into 1-inch lamb casings. (To stuff the sausage into casings, place the sausage in a sausage stuffer and feed casing onto the stuffing tube. Squeeze all of the air out of the sausage casing, then tie a knot at the very end. Begin cranking the handle, assuming you have a manual stuffer, and form 4-inch links, twisting each link several times as each is formed. When you reach the end of your sausage, squeeze the air out of the back end of the sausage and tie the casing off.) These freeze nicely (links or patties) for up to 3 months.

CHORIZO

MAKES ABOUT 2½ POUNDS

Chorizo is a delicious, greasy sloppy mess. I don't even want to know the list of ingredients used to make the store-bought versions of this "sausage," because I am certain it is a laundry list of parts I wouldn't normally consider desirable. But chorizo is, to be very truthful, awesome, and there is nothing that can substitute for it. Period.

I put quote marks around the word *sausage* because it is really a loose blend of ground pork and seasonings that you just scramble in a pan. It doesn't resemble a cased sausage at all, and as far as I can tell, without the addition of a binding agent, there is no way to cook it up so that it sticks together like a patty. Have I mentioned that it is awesome?

This is great for migas, huevos rancheros, queso fundido, a Mexican omelet, and the like. Don't be afraid of the fat or the spices, and trust me when I tell you it is as much the enemy of a hangover as Gatorade or Advil. It is best taken with copious amounts of cheese.

This recipe calls for a meat grinder. If you don't have one, buy your ground pork (a fat-rich mix) from a friendly butcher. You can chop your bacon in a food processor. Blend your sausage by hand, in this case.

Buy the store-bought fatty bacon with as little smoke on it as possible. Fatty bacon is usually cheap bacon with a superhigh fat content. Look for the packages of bacon with as little pink as possible.

2 pounds pork shoulder, cut into 1½-inch cubes

8 ounces fatty bacon, chopped

6 tablespoons red wine vinegar

3 tablespoons minced garlic

⅓ cup minced yellow onion

2 tablespoons chopped fresh oregano

2 tablespoons ancho chile powder

2 tablespoons hot Mexican-style chili powder

1½ tablespoons smoked paprika

1 tablespoon crushed cumin seeds

1 tablespoon salt

1½ teaspoons red pepper flakes

½ teaspoon cayenne pepper

½ teaspoon ground cinnamon

In a large mixing bowl, stir together all of the ingredients with a large spoon until fully combined. Cover the bowl with plastic wrap and refrigerate for 2 hours.

Meanwhile, set up your meat grinder with the smallest die. Grind the chilled meat mixture into a second mixing bowl. Cover and refrigerate again for 1 hour, then grind a second time.

Chorizo can be cooked fresh or rolled into a log in plastic wrap and frozen for later use. Chorizo is most frequently used cooked "loose" and scrambled into eggs, put in tacos or burritos, etc.

LIVERMUSH

MAKES ONE 2-POUND LOAF

I am not going to try and convince anyone that livermush—a weird cousin of meat loaf, boudin, and haggis—is for everyone. That said, it isn't quite as potentially off-putting as headcheese, but it is not what I expect everyone to be dying to make.

Now that I have issued a disclaimer, let me say that good livermush is crazy good. It combines the earthy taste of boudin with sweet spices and the crispy texture of fried bologna. When I was little, my granddad and his buddies would gather at his country store in the mornings to read the paper, drink coffee, and play checkers. At some point he'd plug in his hot plate and griddle white bread and livermush for little half-size sandwiches for his friends. I loved it when he did this because (1) it filled the store with the beautiful smell of spice, and (2) it completely distracted everyone while I stuffed my pockets with penny candy.

There is a little heat to this recipe. Serving it with toasted white bread, a fried egg, and some Red-Eye Gravy (page 198) is a life changer. You can also serve it with toasted white bread with yellow mustard and raw yellow onion slices and fried eggs. Livermush freezes well if wrapped well in plastic or Cryovacked.

This recipe calls for a meat grinder. If one is not available, you can purchase a fatty ground pork from a friendly butcher. Puree your liver in the food processor. Be sure to pulse and not "blend" the liver. It turns to liquid very quickly.

1 pound pork or chicken liver

12 ounces pork shoulder, cut into 1-inch cubes

1½ cups chopped yellow onion

1 cup chicken stock

½ cup cornmeal

3 eggs

1½ teaspoons rubbed sage

1 teaspoon cayenne pepper

1 teaspoon ground rosemary

⅛ teaspoon ground cloves

1 teaspoon salt

2 teaspoons black pepper

Unsalted butter, for cooking

Preheat the oven to 350°F.

In a large stainless steel bowl, stir together the liver, pork shoulder, and onion and set aside. Set up your meat grinder with the medium die attachment. Working in batches, grind the pork mixture into a second stainless steel bowl. Add the stock, cornmeal, eggs, sage, cayenne, rosemary, cloves, salt, and pepper and stir until fully combined. Pour the livermush mixture into a nonstick loaf pan and bake until firm to the touch, about 40 minutes. Remove from the oven, cool to room temperature, then remove from the pan. Cover tightly in plastic wrap and refrigerate for up to 1 week.

To serve the livermush, cut into ½-inch slices. Warm butter in a large sauté pan over medium heat for 45 seconds. Add the slices of livermush 6 or 8 at a time and cook until browned on both sides, about 3 minutes per side. (Livermush is already cooked, so all you are doing is warming it in the pan and giving it a little crunchy texture on the outside.)

GRAVLAX (LOX)

MAKES 1 WHOLE SIDE OF GRAVLAX; SERVES 25

1 (4- to 5-pound) side of salmon, skin on (see Note)

2 tablespoons coriander seeds

2 tablespoons fennel seeds

1 tablespoon black peppercorns

½ cup kosher salt

6 tablespoons light brown sugar

Zest of 2 lemons

Zest of 2 limes

10 sprigs dill

Leaves from 8 sprigs tarragon

Leaves from 6 sprigs thyme

I moved from Chapel Hill, North Carolina, where I had cut my teeth in the kitchen, to my hometown of New Orleans to help a high school friend named Larkin Selman open an amazing little bistro called Gautreau's. Larkin was coming from the kitchens of Alfred Portale, Jonathan Waxman, and Jeremiah Tower. He was a culinary star at a young age with as fine an American cooking pedigree as a young man could dream of.

The kitchen at Gautreau's became known immediately for the most forward-thinking food in New Orleans and the most psychotic, fun-loving, debaucherous circus ever assembled. The sex, drugs, and booze consumed within the four walls of that kitchen while producing five-star food was nothing short of Thompson-esque. How I managed to retain an iota of what I was taught is the definition of miraculous. It was the kitchen that completely cemented my love for restaurants and lit the fire for food and service that still burns in me today.

Almost thirty years later, Gautreau's is still churning out culinary talent who go on to helm the kitchens of New Orleans and beyond. Larkin is long gone from that kitchen, but his spirit has left an indelible imprint, even if all of his contraband has since been scrubbed.

It was at Gautreau's that I first learned to cure gravlax, the Scandinavian quick salt-cured salmon. I remember the first time I tasted a paper-thin slice and how the flavors exploded across my palate. I became the guy in charge of curing the gravlax and we were curing a couple of sides of salmon a day. The scraps frequently came home with me and I would eat it with cream cheese on a local bagel, and it was as good a lox and bagel as I have ever had. Serve on any bread with whipped cream cheese. (Secret: I love this with our Egg Salad, page 179, on toast.)

Lay a large piece of plastic wrap on a flat surface, making sure it is large enough to fully wrap the salmon. Lay the salmon, skin side down, on the plastic wrap.

Place the coriander, fennel, and peppercorns in a small sauté pan over high heat. Warm the pan and spices for 45 seconds, shaking gently. Lower the heat to medium and swirl the spices for another 1 to 1½ minutes, until the spices begin to pop lightly and are very fragrant. Dump the spices immediately onto a small plate and allow to cool until they can be worked by hand. Place the seeds on a wooden cutting board and crush roughly with the bottom of a sauté pan.

In a stainless steel bowl, stir together the coriander seeds, fennel seeds, black peppercorns, salt, sugar, lemon zest, and lime zest. Spread evenly over the salmon, being sure to cover every bit of the exposed flesh. Sprinkle the dill, tarragon, and thyme over the top.

Cover the salmon tightly with the plastic wrap. Set a wire rack in a large baking pan and place the wrapped salmon on it. Refrigerate the salmon, allowing to cure for 3 days. (For a 1-day cure, place another pan on top of the salmon and weight it down with a heavy object.)

Remove the salmon from the refrigerator and press the center with your finger. If it's firm, it's ready. If not, make a little more of the salt-sugar cure mixture, sprinkle it lightly over the salmon, and refrigerate for 1 day more.

When ready to serve, remove the plastic wrap and brush off the cure. (You can rinse it, too, if you feel strongly about it.) Starting at the head, cut thin slices, working down toward the tail. Gravlax will keep for up to 2 weeks in fresh wrap in the refrigerator.

NOTE: You will need to find a "friendly" fishmonger who will sell you a skin-on salmon side *with pinbones removed.* Try to find a wild product. Farm-raised salmon resembles wild in shape alone.

EYE-OPENERS

LET'S GET THIS OUT OF THE WAY. THERE IS LITTLE IN THE WORLD that's more fun than day drinking. Brunch itself is, more often than not, altogether forgettable, but the fact that it is the meal that accompanies weekend day drinking can elevate it to a place of mythical status. Before we proceed, if you take offense to this particular theory, well, we have very little to talk about.

There is little doubt that, as I write this, words like *heathen, irresponsible, immature, immoral, shiftless, depraved,* and *nefarious* will be bandied about as a result of this proclamation, but fortunately for my sleep patterns, I don't give a crap.

Some of the fonder moments in my life have been backlit with a touch of daytime consumption. I loved little more than skipping afternoon class during college with my best friend, Coyt Bailey, mixing cheap interpretations of margaritas and shooting skeet (and occasionally, remote-controlled airplanes or various household appliances). There have been numerous Ole Miss football games that would not have been the same (nor would I have been able to sit through) without a fistful of bourbon and Cokes. A pair of early-morning duck camp zingers, a direct result of swilling from a bottle of something called Hot Damn! with one of my favorite people in the world to drink with, Andy Howorth, left me in excruciating pain from laughing so hard. I was overwhelmed with joy on the back porch of a cocktail joint in Knoxville, with John T. Edge and Ed Lee, among others, where an impromptu gin tasting erupted, as did stories and laughter that left me in tears and with two new lifelong friends, Hunter Lewis and his wife, Ellen. And then there was the day I spent circling Manhattan with my friend Sarah Abell, having drinks in every place we could imagine—from Eleven Madison Park for Champagne to Eataly for whites by the glass to ABC Kitchen for Bloodys to Gramercy Tavern for old-fashioneds—on one of those rare days where nobody had any responsibilities whatsoever.

None of these moments unfolded near the beauty they did without the capricious whim to tipple. No matter how you size it up, night was made for drinking. Darkness cloaks the mischief that can ensue. The late hours are the mistress of high jinks and the seductress of questionable decision making. Shadows are the friend of missteps and the savior of many a silly mistake. To drink among the living and in the full exposure of the sun risks consequences greater than those lurking at night. There is a joy that accompanies it, though, that is a direct result of the counterintuitive nature of its natural place in our lives.

So the next time you have a moment for pause, make the right decision. Dive in and let your hair down. Day drinks are the best drinks, and what's more, they frequently are the precursor to the nap, which is a discussion for another time.

GRAPEFRUIT MIMOSA

SERVES 2

So here's a little admission: I don't like bitter. As a recognized chef of some note (depending who you ask), I am supposed to have this super-refined palate and appreciate all of the esoteric bullshit out there that makes chefs "cheffy." Well, I don't give a crap. I am fifty years old and I don't have to pretend I like flavors that I don't like just to impress some jackwagon that some publicist feels I need to impress. I don't like hoppy beers, amari, pomegranate, cranberry juice, Fernet, grapefruit, or black coffee. I'm also not going to drink Dumpster runoff just because you tell me Its trendy.

Still, I do like weird stuff. I eat lamb testicles, drink pickle juice, love fried chitterlings and haggis, and considering what is in hot dogs, I love eating some really messed-up animal parts. That said, this drink was a real meditation. I have always felt like the mimosa was a drink that either (1) ruined good Champagne, or (2) was just made for crap sparkling wine. The latter makes more sense from the standpoint of someone who loves quality bubbles. But why not use a citrus that might elevate a decent dry Champagne rather than mask everything about it with orangy sweetness? This is what happens . . . And for someone who loathes bitter, it plays, like a boss.

I use ruby red grapefruit because it tends to be a little less bitter than a typical grapefruit, while still capturing the intense citrus flavors that I love.

½ cup freshly squeezed ruby red grapefruit juice, chilled until very cold

⅛ teaspoon pomegranate molasses

Salt

1 cup extra brut Champagne

2 strips lime zest, for garnish

Pour the cold ruby red grapefruit juice into 2 large Champagne flutes. Drizzle half of the pomegranate molasses into each flute, add a small pinch of salt, and stir to combine with a long-handled cocktail stirrer. Top off with the Champagne and garnish with the lime zest.

MICHELADA AND A SHOT

SERVES 2

Hangovers are worse in Mexico. That's all there is to it. But so are fistfights, jail, the exchange rate for buying yourself out of a mess, and the messes you can get yourself into. That said, tequila and beer are the quickest recovery (and by no coincidence whatsoever, the easiest way back into trouble). I speak from experience. Mexico used to be a really fun place to play rough, and as a young man, my brother and a few friends took advantage of that fact and of their very quick remedies.

I stared down my first michelada at a breakfast bar in Mexico City. I don't think it was intentionally a breakfast bar, it was just open at breakfast. Thankfully, because I am still convinced I might not be here today if it hadn't been for that drink that morning. The last intelligible thing I remember uttering the night before was "take me to the bar with the biggest tequila selection in all of Mexico City." We somehow emerged from our misadventures with little more than a scrape or two, but with an enormous hangover on the horizon.

That's where the michelada comes in: all of the minerally goodness of tomato juice, a little acid from some citrus, a touch of salt from the Clamato, Maggi and Worcestershire for earthiness, and beer as a stand-in for the opiate family. On this particular morning, it was an epiphany. With a shot of tequila, it was a divine relief. It would not be the last time I would feel that way, but it would be the last time I ever had to wonder what might be the quickest and most delicious path back to the living.

If you aren't old enough to remember Maggi in your mother's or grandmother's kitchen spice cabinet, get yourself reacquainted. Maggi is close in flavor to soy sauce, though a little sweeter. It also contains a healthy amount of MSG, and if you don't already know how I feel about that, see page 133—I fucking love the stuff.

1 cup Clamato

¼ cup V-8 juice

1 tablespoon freshly squeezed lime juice

1½ teaspoons Worcestershire sauce

1 teaspoon toasted cumin seeds, crushed

¾ teaspoon Maggi sauce

½ teaspoon Valentina hot sauce or your preferred hot sauce

⅛ teaspoon salt

Ice

1 (12-ounce) bottle Pacifico beer

4 sprigs cilantro

2 shots good-quality reposado tequila

In a 1-quart mason jar, combine the Clamato, V-8, lime juice, Worcestershire, cumin seeds, Maggi, hot sauce, and salt. Cover and shake vigorously for 15 seconds. Fill 2 pint glasses halfway with ice. Pour half of the michelada base into each glass and top off with the beer. Garnish with the cilantro sprigs. Pour the tequila into shot glasses, with NO salt and NO lime.

Kick the tequila back in one motion, like your firstborn child's life depended on it. Sip michelada at your leisure. Rinse and repeat.

OJEN FRAPPÉ

SERVES 2

Odds are, if you aren't from the south of Spain or uptown New Orleans, you've never heard of Ojen. It's weird. It's bitter. It's sweet. It tastes like licorice. It fuels a certain segment of the guys who make Fat Tuesday fun and unforgettable. You will likely never have the chance to find this liqueur anywhere else, but when I tell you it is a magical elixir that will surprise and lift you, I mean just that. It combines a number of flavors I am not particularly crazy about (bitterness, anisette), but when balanced nicely, it is amazing.

The giant den on Claiborne Avenue where the Mardi Gras floats for the Rex parade (the grandfather of all Mardi Gras parades) are rebuilt each year will make your head swim with history, pageantry, and tradition. And its denizens, even more so. The Rex Organization, you see, is made up of some of the finest gentlemen in the city, which is not surprising when you consider that each candidate is admitted based on what he has done for the community. The men come from all walks of life, and the love for New Orleans binds them. The Ojen frappé is one of their cocktails of choice, and never is more of the strange liquor consumed on the entire planet than between the hours of 6 a.m. and 2 p.m. each Mardi Gras. And now you know a little NOLA secret.

If you can't find Ojen, any high-alcohol anisette will make a tolerable substitute.

Crushed ice

4 ounces Ojen liqueur or your favorite high-alcohol anisette, like absinthe

2 ounces gin

½ ounce Brown Sugar Simple Syrup (page 243)

½ ounce freshly squeezed lemon juice

8 dashes Peychaud's bitters

2 lemon twists

Fill 2 large old-fashioned glasses with crushed ice. In a cocktail shaker, combine the Ojen, gin, simple syrup, lemon juice, and bitters and shake for 20 seconds. Strain over the crushed ice and garnish with a lemon twist.

OJEN AND NEW ORLEANS: A MYSTERIOUS LOVE STORY

Ojen is a sweetened anisette that used to be distilled in an Andalusian town of the same name. It is similar to absinthe, but without wormwood, so it is not quite as bitter. Mixing it with bitters and sugar triggers a number of desirable results: (1) sugar helps rush alcohol to the brain and eliminates pain, (2) bitters and anisette calm an upset stomach, and (3) combined, the cocktail's ingredients can provide a quick jolt of energy and pluckiness.

It is widely believed that more Ojen is consumed in New Orleans than the entire rest of the world. The connection between this oddly esoteric spirit and New Orleans is a mystery. Nobody I have asked (including the keepers of Carnival lore) and nowhere I have researched suggests any reason why this particular spirit became such a favorite, especially when there are so many other anise-based spirits.

To further complicate matters, in 1999, the last maker of Ojen decided to discontinue production. Before the distillery shut down, a group of New Orleans devotees commissioned one last five hundred–case run (six thousand bottles). Those bottles were produced and shipped to New Orleans, and the last bottle sold off the shelf around 2007.

Rumor has it that a group in Ojen is set to begin producing the eponymous spirit once again, so that the "luck" of Ojen can once again reign over Rex. Until then, anyone hell-bent on the experience can come find me on Mardi Gras morning. I still have several bottles stashed away, and I'll be drinking them for the next ten years.

BIG BAD BREAKFAST BLOODY MARY

SERVES 4

Little paves the way for a responsibility-free day of drinking and laughs like a Bloody Mary. The umami of this cocktail is unsurpassed, and something about the combination of flavors magically alleviates any sort of guilt about consuming them. I stand firmly behind the belief that there is no reason whatsoever that they should be consumed after 2 p.m., and they should be downright criminal after dark.

One of my favorite days was the one I spent with my buddies John Besh and Alon Shaya on the front porch of Big Bad Breakfast in Oxford before a Southern Foodways Alliance dinner. We sat for hours, spreading our charm and wit, guzzling one Blood Mary after another. Few times in my life have I laughed so hard or had as much fun. John and Alon are good company alone, but add a half-dozen Bloody Marys and there is little in the world that's more entertaining.

While I am certain that the purists of the world will be quick to shit on the use of V-8 in this (or any) recipe, I stand firmly by it. V-8 is robust and has an excellent viscosity about it. It has concentrated carrot, celery, beet, spinach, parsley, and watercress juices that make it tomato juice PLUS. It is delicious and has a wonderful texture. Say what you will, but it is as good a starting point as any for a killer Bloody Mary.

2 cups V-8 juice
2 tablespoons freshly squeezed lemon juice
2 tablespoons grated yellow onion
1½ tablespoons prepared horseradish
1½ tablespoons Worcestershire sauce
1 tablespoon soy sauce
1 tablespoon olive brine
2 teaspoons Tabasco pepper sauce

1 teaspoon black pepper
¾ teaspoon minced garlic
¼ teaspoon celery seeds
¼ teaspoon salt
8 ounces vodka
Cracked ice
Pitted green olives, for garnish
Cocktail onions, for garnish
Thin celery sticks, for garnish

In a 1-quart mason jar, combine the V-8, lemon juice, onion, horseradish, Worcestershire, soy sauce, olive brine, Tabasco, black pepper, garlic, celery seeds, and salt. Cover and shake vigorously for 15 seconds. Pack 4 old-fashioned glasses with cracked ice. Pour 2 ounces of vodka into each glass and top off with the Bloody Mary mix. Garnish with olives, cocktail onions, and celery.

THE IDIOT'S CHAMPAGNE COCKTAIL

SERVES 2

Danny Meyer used to throw an earthshaking gathering of the greatest pitmasters from all over the country in Madison Square Park called the Big Apple Barbecue Block Party. About 350,000 people would come to this little postage stamp of soil in Midtown for forty-eight hours every summer and happily wait in line (frequently in the blistering sun) for hours to get a sandwich from Big Bob Gibson, Ed Mitchell, Pat Martin, and the like. Simultaneously each year, Danny held a seemingly VIP gathering in front of Eleven Madison Park to showcase the obscure and relatively unknown whiskey of a buddy of ours named Julian Van Winkle.

It was in the early days of my friendship with Julian when I was still asking freshman questions like, "What kind of heirloom corn varieties are you guys using to make your mash?" Julian is a wonderfully affable man, confident in the quality of his product, keenly aware of shysters trying to ply his affections, and one who enjoys an escape into the placid effects of what his family has distilled for several generations. On a particularly lubricated Saturday afternoon, the two of us leaned on the bar to order a drink as the house band wailed away. Half in the bag and without thinking, I asked the bartender for a glass of twenty-year-old bourbon with a couple of rocks and a twist of lemon, as I had consumed my whiskey for years.

The moment the words escaped my lips, Julian wheeled around, eyebrow cocked, and said, "Did I hear that right?" I was immediately sobered. Terrified I had offended him, I tried to explain how my dad had ordered his Scotch my whole life and how I liked my bourbon. Before I was close to finishing my excuse, he clamped my shoulder and said, "You are the only other person in the world I know who drinks their whiskey like I do!" A man has never known greater relief. For the moment, at least, I was not an idiot. This I drink as a toast to that moment.

2 ounces W. L. Weller Special Reserve bourbon

1 ounce Brown Sugar Simple Syrup (page 243)

1½ teaspoons freshly squeezed lemon juice

2 sprigs thyme

4 dashes Angostura bitters

Dry Champagne, for float

2 lemon twists, for garnish

In a cocktail shaker, combine the bourbon, simple syrup, lemon juice, thyme, and bitters in a shaker with several cubes of ice and shake for 20 seconds. Strain into two Champagne coupes and top off with Champagne. Garnish each drink with a lemon twist.

BLOODY BULL SHOT

SERVES 2

On a rainy Sunday afternoon in about 1969, I was lapping our block on Prytania Street in uptown New Orleans on my brand-new navy blue *badass* Schwinn Stingray. It had a banana seat, a fake car-style gearshift, and metallic streamers that dangled from the ape-hanger handlebars. I was dressed in a yellow slicker with a matching hat and looked just like the Gorton's fisherman. On my umpteenth pass, I was stopped by a group of boys, and one about twice my size stepped forward with a hacksaw and told me to get off my bike or he would cut off my hand. I got off, scared and humiliated, and off he rode, oafishly, on my pride and joy.

I ran home crying to find my mom and dad loaded down in the living room in front of our tiny little black-and-white TV watching the Saints and pressing Reubens in a Sunbeam waffle maker tethered to the wall with an extension cord. My mom deftly prepared sandwiches while my dad lorded over savory ingredients like a mad scientist making this oddly savory Bloody Mary–like concoction. He let me curl up next to him on the sofa sobbing, alternately taking bites of his gooey, crispy sandwich and sipping his drink, both of which he shared with me.

An affair with the Bloody Bull was born in that moment of self-medication. And while I don't remember being particularly comforted or coddled, I do remember immediately not giving a crap. Sometimes alcohol really is the best medicine.

This is a Bloody Bull, heavy enough on the bouillon that it bleeds over into the realm of a Bull Shot, hence the contrived and confusing moniker.

I call for Claussen's dill pickle juice in this recipe. Simply put, there isn't a better mass-produced pickle out there in the world. I have found a couple that approach, but Claussen stands head and shoulders above. A shot of the vinegary brine straight out of the jar is the perfect thing to get a day going at times, and personally, I think it has tremendous medicinal properties. (You're damn right. If I had been alive in 1840, I'd have been selling snake oil.) This needs the shot and Claussen's is all that will do, for me.

Crushed ice

6 ounces V-8 juice

2 beef bouillon cubes, dissolved in 3 tablespoons warm water

1½ tablespoons Claussen dill pickle juice

1 tablespoon freshly squeezed lemon juice

1½ teaspoons freshly squeezed lime juice

2½ teaspoons prepared horseradish

2 teaspoons Worcestershire sauce

1 teaspoon minced garlic

1 teaspoon Kitchen Bouquet sauce

1 teaspoon Tabasco pepper sauce

1 teaspoon freshly cracked black pepper

⅛ teaspoon celery seed

5 ounces vodka

Lime wedges, celery stalks, and quartered Claussen pickles, for garnish

Fill 2 pint glasses with crushed ice. In a cocktail shaker, combine the V-8 juice, bouillon, pickle juice, lemon juice, lime juice, horseradish, Worcestershire, garlic, Kitchen Bouquet, Tabasco, pepper, and celery seed and shake for 15 seconds. Strain over the crushed ice and top with the vodka. Garnish each drink with a lime wedge, celery stalk, and pickles.

If your bicycle has just been stolen, repeat as needed until you don't give a crap or want to go find the guy who stole it and beat his ass. Whichever happens first, go take a nap. Your dad will buy you a new one.

ADVANTAGE: CONNORS
CELERY SODA

SERVES 2

The summer of 1974 was a relatively innocent time. The Vietnam conflict was ending, political criminals were being brought to justice, we were settling into a post–Civil Rights struggle normalcy—the world was, for a moment, somewhat peaceful.

It was peaceful, unless you were my father trapped on a six-hour car ride with my brother and I playing the newly released album by Elton John with the smash hit "Bennie and the Jets" over and over on our portable cassette player, in which case it was a time of measured violence. That cassette tape mysteriously disappeared at some point during that beach trip and the cassette player turned up victim of a heinous and brutal crime.

That same summer, Jimmy Connors would win his first Wimbledon Singles title (in 1973, he won Men's Doubles in an unlikely pairing with Ilie Nastase), and he was the toast of the U.S. tennis world in his fairytale coupling with Chris Evert (who also won the Singles title that year). We all sat around the TV for a week watching the two of them climb their way to the "Lovebird Double."

At the beach that summer, my parents and all of their friends seemed to be mixing everything with soda to put up with the interminable repeat of Elton John, so the drink's moniker seems appropriate. This is a wonderful, light cocktail that's a great alternative to a Pimm's Cup. It's equally English in its subtlety and refinement, and easy on the constitution.

For the garnish, shave stalks of celery with a vegetable peeler for crispy, thin, crunchy curls of celery goodness.

Cracked ice
4 ounces gin
2 ounces Celery Syrup (recipe follows)
1 ounce freshly squeezed lime juice
Zest of ½ lime
6 dashes Angostura bitters
Soda, for topping
Shaved celery, for garnish
2 lime wedges, for garnish
Celery seed, for garnish

Fill 2 collins glasses halfway with cracked ice. In a cocktail shaker, combine the gin, Celery Syrup, lime juice, zest, and bitters with several cubes of ice and gently shake until well chilled, about 20 seconds. Strain over the ice and top off with soda. Garnish each drink with celery, a lime wedge, and a pinch of celery seed.

CELERY SYRUP
MAKES 2 CUPS

2 cups water
¾ cup diced celery
½ cup plus 1½ teaspoons sugar
1½ ounces freshly squeezed lime juice
Zest of 2 limes
1 tablespoon celery seed

Combine all of the ingredients in a small saucepan and bring to a boil over medium heat. Turn the heat to low and simmer for 5 minutes. Turn off the heat, allow to cool to room temperature, and strain. Store in an airtight container and refrigerate for up to 2 weeks.

EGGNOG

I kinda hate that eggnog is relegated to Christmas. It is as arbitrary as compartmentalizing eggs as solely a breakfast ingredient (and that, folks, is an example of irony). Eggnog really isn't anything other than a super-rich version of milk punch—and a version that will kill the worst of stomach ailments, at that. I make a huge bowl at least once a year and intentionally try not to do it around Christmas as my one-man protest of tethering it to that season. This is a great brunch drink no matter what time of year it is.

6 eggs, separated

3 cups bourbon

¾ cup confectioners' sugar

¼ cup sweetened condensed milk

2 tablespoons pure vanilla extract

2½ teaspoons freshly grated nutmeg

Pinch of salt

4 cups whipping cream

Whisk together the egg yolks, 1 cup of the bourbon, ¼ cup of the confectioners' sugar, and the condensed milk in a bowl. Cover and refrigerate for 1 hour. Meanwhile, combine the egg whites, remaining ½ cup confectioners' sugar, vanilla, nutmeg, and salt in the bowl of a stand mixer fitted with the whisk attachment and whip on high for about 2 minutes, until the whites reach stiff peaks. Set aside.

Once the egg yolk mixture is cold, whisk in the cream and the remaining 2 cups bourbon. Gently fold in the egg white mixture. (Note: The whites will continue to try and separate, so you will need to continue whisking them back in as you serve the eggnog.) Serve chilled in a punch cup.

DAD'S MILK SHAKE

SERVES 1

When I was six or seven, there was *nothing* I looked forward to more than when my dad dragged out the old avocado-colored Sunbeam blender from the cabinet next to the sink right before bed. Now that blender saw lots of action, don't get me wrong. It saw the birth of hundreds of true daiquiris and margaritas, and was even the genesis point of some frozen Harvey Wallbangers that may or may not have been the momentary demise of one of our neighbors. But when that sucker made an appearance postdinner, postbath and prebedtime, it meant one thing: Dad was doing his thing.

Dick Currence worked his magic with that machine like he had earned his PhD as a soda jerk. What he coaxed from the hulking prehistoric glass vessel atop that motor was nothing short of manna. I am not sure why I was fed anything else or why my dad needed to ever have any other job in the world than making those milk shakes. This is my version of what he used to treat us to. And, yes, it is fucking excellent with pancakes or a breakfast sandwich, but it's life-changing with a burger.

2 large scoops vanilla ice cream	3 tablespoons Chocolate Sauce (recipe follows)
1 cup whole milk, plus more as needed	1 egg
¼ cup malted milk	1 teaspoon pure vanilla extract

Place all of the ingredients in a blender. Add extra milk as needed until the liquid almost covers the ice cream. Blend until smooth and serve in a tall glass. Thank me later for giving you the excuse to make a milk shake as an adult . . .

CHOCOLATE SAUCE

MAKES 1 CUP

3 tablespoons unsalted butter	½ cup Ghirardelli dark cocoa powder or your favorite brand
¼ cup brewed dark roast coffee	¾ teaspoon pure vanilla extract
½ cup firmly packed light or dark brown sugar	Pinch of salt

Warm the butter, coffee, and brown sugar in a small saucepan over low heat until the butter melts and the sugar dissolves, about 3 minutes. Whisk in the cocoa powder, vanilla, and salt until fully blended. Remove from the heat and cool to room temperature. Store in an airtight container and refrigerate for up to 2 months.

PEACH LASSI

SERVES 1

The lassi is a magical concoction. I am not entirely sure the word isn't a direct translation of "smoothie," because that is essentially what it is, but good yogurt is the key ingredient. I am always tempted to put more sugar in it than I should, yet I am extremely happy when I don't. The natural sweetness of the yogurt and the acids from the citrus and dairy combine to give the fruit an explosive flavor burst. The touch of mint is the cherry on this particular sundae. You can substitute any fruit you like. I just happen to be weak for the peach.

2 cups chopped ripe peaches

1½ cups unsweetened yogurt

1 teaspoon pure vanilla extract

3 tablespoons honey

2 teaspoons freshly squeezed lime juice

1½ teaspoons minced fresh ginger

8 fresh mint leaves, plus 1 mint sprig, for garnish

Zest of ½ lime

2 cups ice

Place all of the ingredients except the garnish in a blender and blend on high until smooth, about 1 minute. Garnish with the sprig of mint.

UPTOWN EXPRESS

SERVES 1

The Dude had it right, though it's highly caloric. The White Russian holds a special place in the hearts of those who (1) like to drink and (2) are prone to bouts of bad indigestion. It soothes and intoxicates, though it soothes more.

After some traveling in the Far East, where condensed milk is the weapon of choice for taking relatively shitty coffee and making it palatable, I was hankering for a coffee breakfast cocktail. And so I hit on this little gem.

In New Orleans, just a few blocks from where I grew up, there exists the Vatican of snowball stands, Hansen's (that's snow cones for those of you not from New Orleans). It has been around for the better part of a century on the same freaking corner. If you know anything about ordering there, you top your slushie delight with a couple of tablespoons of condensed milk. It is like getting kissed on the mouth by God.

This combines my love of drinking with my newfound propensity for getting tired (due to my advanced age), my obsession with flaked ice, and my personal need for sugar. Enjoy. If you think it's hard to eat just one Lay's potato chip, well, you're fucked.

Crushed ice

2 ounces vodka

1½ ounces Kahlúa

2 tablespoons heavy cream

1 single-shot espresso

2 tablespoons sweetened condensed milk

Fill one pint glass with crushed ice. In a cocktail shaker, combine the vodka, Kahlúa, cream, and espresso with several cubes of ice and shake for 30 seconds. Strain over the crushed ice and top with the condensed milk.

DECATUR STREET GUTTER PUNK

SERVES 1

When I lived in the French Quarter in the late 1980s, a population of homeless teens migrated to NOLA, and more specifically to a bar called Keegan's and a coffee shop another block down called Kaldi's. All of this was about one block from where I lived on Decatur. They were vampiric in the hours they kept and the "don't give a fuck about anything but what I want" attitude they exuded.

I frequently started my day at the coffee shop, which meant I had to pass the front of Keegan's, which was completely open to the street, to get there. No matter what time it was, there were angry drunk kids either ending or beginning their day. They zipped in and out of the doors of the bar on skateboards, swung from the arms of the quarter slot machines, drowned themselves in shots of cheap whiskey, and more than anything, harassed and/or spit on everyone who passed in front of the place. They were my people, and I loved everything about them.

I frequently went there after work and had a couple of drinks. I got to know a few of the guys who hung out there and a couple of them even came to work for me, though they were all patently and unapologetically unreliable. Most had run away from perfectly good homes in Dallas, San Francisco, or Kansas City, but all had chosen this perfectly destructive, bohemian lifestyle. Their only motive was to milk every moment out of the day—and hassle people walking by my little neighborhood bar.

I hated loving them and loved hating them. They loved the conflicted natured of our relationship, but ultimately respected that I was a likable part of the establishment. Or at least I bought them shots every once in a while. This cocktail embodies their "don't give a crap, drink, and stay up as long as possible" attitude.

1 double-shot espresso

1 ounce gin

1 ounce heavy cream

½ ounce absinthe

½ ounce Brown Sugar Simple Syrup (page 243)

1 egg yolk

1 teaspoon freshly squeezed lemon juice

1 lemon twist, for garnish

In a cocktail shaker, combine all of the ingredients except the lemon twist with several cubes of ice and shake vigorously for 20 seconds. Strain into an old-fashioned glass. Garnish with a lemon twist.

11 A.M. KICKOFF

SERVES 1

Ask anyone that loves SEC (Southeastern Conference) football, myself included, and they will tell you "11 a.m. kickoff sucks." It is very much a beggars-choosing-to-be-choosers sort of thing. We live for Saturdays. We play football weekly at the highest level of competition and with the highest degree of hatred for our rivals as exists anywhere. As a result, one might think we would be grateful to watch our teams play whenever we were so lucky. But the reality is that folks love to juice it up and have fun the night before a big game, so getting it together to put on a tailgate before an 11:00 kickoff can test the mettle of the best of us. The following contains all of the ingredients to make the morning after easier.

1 double-shot espresso

2 ounces bourbon

1 ounce Brown Sugar Simple Syrup (recipe follows)

1 ounce honey

⅛ teaspoon ground nutmeg

2 dashes of orange bitters

1 orange twist, for garnish

In a cocktail shaker, combine all of the ingredients except the orange twist with several cubes of ice and stir with a long-handled barspoon until chilled, about 1 minute. Strain into a Champagne coupe and garnish with an orange twist.

BROWN SUGAR SIMPLE SYRUP
MAKES ½ CUP

½ cup brown sugar

4 tablespoons hot water

Stir together the sugar and water in a small sauté pan. Place pan over medium heat and swirl until the sugar has dissolved, about a minute. Remove from the heat. Cool to room temperature. Store in glass or plastic at room temperature for up to 2 weeks.

FALLING DOWN BROWN COW

SERVES 1

Since it has been established that bourbon goes well with Coca-Cola *and* if you will trust me that it goes well with vanilla ice cream, then it would make sense that the three together would work equally well, right? Well, you can bet your sweet ass on it! And I will not lie to you. I found this Dad's Root Beer mug when we were looking for props for the book's photographs, and the minute I saw it, I snatched it up and said, "I know *exactly* what we are doing with this." You see I am a little bit . . . no, I am totally a child that way.

I will find something I loved as a child and I will find a way to put booze into it as an adult. I will capture that childhood joy and mash it up with adult pleasure-seeking tendencies.

So here it is. Should you choose to get overserved on ice cream, there is no better way to do it, unless you can get your hands on a tank of liquid nitrogen, make an ice cream base with about two-thirds whiskey in it, and freeze it into Dippin' Dots. Then you can completely waste an entire Sunday afternoon eating ice cream and trying to explain the effect it is having on you to people who are entirely uninterested in hearing about it. And then fall asleep into the most beautiful slumber you have ever known. Trust me, I've done it, if that wasn't clear. Call me anytime you want to spend a Sunday together. We'll totally put a car into a ditch.

2 scoops vanilla ice cream

2 ounces bourbon

Pinch of ground cinnamon

Coca-Cola, to float

1 cinnamon stick, for garnish

Place the ice cream in a large frosted mug. Pour the bourbon over the top and sprinkle with ground cinnamon. Top off with the Coke and garnish with a cinnamon stick.

DONKEY PUNCH

SERVES 12

I love punch. I have loved punch since my brother and I, in our teens, started mixing cheap vodka and rum with copious amounts of sugar and the unapologetic, artificially flavored Kool-Aid mix (the shrub of our teen years) and dispensing our elixir to our thirsty friends. There was a particularly notorious pool party that went on one weekend when my parents were out of town. We were left to our own devices for seventy-two hours after my parents departed and before my grandparents showed up. As my parents were going out the front door, my friends were sneaking in the back with wheelbarrows full of stereo equipment and contraband. The next two days are a little bit of a blur, thanks to our crude punch. Suffice it to say, I ended up in the hospital having my head stitched up after it was busted open by a chair.

It achieved then, as it does now by more sophisticated measure and ingredients, the desired effect. A punch breaks the ice in a hurry, and it is easy to scoop-and-serve with little fuss. This one is a slight departure from the French 75, but of the same genus. I have not been back to the hospital, but it is *only* because I am now, three decades later, more respectful of the punch's punch. But beware, the donkey *will* kick you in the head if you aren't careful.

8 cups distilled water

Lemon slices, edible flower petals, and fresh herb sprigs (optional)

2 cups gin

1 cup Berry Lemon Shrub (recipe follows)

2 cups Champagne

Assorted fresh berries

Orange slices

Bring the water to a boil. Allow the water to cool to room temperature, fill 1 or 2 ice cube trays with the cooled water, and freeze. Reserve the remaining water. Layer several slices of lemon, flower petals, and fresh herb sprigs in the bottom of a Bundt pan. Unmold the ice cubes and place them on top of the lemon, petals, and herbs to keep them from floating. Add more lemon, petals, and herbs on top of and tucked around the sides of the ice. Pour just enough reserved boiled and cooled water into the mold to barely cover the ice cubes, but not cause them to float. Freeze the Bundt pan for 4 hours or overnight.

Stir together the gin and shrub in a punch bowl. Add the Champagne and gently stir to combine. Float the berries and orange slices in the punch bowl. Remove the Bundt pan from the freezer and submerge the outside of the pan in warm water to loosen the ice ring. Turn the ice ring out into the punch bowl and let the games begin.

BERRY LEMON SHRUB
MAKES ABOUT 3 CUPS

2 cups assorted fresh berries, such as blueberries, raspberries, and blackberries

Peels from 3 lemons

1½ cups sugar

2 teaspoons fresh rosemary leaves

½ cup apple cider vinegar

Combine the berries, lemon peels, sugar, and rosemary in a large bowl. Smash the berries to help extract their juice more quickly. Cover and refrigerate until the sugar is completely dissolved, 24 to 36 hours. Remove from the refrigerator, stir together until well combined, and mash up any remaining pieces of fruit that may still be intact. Strain the shrub into a 1-quart mason jar and stir in the vinegar. Allow to sit again to let the flavors combine for several hours before using. Store in an airtight container, refrigerated, for up to 2 months.

THE VACATION WIFE

SERVES 1

This drink is named for the fact that my wife, Bess, calls chef Ashley Christensen my "vacation wife" due to the amount of time we spend on the road cooking at different events together. There are very few people I like to day drink with as much as my dear, sweet, wonderful, beautiful friend Ashley. And let me make it perfectly clear, in this instance at least, it isn't because I am a complete lush, it is because of the joy that she, in particular, gets from knowing that if she can disengage for a moment from the rigors of responsibility while the sun is up, then *that* is reason to celebrate and *that* moment is frequently marked with a thoughtful and well-crafted cocktail. While I will just throw whatever I can get my hands on over some ice and settle into the most comfortable chair that is in closest proximity to my doughy white ass, Ashley will go out and collect berries, herbs, and shrub stems to turn cheap vodka into a flavorful gin. So this is to celebrate my amazing friend who truly knows how to milk the most from every moment on this planet and uses most of those moments to distill joy for everyone else around her. My baby girl could not have a better godmother.

4 ounces ruby red grapefruit juice

2 ounces gin

1 ounce Lillet Rosé

½ teaspoon Lime Bitters (recipe follows) or store-bought

Small splash of grenadine

1 sprig fresh savory or thyme

1 lime twist, for garnish

In a cocktail shaker, combine all of the ingredients except the lime twist with several cubes of ice. Pour back and forth with another shaker until well combined, 6 to 8 times. Strain into a Champagne coupe and garnish with the lime twist.

LIME BITTERS
MAKES ABOUT 2 CUPS

Peels from 9 limes

2 cups vodka

1 tablespoon gentian root

2 whole star anise

5 black peppercorns

1 green cardamom pod

Pinch of dried wormwood

Place the lime peels on a baking sheet in an unlit gas oven and allow to sit until dried out, at least 12 hours and preferably overnight, or place in an electric oven on the lowest setting for 1 to 1½ hours, checking constantly, until the peels have dried but are not crispy.

Combine the dried lime peels, vodka, gentian root, star anise, peppercorns, cardamom, and wormwood in a sealable container. Allow to sit at room temperature in a cool, dry place for 4 to 6 weeks. Strain and store in glass bottles for up to 3 years.

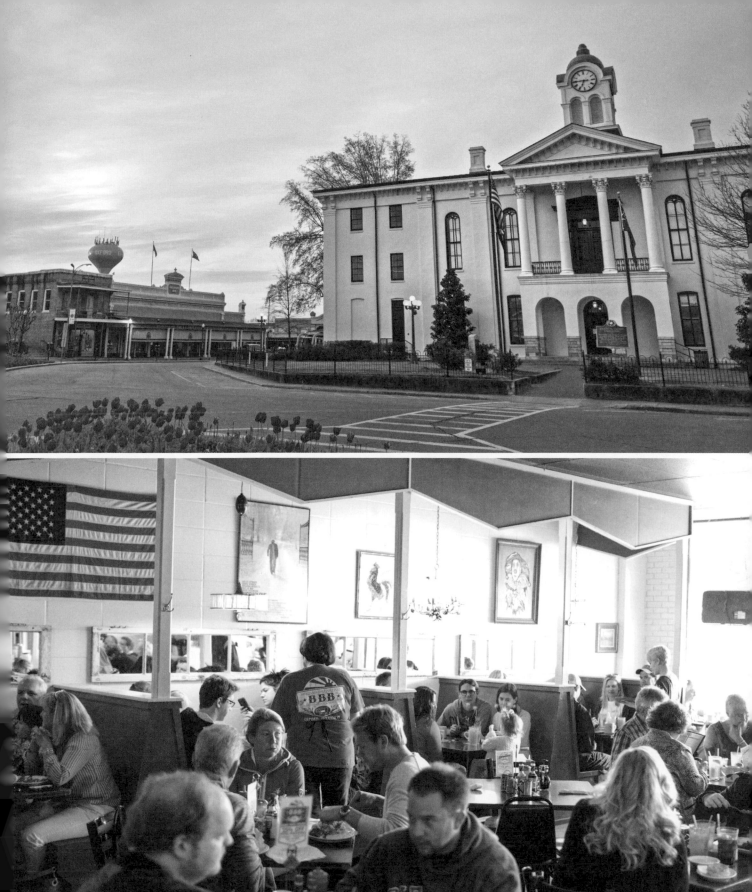

ABOUT THE AUTHOR

JOHN CURRENCE was born and raised in New Orleans, Louisiana, and had his first cooking job while working offshore as a deckhand on a tugboat in the Gulf of Mexico. His love for the kitchen was ignited during his first restaurant job at Bill Neal's Crook's Corner while at the University of North Carolina. That job along with several others he curated during those years (baking bread at an Italian restaurant, working at a butcher shop, cutting salmon and bluefish at a local smokehouse, and working a short-order line at a bookstore/cafe) cemented his love for the industry. Currence returned to New Orleans to help his childhood friend Larkin Selman open Gautreau's, where he worked as sous chef. After several years, Currence moved on to the Brennan family of restaurants to help open Bacco, before finally settling in Oxford in 1992 and opening City Grocery. Since then, the City Grocery Restaurant Group has opened a number of restaurants, including Ajax Diner, Nacho Mama's, Kalo's Tavern, Big Bad Breakfast, Bouré, Lamar Lounge, The Main Event, and Snackbar.

Currence is the recipient of the 2009 James Beard Award for Best Chef South and the Southern Foodways Alliance Guardian of the Tradition Award. He has appeared on television programs such as *Parts Unknown*, *Mind of a Chef*, *Bizarre Foods*, *Treme*, and *Top Chef Masters* and his writing has appeared in *Food & Wine* and *Bon Appétit*, among many others. He is a contributing editor for *Garden & Gun* magazine, a board member of No Kid Hungry (a project dedicated to eradicating childhood hunger in the United States), and an organizer and past board member of the prestigious annual Southern Foodways Symposium.

During his tenure as president/chairman of the Mississippi Restaurant Association, the Association was one of the first in the country to establish a statewide culinary educational program in Mississippi public schools. He worked for years as organizer of a local farmers' cooperative and market which established a bi-weekly venue for local farmers to sell their goods in the Oxford community. A deep interest in the arts led to five years as president of the local arts council and a nine year project assembling funds and overseeing the construction of a community performing arts center. The eighteen months following hurricane Katrina found Currence mostly in New Orleans leading the rebuilding of Willie Mae's Scotch House in the Treme neighborhood of the city, which was the subject of a feature-length documentary called *Above the Line: Saving Willie Mae's Scotch House*. An avid hunter and fisherman, Currence lives in Oxford with his wife, Bess, and extremely strong-headed but amazing daughter, Mamie. If you need him, he's the chubby guy at the end of the bar, sipping whiskey and bitching about the current state of American politics, entitlement, and/or commercial air travel. Just keep your hands and feet away from his mouth and cover your children's ears . . .

INDEX

Copyright © 2016 by John Currence
Photographs copyright © 2016 by Ed Anderson

All rights reserved. Published in the United States by Ten Speed Press, an imprint of the Crown Publishing Group, a division of Penguin Random House LLC, New York.
www.crownpublishing.com
www.tenspeed.com

Ten Speed Press and the Ten Speed Press colophon are registered trademarks of Penguin Random House LLC.

Library of Congress Cataloging-in-Publication Data
Names: Currence, John, author. | Anderson, Ed (Edward Charles), photographer.
Title: Big bad breakfast : the most important book of the day / John Currence ; photography by Ed Anderson.
Description: First edition. | Berkeley : Ten Speed Press, [2016] | Includes bibliographical references and index.
Identifiers: LCCN 2016007212 (print) | LCCN 2016009379 (ebook)
Subjects: LCSH: Breakfasts. | LCGFT: Cookbooks.
Classification: LCC TX733 .C87 2016 (print) | LCC TX733 (ebook) | DDC 641.5/2—dc23
LC record available at http://lccn.loc.gov/2016007212

Hardcover ISBN: 978-1-60774-736-9
eBook ISBN: 978-1-60774-737-6

Printed in China

Design by Betsy Stromberg
Coffee ring art on page 181 by Olga Popova/Shutterstock
All other coffee ring art by S.Noree Saisalam/Shutterstock

10 9 8 7 6 5 4 3 2 1

First Edition